A History of Banking in Antebellum America

Previous banking histories have focused on the money supply function of early American banks and its connection to the recurrent boom-bust cycle of the antebellum era. This history focuses on the credit-generating function of American banks. It demonstrates that banks aggressively promoted develop- ment rather than passively followed its course. Using previ- ously unexploited data, Professor Bodenhorn shows that banks helped to advance the development of incipient indus- trialization. Additionally, he shows that banks formed long- distance relationships that promoted geographic capital mobility, thereby assuring that short-term capital was directed in socially desirable directions, that is, where it was most in demand. He then traces those institutional and legal developments that allowed for this capital mobility. The result was that America was served by an efficient system of financial intermediaries by the mid-nineteenth century.

Howard Bodenhorn is Associate Professor in the Depart- ment of Economics and Business, Lafayette College, Penn- sylvania. He has also taught at St. Lawrence University, received a John E. Rovensky Dissertation Fellowship (1989–90), was the recipient of the Arthur H. Cole Award for the best article in the *Journal of Economic History* for 1993, and was a John M. Olin Junior Faculty Fellow (1995–96). Professor Bodenhorn has published numerous articles on early American banking, which have appeared in the *Journal of Economic History, Review of Economics and Statistics,* the *Journal of Money, Credit and Banking*, and the *Business History Review*, among other leading journals.

Advanced Praise for

A History of Banking in Antebellum America

"For years scholars interested in understanding the sources of growth in the antebellum economy largely ignored the financial sector and focused instead on measuring and explaining trends in 'real' magnitudes. Bodenhorn redresses this imbalance and argues convincingly that banks played a fundamental role in the period's acceleration of economic growth. In my opinion, this would be a great book to use in a course on American economic history. Bodenhorn provides clear, succinct introductions to the major scholarly debates over the pace and pattern of economic growth and the importance of the financial sector. At the same time, he brings to bear such a range of different types of evidence (from the macroeconomic and quantitative to the micro and anecdotal) that students would obtain a good sense of the many ways in which economic historians can explore and test alternative hypotheses."

– Naomi R. Lamoreaux, *University of California,*
Los Angeles

"Traditional assessments of American banking before the Civil War highlight its passivity, its instability, and its anti-manufacturing bias. Bodenhorn's revisionist account argues instead for a pro-active role for U.S. banks in this period. Through the masterly application of economic theory to a broad range of old and new sources, he convincingly depicts the banks as flexible and effective allocators of capital between sectors and regions. This promises to be a landmark in U.S. banking historiography, and deserves to be read by economic and monetary historians everywhere."

– Cormac Ó Gráda, *National University of Ireland, Dublin*

"Bodenhorn provides an eloquent and convincing analysis of the financial system in antebellum America which challenges established theories of early U.S. banking by contending that these institutions played a positive role in their country's economic development during this period. Drawing upon a wealth of primary material, the book is a must for financial and economic historians or anyone interested in nineteenth century U.S. history."

– Lucy Newton, *University of Reading, United Kingdom*

Studies in Macroeconomic History

SERIES EDITOR: Michael D. Bordo, *Rutgers University*

EDITORS: Forrest Capie, *City University Business School*
Barry Eichengreen, *University of California, Berkeley*
Nick Crafts, *London School of Economics*
Angela Redish, *University of British Columbia*

The titles in this series investigate themes of interest to economists and economic historians in the rapidly developing field of macroeconomic history. The four areas covered include the application of monetary and finance theory, international economics, and quantitative methods to historical problems; the historical application of growth and development theory and theories of business fluctuations; the history of domestic and international monetary, financial and other macroeconomic institutions; and the history of international monetary and financial systems. The series amalgamates the former Press series *Studies in Monetary and Financial History* and *Studies in Quantitative Economic History*.

Other books in the series:

The Gold Standard and Related Regimes
Michael D. Bordo
0-521-55006-8

Monetary Regimes in Transition
Michael D. Bordo and Forrest Capie, editors
0-521-41906-9

Elusive Stability
Barry Eichengreen
0-521-44847-6

A Monetary History of Italy
Michele Fratianni and Franco Spinelli
0-521-44315-6

Managing the Franc Poincaré
Kenneth Mouré
0-521-39458-9

Between the Dollar-Sterling Gold Points
Lawrence H. Officer
0-521-4546-2

Japanese Banking
Norio Tamaki
0-521-49676-4

The Strategy and Consistency of Federal Reserve Monetary Policy, 1924–1933
David C. Wheelock
0-521-39155-5

Canada and the Gold Standard
Trevor J. O. Dick and John E. Floyd
0-521-40408-8

Europe's Postwar Recovery
Barry Eichengreen
0-521-48279-8

The Economics of World War II
Mark Harrison, editor
0-521-62046-5, 0-521-78503-0

The Rise of Financial Capitalism
Larry Neal
0-521-45738-6

The Credit-Anstalt Crisis of 1931
Aurel Schubert
0-521-36537-6

Competition and Monopoly in the Federal Reserve System
Mark Toma
0-521-56258-9

Banking Panics of the Great Depression
Elmus Wicker
0-521-56261-9, 0-521-66346-6

A History of Banking in Antebellum America

Financial Markets and Economic Development in an Era of Nation-Building

HOWARD BODENHORN

Lafayette College

CAMBRIDGE
UNIVERSITY PRESS

PUBLISHED BY THE PRESS SYNDICATE OF THE UNIVERSITY OF CAMBRIDGE
The Pitt Building, Trumpington Street, Cambridge, United Kingdom

CAMBRIDGE UNIVERSITY PRESS
The Edinburgh Building, Cambridge CB2 2RU, UK http://www.cup.cam.ac.uk
40 West 20th Street, New York, NY 10011-4211, USA http://www.cup.org
10 Stamford Road, Oakleigh, Melbourne 3166, Australia
Ruiz de Alarcón 13, 28014 Madrid, Spain

First published 2000

Printed in the United States of America

Typeface Times Roman 10.5/13 pt.   *System* QuarkXPress [BTS]

A catalog record for this book is available from the British Library.

Library of Congress Cataloging in Publication Data

Bodenhorn, Howard.
     A history of banking in antebellum America: Financial markets and economic
development in an era of nation-building / Howard Bodenhorn.
          p.   cm.
     Includes bibliographical references and index.
     ISBN 0–521–66285–0. – ISBN 0–521–66999–5 (pbk.)
     1. Banks and banking–United States–History.   I. Title.
HG2472.B63   2000
332.1'0973 – dc21   99–13089
                                                                          CIP

ISBN   0 521 66285 0   hardback
ISBN   0 521 66999 5   paperback

To Nadine, Elmetta, Fay, and Irene, who never let me doubt the importance of learning

Contents

ix

It is not possible to introduce into a single volume all that is curious or interesting about banks; and scarcely less difficult to avoid some things that may appear trifling or impertinent.

J. S. Gibbons, 1859

List of Tables and Figures

Tables

xi

Figures

Preface

In *Enterprise*, his comprehensive history of the American economy, Stuart Bruchey laments that the relationships between money, bank credit, and economic growth raise a host of intriguing questions that historians, economic or otherwise, have largely ignored. He attributes the lack of attention given these complex interactions with a preoccupation with the politics of early American banking, particularly with the politics of the Second Bank of the United States. Despite his lamentation, the Bank War and the politics of banking take center stage in Bruchey's chapter on pre–Civil War banking. This observation is not offered as criticism, but to indicate the state of current knowledge on antebellum banking. Bruchey's book, in fact, little differs from any other economic history textbook. All those with which I am familiar focus on the activities of the Second Bank and so-called wildcat banking. But then that is not particularly surprising as those are the topics that have fascinated generations of banking historians, and it is the textbook writer's task to summarize and synthesize the existing state of knowledge.

Despite the lack of attention it has received, one of the most important questions in the study of financial institutions – if not the single most important question – is the effect financial intermediaries have on economic growth and development. Does, for example, the size and scope of a country's financial superstructure relative to national income or product exert a measurable influence on the pace or pattern of economic development? How rapidly does a country's financial superstructure expand? What fraction of a country's investment is financed with the assistance of the financial sector compared to internal finance? What types of financial instruments are available to borrowers and savers? How far do they penetrate into the economy? How specialized are intermediaries? What is their geographic distribution, and is it optimal in some sense? What effect does the geographic distribution of financial intermediaries have on the geographic allocation of capital? Though these are easy questions to ask, answers are difficult and precarious. Although the pages that follow offer answers to many of these questions, the reader who is looking for universal and immutable answers may be well advised to stop here.

To those already well versed in the literature and comfortable with the historiography of early American banking, this book will be, I hope, both informative and troubling: informative because a wealth of sources not previously tapped are employed; troubling because the interpretations differ in many respects from the most notable writers, namely, Bray Hammond and Fritz Redlich. In both intent and tools, this study is substantially different from theirs. Redlich approached the subject from a biographical perspective, providing a study of the people and personalities that shaped banking theory and banking policy (which, according to Redlich, had little effective overlap) in nineteenth-century America. It differs from Hammond's too. Hammond noted that American banking has traditionally been studied primarily as a source of instability in the American economy. And while he objected to that approach – at least he said he did – it was that tradition that shaped a great many of his impressions, helped select a great deal of his subject matter, and generated a great many of his conclusions. But such is not to discount the value of Hammond's magnum opus, as few books in economic history have rivaled it for both longevity and influence. Hammond's interpretations, of course, have not gone unchallenged, but they set the tone for a host of subsequent banking studies. Most of the research on the banking industry appearing in the two decades following the publication of his book accepted the notion that banks were "quasipublic" enterprises that competition would not and could not keep in check. Even Milton Friedman and Anna Schwartz, advocates of laissez-faire in nearly all other economic activities, accepted the notion in their classic *Monetary History of the United States* that banks were fundamentally different and required close oversight and regulation.

Hammond's "lesson from history," if you will, provided an intellectual underpinning to the notion that the government should regulate banking and the more centralized the system, the better.

While not wishing to tread too far into the murky waters of policy prescription, this endeavor does, at several points confront Hammond's implication that regulation is always necessary and usually beneficial. Relevant policy prescriptions are, in fact, largely beyond the pale for economic historians, who have a difficult enough time drawing plausible and reasonable interpretations from scattered, disconnected, and incomplete bits and pieces of information. Economic historians are often spared the onus of offering policy prescriptions, but that advantage is generally offset by the disadvantage of having less than complete information. And of all the various subdisciplines of economic history, few offer a more frustrating paucity of data than financial history, a complaint repeated by scholars since the inception of the study of American financial markets. In 1816 Mathew Carey expressed his frustration when he wrote that the "arcana of banking are guarded with Masonic rigour and rarely come before the public in such an authentic and tangible form as to admit to being the basis of argument."

Although considerable amounts of data (like D. N. McCloskey, I prefer the term *capta* – things seized – as opposed to *data* – things given) have become available since 1816, there remain yawning gaps in our understanding of early American banking, not always because historians have failed to ask the appropriate questions, but because they have failed to uncover the information necessary to formulate defensible answers. At more junctures than would have been preferred, the same problems were confronted in the present study. We are left therefore to remain patient and accept the unpleasant reality that statistical dark corners are illuminated only gradually.

The centerpiece of this work is the *domestic* capital market – more specifically, the commercial banking industry and the short-term capital market – and its relation to the pace and pattern of economic growth observed in antebellum America. In this, the present study differs from most previous work in that it does not deal explicitly with the monetary function of banks. Instead, I concern myself with the credit-generating function of banks. The questions of interest are: Did the establishment of banks represent a necessary precondition for economic growth? Did banks effect an efficient allocation of funds between sectors? Did they effect an efficient geographic allocation of funds? And if they did, what were the organizations and institutions fostering these efficient allocations? The answers, briefly, are that while banks may not have been a necessary precondition, their presence or absence certainly influenced the subsequent rate of growth; that they did promote an efficient sectoral and geographic allocation of funds; and that a complex institutional structure arose, sometimes influenced by exogenous technological advances, to mobilize capital and move it into its most productive employments.

The reader will quickly become aware that a variety of data from a broad spectrum of sources has been compiled to address these issues. In some cases, the work is decidedly macroeconomic in approach; in others, it is decidedly microeconomic. Satisfactory answers often require a multitude of approaches, and both were used here. Fritz Redlich noted long ago that there are two kinds of scholars: those who like to dig up little treasures and those who like to climb mountains and paint a sweeping landscape. In my own case, there is a general preference for the former. Finding interesting facts in dusty ledgers has provided me with an innumerable number of scientific "aha's" of unmeasurable personal utility. But then, climbing mountains also holds a special appeal. There is, of course, no reason why the two need be mutually exclusive – efficient division of labor notwithstanding. What follows may, in fact, be characterized as a climb up a mountain interrupted by an occasional archaeological dig along the way.

D. N. McCloskey argues that female scholars, for whatever reason, develop an intimate relationship with their subject. It is, as she says, a thing that becomes dear to them for a period of time. Her assertion may be true – it deserves, as McCloskey would undoubtedly admit, more than casual empiricism before a firm conclusion can be reached. It is my belief, however, that historians, and economic historians particularly, do in fact develop a deep and lasting affection for their favorite subject. (Note, for example, Robert Fogel, for whom two volumes and a ream of papers on slavery did not suffice – two more volumes were called for before he could still his pen on the subject; or McCloskey on Britain's industrial (non)failure; or Robert Gallman on pre-1900 economic growth and capital formation; or Douglass North on the role of institutions; or Lance Davis on capital markets.) Such has certainly been true in my case. For the better part of a decade, early American banking has absorbed my thoughts, sometimes to my colleagues' and certainly to my wife's chagrin.

My interest in the subject began in Eugene White's economic history course. Eugene asked us to read several articles on free banking, as well as a section of Hammond's classic study, and write an essay addressing some topic Eugene believed to be important (I do not remember exactly the topic, and the essay has since fallen by the wayside). Of course, the question he asked could have been answered from the material contained in those readings, but the question he asked was not the one that interested me. Hunting down some original sources (a couple of U.S. House documents and the 1860 census compendium, if memory serves), I gathered some data and asked and answered a completely different question. Eugene, of course, gave me a "B" on the essay because I had wandered off into what he believed to be a tangential and necessarily less interesting issue than the one he proposed.

Nevertheless, my interest in nineteenth-century banking was piqued, and I have stayed the course ever since. Had I known at the time what I was getting into, I may not have followed this path – the sheer volume of work on antebellum banking is astoundingly large and seemingly growing at a nearly exponential rate. Hugh Rockoff, of course, knew this and tried to persuade me to follow some other course, but I persisted. What follows is the result of that persistence. I can only hope that the reader will give it a better mark than Eugene gave me on my first foray into the subject and that Hugh will not consider it time ill spent. I must admit that, at times, I have considered the pond of antebellum American banking history pretty well fished out, but many previous interpretations I have found not to my liking or less than convincing and have continued casting my linc. I now leave it to the reader to determine if it was, in fact, time well spent. And, upon reflection, I now realize that many good-sized fish remain in this pond. There remain a multitude of unanswered questions. But those, regrettably, are left to others.

My travel to various archives was funded with several grants. A John E. Rovensky Dissertation Fellowship supported collection of data at the State Library of Kentucky in Frankfort and the University of Tennessee Library at Knoxville. A graduate study grant from Rutgers funded the collection of materials at the State Library of Pennsylvania. Financial support from St. Lawrence University and

Lafayette College funded several research forays into the archives at the Library of Virginia and the Virginia Historical Society. A Cole Grant-in-Aid from the Economic History Association funded the collection of the data on the private banking house of Branch & Sons of Petersburg, Virginia and the Bank of Cape Fear. A John M. Olin Faculty Fellowship, however, was critical to the completion of this manuscript as it afforded me a year away from my teaching responsibilities and it was during that year that the manuscript was completed.

Many of the issues dealt with below have appeared in several articles, but the present study expands considerably on them and reflects some changes in my thinking. Some of the issues addressed in Chapter 3 appeared in "Private Banking in Antebellum Virginia: Thomas Branch & Sons of Petersburg," *Business History Review* (forthcoming). Chapter 4 pulls together much of the material first reported in "Capital Mobility and Financial Integration in Antebellum America," *Journal of Economic History* 52 (September 1992), pp. 585–610 and in "Regional Interest Rates in Antebellum America," (coauthored with Hugh Rockoff) in Claudia Goldin and Hugh Rockoff, eds., *Strategic Factors in American Economic History: A Volume to Honor Robert W. Fogel* (Chicago: University of Chicago Press, 1992). Chapter 5 represents a more complete discussion of issues first raised in the 1992 *Journal of Economic History* article. Some of the issues raised in the Epilogue were first published in "A More Perfect Union: Regional Interest Rates in the Twentieth Century United States," in Michael Bordo and Richard Sylla, eds., *Anglo-American Financial Systems: Institutions and Markets in the Twentieth Century* (Burr Ridge, IL: Irwin, 1996).

In the process of writing this book and the host of earlier articles wherein preliminary answers to some of the questions posed here were offered, I have received helpful comments from too many people to acknowledge them all. Seminar participants at Rutgers University, Miami University (Ohio), St. Lawrence University, Wellesley College, and the University of Akron, as well as participants at the 1990 Cliometric Society Conference, the NBER conference honoring Robert Fogel (1991), and the NYU/Salomon Brothers Conference on Anglo-American Finance (1993), offered many helpful comments. Special thanks, however, go to Charlie Calomiris, Lance Davis, Mike Haupert, John James, Larry Schweikart, Gene

Smiley, and Dick Sylla, all of whom offered constructive criticisms along the way. My deepest appreciation goes out to Michael Bordo, Stanley Engerman, Richard Grossman, Naomi Lamoreaux, Kerry Odell, Angela Redish, Hugh Rockoff, and Eugene White, who read and commented on earlier drafts of this monograph. Because the work has evolved and is much changed since they first read it, however, they should be absolved from any responsibility for errors of fact or interpretation.

1 Introduction: Historical Setting and Three Views of Banking

Credit, in some form or other, is the principal lever of business operations
New York Bank Commissioners (1831)

The banker, therefore, is not so much primarily a middleman in the commodity
"purchasing power" as a producer of this commodity. . . . He stands between those
who wish to form new combinations and the possessors of productive means. He
is essentially a phenomenon of development. . . . He makes possible the carrying
out of new combinations, authorises people, in the name of society as it were, to
form them. He is the ephor of the exchange economy.
Joseph Schumpeter (1934)

SETTING THE STAGE

The hallmark, some may even argue – as many did during the era of
Manifest Destiny – the birthright, of America is growth: growth in
population, geography, economy. When Robert R. Livingston and
James Monroe, under President Thomas Jefferson's direction, nego-
tiated the purchase of the Louisiana Territory from Napoleon for the
paltry sum of four cents per acre, the United States was, with a population of about five million souls, confined to a tiny strip of land
bounded by the Atlantic to the east and the Appalachians to the west.
It was a marginal nation – marginal militarily, politically, and economically – on the periphery of the Western world. But it was not to
remain so. The Louisiana Purchase, which Jefferson believed would
accommodate the next one hundred generations of Americans, nearly

1

doubled the nation's territorial expanse. The error of Jefferson's expectations soon became apparent, however. A birthrate half again as great as Europe's and unprecedented waves of immigration produced a population that grew by about 35 percent every decade, and one that rapidly peopled Jefferson's territorial legacy. Through a series of treaties and military conquests, the nation again nearly doubled in size between 1804 and 1850, a broad expanse also quickly peopled by a population that doubled between 1800 and 1820 and more than doubled again between 1820 and 1850.[1] On the eve of the Civil War, the United States was home to nearly thirty-two million people strewn across more than three million square miles.[2]

Within a half-century of the ratification of the Constitution the United States clearly underwent a remarkable transformation and became something more than an "insignificant nation on the European periphery."[3] Population increase and the opening to immigration of a vast new territory prompted wave upon wave of internal (and international) migration. In 1790 the geographic center of the American population lay in Kent County, Maryland some twenty-three miles *east* of Baltimore. By 1850 the center of the population had shifted to about twenty-three miles southeast of Parkersburg, Virginia (now West Virginia).[4] Over the subsequent decade the population continued its inexorable westward march and the geographic center crossed the Ohio River, establishing itself a few miles east of Chillicothe, Ohio.[5] Ohio, which itself had been an insignificant region on the periphery of the American economy in 1790, had by the Civil War become the third most populous state in the republic. By 1860 Illinois, Indiana, and Missouri, each inhabited mostly by native Americans and itinerant hunters and trappers in 1790, had more than one million souls.[6]

Accompanying these increases in population and geography was an equally, possibly more, impressive increase in economic output, both in the aggregate and per capita. Between 1840 and 1860 the population increased at a rate that implied a doubling every twenty-three

1. McPherson, *Battle Cry of Freedom*, pp. 6, 9.
2. Foner and Garraty, *Reader's Companion*, pp. 681–2.
3. McPherson, *Battle Cry of Freedom*, p. 9.
4. U.S. Department of Commerce, *Statistical Abstract*.
5. Norris, *R. G. Dun & Company*, pp. 4–5.
6. U.S. Census Bureau, *Population* (1870), p. 3.

years, yet real aggregate economic output expanded at a rate that implied a doubling every fifteen years.[7] To some economic historians, most notably Walt Whitman Rostow, such large and sustained increases in real per capita output signified that the United States had, sometime between 1840 and 1860, achieved "take-off" – that is, a "decisive interval in the history of a society when [economic growth] becomes its normal condition."[8]

For Rostow and others sympathetic to his interpretive framework, take-off results from three convergent influences: (1) a rapid rise in the rate of productive investment, (2) the development of one or more leading, technologically sophisticated industries, and (3) the "emergence of a political, social, and institutional framework which exploits the impulses to expansion in the modern sector . . . and gives growth an on-going character."[9] As appealing as Rostow's grand space-age metaphor may be, many remain skeptical and recent research into the pace and pattern of American economic growth suggests that few developed or developing countries experienced anything like true take-off. This was particularly true for the United States. Paul David, for example, by pulling together scattered scraps of evidence from a variety of sources and employing an ingenious estimating technique argued that there was little support for the notion that the U.S. economy experienced a Rostovian take-off in the 1840s or thereabouts. Instead, David's conjectural estimates point to an average annual increase in real per capita income between 1800 and 1835 of about 1.2 percent. Between 1835 and 1860, real per capita output grew by about 1.3 percent annually. David's conjectures imply a very slight acceleration, but suggest an economic transformation something less dramatic than a take-off.[10]

Utilizing data uncovered since David's conjectural estimates first appeared, Thomas Weiss recently revisited David's procedures, producing new conjectures concerning the pace of economic growth in the first half of the nineteenth century. Weiss's conjectures provide a somewhat different portrait of antebellum America. His estimates suggest a pattern of slightly accelerating economic growth. Between

---

7. Engerman and Gallman, "U.S. Economic Growth," p. 10; and U.S. Census Bureau, *Population* (1870), p. 3. The number of years required for a given series to double can be approximated by dividing 72 by the average annual growth rate of that series.
8. Rostow, *Stages of Economic Growth*, pp. 36, 38.
9. Ibid., p. 39.
10. David, "Growth of Real Product," pp. 155–7.

1800 and 1820, for example, real per capita output increased by about 0.4 percent per annum. Between 1820 and 1840, by 1.2 percent; and by 1.6 percent between 1840 and 1860.[11] Clearly, then, real economic activity was accelerating throughout the antebellum period, but that acceleration occurred prior to Rostow's dating. There is, in fact, little evidence of take-off per se, though the United States did experience a gradual upward trend in growth rates of economic output. Viewed from a longer-term perspective, noted Barry Poulson, "the transition to modern economic growth was not sharp and discontinuous, but rather covered a long period marked by episodes of economic growth and retardation."[12]

To date no general consensus has been reached concerning the nature and timing of economic growth and development in the antebellum economy.[13] Stanley Engerman and Robert Gallman, in their survey of the empirical literature, concluded that the decades encompassing 1807 to 1837 were, in fact, ones of economic growth and structural change (generally referred to as economic development).[14] During these decades, production was moving from the home and the artisan's shop to the factory. Real per capita output was expanding rapidly as was real per capita income. Though rising at rates that seem low by modern standards, the increases were impressive relative to the preceding half-century or so. While most might accept this characterization, debate begins when discussions about relative rates of growth and their timing arise. "Some scholars," as Engerman and Gallman noted, "would argue that acceleration was in evidence before the Civil War; others, only after it. But neither group would hold that acceleration was sudden; both see it as a fairly gradual process."[15] And this seems, for the time being, to be the best way of looking at things.

The issue yet to be resolved, and the one with which this book is chiefly concerned, is the role of banks and financial intermediaries in this "fairly gradual process." While mountains of work have been

11. Weiss, "Economic Growth before 1860," table 1.6, p. 24.
12. Poulson, "Economic History and Economic Development," p. 73.
13. The one exception to this statement might be a general antipathy toward Rostow's take-off schema. Though his notion of the process of growth and development has been largely abandoned, it remains as a monument (though often unrecognized as such) of the cliometric revolution. It was the provocative nature of his interpretation that spawned the search for answers that ultimately uncovered its shortcomings.
14. Engerman and Gallman, "U.S. Economic Growth," p. 17.
15. Ibid.

amassed considering the effects of increases in the traditionally defined, tripartite factors of production (land, labor, and capital – even technology), considerably less work has considered the role of financial intermediaries despite Douglass North's assertion that "capital formation in the nineteenth century is a story of successive improvements in financial mediation by organizations taking advantage of the opportunities created by the basic institutional framework."[16]

BANKS AND CAPITAL, REAL AND FINANCIAL

Prior to, or at least concurrent with, the onset of modern economic growth in most developed countries was an increase in the productive capital stock. While Kenneth Sokoloff has disputed the notion of capital deepening in early antebellum America, substantial capital accumulations were required to maintain even a given capital/labor ratio with an increasing share of the labor force engaged in manufacturing, however defined.[17] And estimates of the nineteenth-century American capital stock imply a pattern of economic development similar to that implied by research on real wages and per capita income. Gallman's research suggests that between 1800 and 1840 the domestic capital stock increased at an average annual rate of about 4 percent. Between 1840 and 1860, it increased at about 6 percent. To Gallman this was clear evidence of a "broad pattern ... of an early [pre-Civil War] acceleration" in the pace of economic growth and the onset of modern development.[18]

Not only did increases in the capital stock, both in aggregate and per capita, suggest a quickening of economic growth in the mid- to late-antebellum years, but the changing composition of American capital also supports that conclusion. Like Sokoloff, Gallman noted that prior to 1840 the nature of capital investment changed very little, implying an expanded utilization of existing technologies. The period after 1840, however, witnessed a change in the nature of capital investment. The share of animals in the total dropped sharply, the

16. North, "Institutional Change in American Economic History," pp. 97–8.
17. Sokoloff, "Invention, Innovation, and Manufacturing," pp. 346, 358; Sokoloff, "Productivity Growth in Manufacturing," p. 681.
18. Gallman, "American Economic Growth before the Civil War," table 2.4, pp. 88–9.

share of structures increased modestly, but most notably the share of equipment rose markedly. The United States in the late antebellum era, wrote Gallman, was "an economy shifting in the direction of industrial activity and modern economic growth."[19]

Capital accumulation, like that occurring during the antebellum era, required increased rates of investment and savings. Lance Davis and Gallman's research suggest a general rise in the rate of capital formation in the early nineteenth century that predated the transition to modern economic growth, and that capital formation followed a pattern of long swings or Kuznets cycles similar to overall economic activity. The underlying cause of the increased rate of capital formation remains clouded, but Davis and Gallman suggested two possible explanations. One, that the investment function shifted in response to changes in aggregate demand.[20] The second, and the one they preferred, was that the savings function shifted out (relatively more, at least, than the investment function) largely as a result of increased savings rates among households. They offered four potential explanations of this shift in the savings function: (1) a simple change in consumer preferences toward future over present consumption; (2) an increase in per capita income with savings being income-elastic; (3) an increase in the returns to savings with savings being interest-elastic; and (4) a change in the composition of the group constituting the personal savings sector.[21]

Davis and Gallman focused on the last of these explanations and, in effect, argued that the apparently rapid rise in the savings rate was just that – more apparent than real, largely because savings took a different form in the latter half of the antebellum era. Farmers, they argued, tended to save more from current income than their urban counterparts, which would suggest that as labor migrated from agriculture to manufacturing in the nineteenth century the savings rate should have diminished. The noted rise in the savings rate was an increase in the *measured* savings rate not the actual savings rate. Early in the nineteenth century, before reasonably modern financial markets had penetrated the hinterlands, farmers had a single outlet for their savings – more labor and less leisure, particularly more labor invested in such nontraditional and unmeasured forms as land and

19. Ibid., p. 93.
20. Davis and Gallman, "Capital Formation," p. 25.
21. Ibid., pp. 48–9.

building improvements. Off-season labor became embodied physical farm capital. Once the financial sector extended its reach into the hinterlands, as it did after 1820 or so, financial instruments became an outlet for rural savings. No longer reliant only on capital improvements to their farms as a retirement fund, farmers faced a choice between physical and financial capital as alternative repositories for their savings.

Realizing this shift in the composition of capital required changed attitudes toward the exchange of physical for financial capital, and Davis and Gallman argued that this shift occurred in the nineteenth century. "Traditionally willing only to invest in assets he could touch," they wrote, "the saver . . . gradually became willing to hold scraps of paper representing real assets located far away in both space and experience."[22] Davis and Gallman believe these attitudes changed little by little, reaching full flower only in the postbellum era. The demands of Civil War finance followed by massive railroad and other corporate debt and equity issues in the postbellum era extended the scale and scope of financial markets and brought about the transformation. It seems likely, however, that the saver's willingness – even the rural saver's willingness – to hold these scraps of paper, symbolic capital as Davis and Gallman labeled it, arose considerably earlier. Banknotes were scraps of paper – symbolic capital – backed as they were by a simple corporate promise to deliver a physical asset at a future date, which from many people's point of view was something beyond the pale in both space and experience.

Not denying the importance of the fourth factor suggested by Davis and Gallman, their latter argument suggested that the third factor they identified – an increase in the returns to savings with savings being interest-elastic – was of equal importance. In the earliest stages of development financial saving was not nearly as sophisticated as it was to become. Savings, instead of taking form in the shape of corporate securities, government debt and the like, was embodied in money holdings. To the earliest American savers, the choice was not between a sophisticated, well-diversified mutual-fund and land improvements. It may have been, and most likely was, a choice between money holdings and additional physical assets. In 1800 banks and thus bank-supplied currencies were relatively

22. Ibid., p. 62.

unknown in the hinterlands. By 1820 banks had extended their reach and were monetizing at least some parts of the rural economy. And as banks became better known, more reputable, more established, and therefore more trusted, the return to holding real balances increased as a result of relatively low inflation rates, the increased ease of transacting with currency, and its increasing stability in expected value. Increases in the real return on money increased the demand for it and hence the equilibrium stock desired at any income level.[23] The economy experienced, to borrow Edward Shaw's terminology, monetary and financial deepening.

Both Shaw and Ronald McKinnon argued that money holdings and real capital accumulations were highly complementary in the early stages of economic development.[24] That is, conditions that made an increase in holding real cash balances attractive enhanced rather than inhibited private incentives to accumulate capital. The Shaw-McKinnon conclusion stands in sharp contrast to both the dominant Keynesian and monetarist models, which both hold that real cash balances substitute for capital accumulation. That is, both schools view money as a form of wealth that competed with other assets in wealth portfolios. But Shaw and McKinnon believed that such models were inappropriate vehicles for analyzing events in a developing country. Instead, the dominant paradigm was designed to highlight the implications of money holding on growth in a mature economy with well-functioning markets and a fiat currency issued by a monopoly central bank. Few, if any, of these prerequisites held in early nineteenth century America or most other developing countries. Eliminating, or even reversing these assumptions, leads to a world in which real cash balances were held because money was the only available financial instrument that could be freely bought and sold. Given this, if the

23. The return on money holdings need not be pecuniary. Money holdings were another form of asset accumulation (that is, they could be held as an alternative to physical assets, which tend to decay or depreciate depending on the exact form of the asset), which served as a store of value. In addition, money holdings decreased the costs of transacting – a benefit that could, theoretically at least, be measured and included in the real return to money holding. Modern monetary theory assumes that the real return on money is the negative of the inflation rate. This may be reasonable in an economy with a host of financial securities with a positive (nominal) return. Financial markets in developing countries, on the other hand, are not so sophisticated and money may be the only nonphysical asset widely available to small savers.
24. McKinnon, *Money and Capital*, pp. 43, 56–7 and chapter 5; Shaw, *Financial Deepening*, chapter 2.

desired level of investment increased for any given level of income, the average ratio of real cash balances-to-income would also increase. The emergence of banks and bank-supplied currency then directly affected the rate of capital accumulation. Bank-supplied currency performed its dual role as both a medium of exchange and a store of wealth. And as real cash balances were debt in that they represented liabilities generated in the intermediation process, money holding was not a distinct form of wealth, but was part and parcel of the process of capital accumulation.

A second crucial factor in the mobilization of capital – of drawing it from hoards and shifting from familial to impersonal lending – was the emergence of market-determined interest rates after about 1780. Winifred Rothenberg found that before the American Revolution debt documents rarely reported rates of interest. Interest, if it was charged at all (a debatable point according to Rothenberg) was reported simply as "lawful interest," or 6 percent in Massachusetts. Beginning in the 1780s, interest rates began rising sometimes as high as 9 percent, "floating free of their ancient and customary restraints."[25] Setting rates free of customary restraints allowed rates of return on financial instruments to compete with returns on physical capital, thereby making paper assets an attractive substitute for physical assets. This simple change was, as Rothenberg noted, "a phenomenon critical to the historical development of capital markets."[26]

To Shaw and other scholars who have studied the relationship between financial and economic development, the appearance of free-floating interest rates was necessary for a shift in economic momentum. Low effective interest rates, whether set by custom, law, or religious conviction, made bankers and money lenders "inert, content to service traditional borrowers and extract [their] monopoly profits from wide margins between low real loan rates and much lower real" returns on cash balances.[27] Freeing interest rates from their traditional limits, in combination with the development of a more competitive financial sector, encouraged lending to nontraditional borrowers whose projects may have been riskier than traditional enterprises, but were the ones most likely to encourage mercantile and industrial innovation and, hence, growth and development.

25. Rothenberg, "Emergence of a Capital Market," p. 790.
26. Ibid., p. 790.
27. Shaw, *Financial Deepening*, p. 123.

While the initial stirrings of financial modernity first appeared in the late eighteenth century, it was in the initial decades of the nineteenth century that they became broadly evident. Richard Sylla, Jack Wilson, and Charles Jones developed an impressive time series of financial returns on various financial instruments (corporate stocks, government bonds, and commercial paper) and suggested that "stock and bond data indicate that something like a financial watershed occurred around 1815."[28] The break was most evident in the stock market, where returns in the period 1815 to 1850 were substantially higher than in preceding decades. The 1815 to 1850 period, as well, demonstrated the least variability in stock returns in the 200 year period covered. It was, they noted, the longest and strongest bull market ever experienced in the United States. Although inferences drawn about general economic growth from admittedly small scraps of financial data should be taken with caution, they note that the "financial watershed that is evident around 1815 is consistent with other evidence that the pace of economic development quickened around that time."[29]

It was surely no coincidence that growth in the American commercial banking industry experienced one of its most fecund periods in the decades preceding and surrounding the great bull market. In 1790 there were only three chartered commercial banks in the United States. By 1815 there were 212; by 1835, 584; and that despite a war, an embargo, and a deep recession in the late 1810s and early 1820s. The question that naturally arises is: Which was the driving force? Did banks simply tag along on the coattails and capture the benefits of broader economic change? Or, did the arrival of banks predate – in some broad sense – the accelerating pace of economic growth occurring some time after 1820?

If the dating provided by David and Weiss's conjectures and those of Sylla, Wilson, and Jones are even approximately correct, there are two interpretations. One, and the one probably most appealing to most economic historians, is that the changes were largely concurrent, as concurrent, at least, as historical events approximately dated can be believed to be. The other, assuming that the dating of a financial watershed around 1815 is approximately correct and accepting that the 1820 to 1840 economic watershed occurred closer to 1840

28. Sylla, Wilson and Jones, "U.S. Financial Markets," p. 34.
29. Ibid., p. 40.

than 1820 (which Gallman's research on the domestic capital stock suggests), is that the initial rumblings of modern financial development predated the initial stirrings of modern economic growth by a decade or two or more.

As with many issues in economics and economic history, there is nothing like consensus on the question of which came first – financial or real sector growth and development. Many believe that broader economic development leads narrower financial development. Joan Robinson, summarizing this view quite succinctly, wrote that "where enterprise leads finance follows."[30] Other notable economists posited an alternative line of causation. Joseph Schumpeter and Alexander Gerschenkron, for example, suggested that financial development was a necessary prerequisite for general economic development. Financial development must occur first in order to siphon financial capital from the equilibrium circular flow and channel it to innovative entrepreneurs.[31]

Hugh Patrick labeled these competing views the "demand-following" and "supply-leading" theories of the relationship between financial and economic development. The demand-following thesis posits that as the economy developed the demand for financial services increased, which provoked a supply response. The demand for banking services depended on growth of real output and income which depended, in turn, on the commercialization of agriculture, the expansion of trade, and the development of a protomodern industrial sector. The more rapid these developments, the greater the demand by enterprises for external finance and, therefore, financial intermediation as high-growth industries could not rely on internal funds to finance fixed or working capital. "In this case, the evolutionary development of the financial system is a continuing consequence of the pervasive, sweeping process of development."[32]

The demand-following position implies that financial intermediaries were passive agents, permissive of growth. As economic growth and development intensified, financial markets arose, grew and matured, and their increasing sophistication, in turn, fed back as a

---

30. Robinson, "Generalizations of the General Theory," p. 86.
31. Schumpeter, *Theory of Economic Development*, chapter 3; Gerschenkron, *Economic Backwardness*, chapter 2. See also Cameron, *Banking in the Early Stages*; Cameron, *Banking and Economic Development*; and Goldsmith, *Financial Structure and Economic Development*, p. 48 for similar conclusions.
32. Patrick, "Financial Development," pp. 174–5.

stimulant to further economic growth. This view follows from two rather large, typically unstated, assumptions. One, that the supply of financial entrepreneurship was highly elastic relative to the industry's profit potential. The second, that a favorable legal, institutional, and economic environment conducive to the founding of banks and other financial intermediaries existed at the onset of economic development.[33]

The first condition was apparently met in antebellum America. Most states were required to enact statutes with rather severe penalties to curb the formation and operation of private banking in order to protect the monopoly or oligopoly positions of state-chartered banks. And free banking, where it was encouraged, was typically followed by an influx of new banks. Clearly, financial entrepreneurship was alive and well in early America. As for the second condition, a hospitable institutional environment, America too excelled. Douglass North has repeatedly pointed out America's acceptance, even encouragement, of entrepreneurship and risk-taking. To North it was the adaptability of both the society's formal rules and informal constraints embodied in attitudes and values that produced an economic environment that rewarded economic adventurism.[34] Similarly, a decentralized, federal, Madisonian polity encouraged experimentation and adaptation of institutions to local needs or preferences. Nowhere were the results of this decentralized federalism more evident than in banking policy. With the exception of the First and Second Banks of the United States, antebellum banks were creatures of the individual states themselves, reflecting the desires, even the whims, of local residents. Banks in New England little resembled banks in the Deep South in terms of size, organization, charter requirements, and whatnot. Nevertheless, they all were designed to pursue the same goals – the provision of monetary and intermediation services. The decentralized nature of the polity allowed for a regional flexibility with the result that banks "grew more and more different over time, like the beaks of Darwin's finches."[35]

The supply-leading hypothesis, most closely associated with the seminal works of Schumpeter and Gerschenkron, has until quite recently, received considerably less attention. Strong versions of this

33. Ibid., p. 174.
34. North, "Institutional Change in American Economic History," p. 96.
35. Friedman, *Crime and Punishment*, p. 263.

hypothesis hold that the creation of financial institutions and the supply of financial services must arise prior to the demand for them, especially prior to the demands of entrepreneurs in modern, growth-inducing industries. A fundamental shortcoming of the supply-leading view was its narrowness in conception, based as it was on a model of German universal banking, and not widely applicable to many other countries' emergent banking sectors. For this reason, their supply-leading hypothesis has either been rejected or dismissed as inapplicable to a study of most early banking sectors. The result has been a wide acceptance of the competing demand-following hypothesis. Henrietta Larson, to cite but one example, argued that early Anglo-American bankers were largely passive players in the inter-mediation process. They did not, like the German universal banks, actively promote new enterprises. They simply serviced the needs of existing, well-established, highly reputable firms, mostly mercantile concerns. "The *Credit Mobilier* idea was slow to gain support in London [or America]," she wrote, "where the banking traditions made the banker the passive agent in the movement of capital."[36]

A fundamental shortcoming of the supply-leading hypothesis is that a supply-leading financial system may not have been, and prob-ably could not have been, profitable at the outset. Because few nascent modern industries existed, there were few available lending opportunities. As a result, such institutions would typically either be government enterprises or be heavily subsidized, either directly or indirectly, by the government. While Schumpeter and Gerschenkron imagined the Credit Mobilier as their archetype supply-leading bank, several early American banks fit into their framework in a rudimen-tary, somewhat anachronistic, way not envisioned by them. The Bank of the Commonwealth of Kentucky or the Bank of the State of Ten-nessee represented but two examples of banks formed in the early nineteenth century, either wholly owned or heavily subsidized by the state to make low-interest loans to farmers and others to realize those states' agricultural potentials. While not the type of banks envisioned by proponents of the supply-leading hypothesis, these banks nonethe-less promoted the development of commercialized agriculture – a step recognized by most to be the first step on the long path toward economic modernity.

36. Larson, *Jay Cooke*, pp. 86–7.

A *modified* supply-leading hypothesis and one that fits the American experience at several turns is one in which financial institutions arose prior to the development of a modern industrial, manufacturing sector. Picture, if you will, a bank like the Bank of Kentucky or its equivalent chartered in many southern and western states. This bank was initially envisioned by its proponents to aid and support the development of the state's agricultural possibilities. Branches were initially placed in centers of agricultural production, in towns like Maysville, Bowling Green, and Lexington, or places of political clout, like Frankfort. Those men more financially sophisticated than legislators responding to purely political considerations recognized that pure agricultural lending would lead to unbalanced, undiversified, and illiquid portfolios. Through their lobbying activities, the main office was located in Louisville where the directors and principal officers with a controlling voice in the operations of the bank were men with mercantile and manufacturing backgrounds. Once in control of the bank, they bowed to the political reality that the bank must accommodate farmers, but they required that even rural branches invest a large portion of their loanable funds in commercial bills of exchange drawn against shipments of agricultural produce bound for Louisville, New Orleans, New York, or even European cities. The portfolio of the head office in Louisville, on the other hand, was nearly the opposite of those held at the bank's branches. The Louisville office directed most of its credit to established merchants, doling out but small amounts to agriculture. And being in a commercial center, it was also in a position to lend to emerging manufacturing firms.

Institutions such as these initially loaned the lion's share of their funds to traditional – primarily agricultural and commercial – sectors, but gradually altered their portfolios as new industries arose and more profitable or less risky lending opportunities emerged. In this way, banks were profitable from the outset without the need of direct government subsidies. But governments, nevertheless, encouraged the establishment of financial intermediaries by granting them special privileges. These privileges included such things as corporate status with its attendant limited liability, the right of summary diligence whereby lenders could foreclose on delinquent debtors without the formality of court pleadings which lowered the expected costs of lending and risk taking, the right to create liabilities (deposits and banknotes) under unusually favorable circumstances, or simply by granting them local, regional, or even state-wide monopolies until their business was sufficiently entrenched to more easily withstand the rigors of competition.

If this modified supply-leading hypothesis is even approximately applicable to the antebellum experience, the choice of banking structure and policy made by state legislators would have affected each state's subsequent economic growth – given the highly federalist structure of early American polity and assuming that events in one state were slow to spill over into neighboring regions. It is not presumed that supply-leading finance represents a necessary precondition for inaugurating self-sustained economic development. Rather, that choices made at the state level affected the potential for growth through financial intermediation. The sources of growth and development, as Goldsmith noted, were simply too many and too varied for financial intermediation alone to have been its wellspring. But financial development was likely to have been a contributing factor, and probably much more so at the beginning of the process. That view was common among a great many contemporary Americans. In 1835, for example, New York's bank commissioners wrote that:

Banks have justly been esteemed as among the most useful and powerful agents in developing the resources and stimulating the industry of the country.... [Without them, the country] could not have spread half the canvass which now whitens the ocean, or given motion to half the spindles which are now in operation ... and it is to the increased use of credit in its various shapes during the last half century, that the world is mostly indebted for the astonishing rapidity with which manufacturing, commercial and even agricultural improvements have advanced.... It is less than half a century since banks of issue to any considerable extent have been brought into use as parts of this great system of credit, and ought we not to attribute their influence, some portion of the amazing impulse imparted to business during this period.[37]

Banks, it seems clear, were attributed leadership status by contemporary Americans. The issue at hand is to determine just how correct their convictions were.

37. New York General Assembly, *Assembly Document No. 74* (1835), p. 9. See also Gibbons, *Banks of New York*, pp. 12–13 for a similar conclusion.

MONEY AND CREDIT: THE TWIN FUNCTIONS OF BANKS

Given the intensity of the debate surrounding the role of financial intermediation in the process of growth and development, it is clear that banks did something. But it is not clear how important that something was or when, if ever, it became critical. What was that something? Banks in antebellum America, as in other places at other times, served two functions. They supplied the country with a circulating medium (banknotes and deposits) and intermediated between savers and investors. Noting again the importance of capital in realizing the potentials of economic growth, William Parker noted that capital "leads a complicated and curious life."[38] Capital must be financed; that is, it must be paid for before or during the periods during which it is produced. The unique feature of capitalist economy, argued Parker, is that this financing function is provided by one or more of three distinct groups: (1) private individuals who may lend resources to one another; (2) a financial institution that takes in money from one group of people and lends it to another group; and (3) the state, which coins or prints money that it inserts into the circular flow of exchange occurring in the private economy.[39]

Setting aside the first of these three for the moment (it was, of course, an important source of funds, but notoriously difficult to quantify) antebellum America depended on the second – financial intermediaries – in financing its capital and providing its money. The United States Mint was slow in producing an adequate circulating coinage and the various governments' emissions of paper instruments that acted as money were slight to nonexistent. It was bank-issued money that served as the predominant domestic medium of exchange. Peter Temin estimated that there was about $41 million in specie in the United States in 1820 with more than one-half that amount held as bank reserves, leaving then about $20 million of specie in circulation.[40] By comparison, aggregate issues of circulating banknotes, while difficult to estimate for earlier periods in American history, exceeded $36 million by J. Van Fenstermaker's calculations

38. Parker, "Finance of Capital Formation," p. 168.
39. Ibid., p. 168.
40. Temin, *Jacksonian Economy*, table A.2, pp. 186–7.

(probably an underestimate) and bank deposits exceeded $27 million (probably an overestimate).[41] Economic transactions in early America, clearly, were carried out through the medium of bank-supplied currency. Of the $83 million in currency chasing goods around the economy, about 76 percent was bank-supplied.

Bank currency, then, was the lifeblood of commerce in early America and nowhere was its animating influence more profound than in areas of recent settlement. "Each region," wrote Parker, "as it opened up, desperately needed something to use as money to replace the inconveniences and clumsiness of barter trade. Supplying that need could permit wealth to grow and production to increase so that a price level and the liquid means for savings and investment could form."[42] In addition, replacing barter or commodity money with bank-supplied currency reduced the costs of transactions, freed resources to be redirected toward productive ends, and allowed consumers and producers to smooth intertemporal imbalances between receipt and expenditure inherent in a commercial economy.

Besides creating prices and creating liquid forms of investment, there were direct and not inconsequential social savings arising from the appearance of bank-issued currencies. One benefit of the arrival of financial institutions was that individuals could release their holdings or hoards of relatively unproductive precious metals whose value in exchange typically reflected their true opportunity costs (that is, $100 in gold exchanged for $100 in cattle). In the alternative, once money-creating institutions arose, precious metals could be replaced by paper certificates with far lower resource costs (that is, less than 1 cent in paper and ink exchanged for $100 in cattle), which carried promises to be exchangeable into specie at their stated value. This

41. Fenstermaker, *Development*, tables 10 and 11, pp. 66–8. Fenstermaker reported aggregate figures for 145 banks for which he could locate balance sheets for 1820. There were, however, 341 banks in operation. The circulation and deposit figures reported in the text were calculated by taking the average for the 145 reporting banks and multiplying by 341 operating banks. As a result the figures are, at best, rough approximations and because early figures are dominated by reports of urban banks, the estimates probably underestimate banknote circulation and overestimate deposits because urban banks had lower circulation-to-deposit ratios than country banks. Despite the difficulties and biases of this simple calculation, the numbers remain, broadly speaking, informative. An informed and reasonable estimate would place the ration of bank-supplied to total currency in the range of 70 to 80 percent in the 1820s.
42. Parker, "Finance of Capital Formation," pp. 168–9.

process freed up metals to be used in alternative productive uses, whether religious icons, yachting cups, jewelry, or the settlement of foreign exchange claims.

Clearly, the resource costs of fractional-reserve currency carrying a redemption guarantee did not reduce the resource costs of bank-supplied currency to zero as does a fiat currency issued by a central bank. Transactions were still based on specie convertibility and banks were forced to hold bullion and coin to meet redemption demands. But a fractional reserve system remained a cheaper way to provide a given volume of money than did a pure specie basis. Additionally, the use of specie was not reduced to its theoretical minimum because many people remained wary of banks because some banks occasionally failed to meet their redemption promises.

That redemption guarantees were not always honored does little to change the essence of the argument. Occasional reneging on the redemption guarantee may have diminished the use of paper money below its socially optimal level in a risk-free world, but even contemporaries knew that such a place was not and could not be. "Every one knows," wrote one, "that the banking system, wherever and however pursued, is not unattended with the possibility of loss. . . . [But] [i]f our policy is to be founded on indefinite apprehensions, let us extinguish the banking system altogether, and when we have returned to a pure metallic currency, we shall find that the perils of false brethren, of thieves and counterfeiters, of negligence and accident, are yet to be encountered."[43]

Whatever the risks of a bank-supplied currency, it was apparent that most Americans were willing to accept them. They could have done away with banks at any time had the perceived risks and expected costs of bank-supplied currency outweighed the social savings it generated. That Americans chose not to and that they, in fact, continued to accumulate ever larger bank-supplied currency balances should tell us something about their perception of the utility of banks.

Money creation by banks, however important it may have been, was incidental to their most fundamental task – that of intermediating between borrowers and lenders, savers and investors. What is the business of financial intermediaries generally? Early Americans, like

43. Anonymous, *Defence of Country Banks*, p. 15.

Nathan Appleton, believed that banks acted "merely as convenient brokers between the owners of capital, and the persons employing it."[44] One could quibble with his choice of words, but he understood the basic point, that financial intermediation involved a redirection as well as a transformation of funds – twin functions that distinguished intermediaries from other types of economic units.[45] They redirected funds by taking them from the hands (or hoards) of savers and placing them in the hands of investors. And they transformed those funds by taking up one kind of debt instrument (primary debt issued by the ultimate investor) and offering their own debt instruments (banknotes and deposits) in return.

Modern research has laid out a number of reasons why banks were called on to perform these coincident tasks. Scholars such as Eugene Fama, Ben Bernanke, and Mark Gertler, among others, have argued that banks supplied critical intermediary roles to overcome information asymmetries with their resulting agency problems, to minimize monitoring costs, and to resolve differing preferences for maturity, liquidity, and divisibility between savers and investors. Though modern research has offered formal and sophisticated models to support their claims, the basic intuition underlying them was not unknown to nineteenth century Americans. One, writing in the *North American Review* in 1827, noted that "individuals with loanable funds would hardly know who merited their confidence . . . and would frequently allow their funds to lie idle were it not for the intercession of banks. These institutions 'assume the responsibility of the debtor; they relieve the creditor of his anxiety and doubt; they enable him to divide into small portions and transfer some of his risk to those with whom he deals.'"[46] In other words, through their intermediation services banks allowed individuals to lend relatively small sums in relatively liquid form. In addition, banks assumed a greater part of the risk even while reducing it substantially through broad diversification and performed the critical monitoring of the borrowers' behavior. By pooling the funds of hundreds of small savers, banks were able to

---

44. Appleton, *An Examination*, p. 43.
45. Goldsmith, *Financial Institutions*, p. 5.
46. Porter, *North American Review* (1827), quoted in Miller, *Banking Theories*, p. 81. For useful introductions to modern research on the role of banks as intermediaries, see Fama, "What's Different About Banks"; Bernanke and Gertler, "Agency Costs;" Gertler, "Financial Structure"; and sources therein. The applicability of modern research into antebellum institutions is dealt with in greater detail in Chapter 2.

perform these tasks at a much lower aggregate cost than had each of these individuals attempted to lend on their own.

The issue at hand, and one whose consideration will consume the pages that follow, was the importance of banks in their dual roles of money supplier and credit intermediator in promoting economic growth in the first half of the nineteenth century. The theoretical justification that the appearance and development of a financial superstructure facilitated growth is, Goldsmith noted, roughly analogous to the textbook explanation of the advantages of indirect exchange over simple barter. The creation of a gamut of widely available financial instruments (whether they be as simple as fractional reserve banknotes or as complex as inflation-hedged derivative mutual funds) frees households and other economic agents from the "indissoluble tie between their own saving (unconsumed income) and their investment (expenditures on durable assets)."[47] In the absence of widely available, freely exchangeable financial assets each economic unit's savings is necessarily equal to its investment, as seen earlier in the case of farm labor expended in improvements becoming embodied physical capital. Once various financial instruments can be substituted for internally generated capital in a more diversified portfolio of earning assets, each individual's investment may be either larger or smaller than his or her savings.

But the possibility that the introduction of financial instruments may accelerate economic growth requires two additional Schumpeterian assumptions. The first being an unequal distribution of entrepreneurial talents and opportunities. That these differential opportunities are distributed normally, or along any other conceivable nonuniform distribution is not the important point. If all individuals had similar talents and faced similar opportunities, there would be no scenario under which it would be utility-enhancing for society generally to transfer savings from one individual to another. Each person's expected net returns and risks would be equal and, hence, no transfers would occur.[48] Once differential abilities and willingnesses to accept risk are introduced, resource transfers may be utility-enhancing.

The second critical assumption is the indivisibility of many investment projects. Scale or scope economies in large-scale investments

47. Goldsmith, *Financial Structure*, pp. 392–3.
48. Ibid., p. 393.

may, and probably do, exist. Some investors' projects are simply too large to be financed by an individual saver/lender. Instead, they require the combined savings of a number of individuals, each of which may have different preferences toward liquidity, maturity, and risk. Financial instruments of various kinds can be developed that allow for the pooling of scattered pockets of savings while meeting the preferences of various classes of savers. Why else would modern corporations finance themselves through various combinations of bank loans, commercial paper, common stock, preferred stock, bonds, and subordinated debt? Clearly, they are tapping into as large a pool of savings as possible by offering different classes of savers with different preferences a financial instrument that matches their preferences toward liquidity, maturity, and risk.

In antebellum America the range of potential savings vehicles was considerably narrower than in the late twentieth century. Nevertheless, financial intermediaries were critical to the process of creating financial instruments to meet the needs of various classes of savers. Savers faced several alternatives. One was to hold their savings in unproductive hoards, either as inventories of physical assets (say, corn or salt pork) or full-bodied metallic currency. A second was to lend directly to investors and hold the primary securities thus issued by them (say, commercial paper). The presence of banks, however, afforded savers a number of indirect saving vehicles. Those with relatively large amounts of unexpended income could buy bank shares and earn a return reflecting the average return on the bank's portfolio of primary securities while simultaneously accepting risks reflecting the average quality of the portfolio. Those with small amounts of savings, on the other hand, could substitute banknotes or deposits for physical assets, carrying smaller (but still positive) risks.

Banks, in turn, used these funds to invest in primary securities issued by ultimate investors; securities not necessarily suitable to the preferences of small savers. Banks were, as Appleton noted, "convenient brokers" between ultimate savers and ultimate investors that redirected and transformed funds, offering one kind of debt instrument to savers while taking up debt instruments of an altogether different character from investors. In the absence of banks, capital accumulation would certainly have been a slower, more grinding process than it actually was and the pace of economic growth and the process of development may well have taken on a quite different hue;

something that both contemporary and modern writers recognized. Common to all theories of economic growth is an emphasis on capital accumulation and savings and the notion that these must increase if an economy is to experience real growth. While many theories ignore the role of financial institutions, they are an integral component of a market economy as they encourage both savings and investment. And Rondo Cameron argued that "[w]hatever social, psychological, or economic changes may take place to persuade society to desire to save a significantly larger proportion of its net product, the existence or introduction of financial institutions will be necessary to make that decision effective."[49] George Tucker, the first professor of political economy at the University of Virginia, was considerably more blunt. "Credit," he argued, "enters so largely into the dealings and concerns of every civilized [read developed or developing] community, that, if any large part of its operations were suddenly suspended, the whole machinery of society would be at a stand."[50]

PLAN OF THE BOOK

The centerpiece of this book is the *domestic* capital market; more specifically, the commercial banking industry and the short-term capital market. Even here, it differs sharply from previous studies. Earlier studies of early American banking have tended to focus on the money-supply function of banks. This study is not much concerned with those monetary functions. Rather, its principal concern is with their credit-generating and credit-intermediating role. This is not to say that it is safe to ignore their monetary functions. Clearly it is not. Banks, as previously noted, supplied the bulk of the country's circulating media. But their creation of money was incidental to their intermediating of credit. Too often, scholars have not appreciated this link and incorporated it into their analyses. Bray Hammond, at some level, did. He noted that "banks were so often spoken of as 'putting their notes in circulation' that it sounds as if their doing so were an end in itself and presupposed nothing more than perhaps their thrusting notes out the window to be caught by the wind."[51] This analogy

49. Cameron, "Theoretical Bases," p. 4.
50. Tucker, *Theory of Money and Banks*, p. 127.
51. Hammond, *Banks and Politics*, p. 694.

may hold in a simple monetarist theoretical construct with a central bank supplying additions to a fiat currency through helicopter drops or with the morning paper. But such a conception is inapplicable to a world of redeemable bank-supplied currency with no central bank. Currency creation was part and parcel of the intermediation process, of standing between and bringing together savers and investors. Note issue "was necessarily incidental to the accomplishment of loans, purchases, or other transactions that gave the bank earning assets in return."[52]

Chapter 2 turns to the issue at hand, the direct contribution of banks to the development of the American economy. This chapter may be best characterized as macroeconomic in approach. It proceeds by filling in the outlines of the relationship between financial development and economic growth sketched out above. A highly stylized growth model is presented designed to highlight the two paths through which financial development may influence economic development. Simply put, banks can affect economic development either by increasing the pool of savings available to potential investors or by directing capital into more efficient investments than could individual investors seeking out profitable opportunities on their own. Chapter 2 principally addresses the first of these factors; that is, did the size of the financial sector influence economic growth? Using data that are admittedly imperfect, empirical tests nevertheless suggest that initial financial development was an important impetus to subsequent economic growth. While the results suggest a causal mechanism, it must, as was previously noted, be remembered that the causes of growth are simply too many and too varied for a single factor – financial intermediation in this case – to have been the lone wellspring. Nonetheless, its seems clear that financial intermediation was an important factor. Still, "it is not unfair to characterize virtually all of the statements on the causal relationship, if any, between financial development and economic growth as impressionistic."[53] More satisfying, more complete answers await further research utilizing more complete data sets than can be constructed for antebellum America.

Whereas the approach in Chapter 2 is best characterized as macro-

---

52. Ibid.
53. Goldsmith, *Financial Structure*, p. 403.

economic or aggregative in approach, Chapter 3 is decidedly micro-economic in nature. In the course of reviewing the records of ante-bellum banking it very early became apparent that Goldsmith was onto something when he wrote that "I have come more and more to feel that a highly aggregative approach . . . may produce good leads, but is not likely to provide answers to the most interesting questions in the field."[54] In a sense, the data pulled together in Chapter 3 are designed to test the second causal mechanism – increased efficiency of investment – quite possibly the most interesting question. Yet, here again, the test must be indirect and roundabout. For economic development to have proceeded, manufacturing enterprises needed to arise and grow, both in absolute size and in proportion to economic activity generally. For that growth to occur in a timely manner, manufacturers needed access to external finance, notably bank credit. Following the modified supply-leading hypothesis outlined above, bankers – typically being merchants themselves – tended to lend to enterprises and entrepreneurs with whom they were familiar, namely other merchants. As the century wore on, however, and as manufacturing produced a larger share of value added in GDP, the sector's credit demands increased. Banks responded by providing them with more of it. True, it tended to be short-term credit, but much recent research has suggested that short-term or working-capital credit was of far greater importance than long-term fixed capital. With the possible exception of railroads, the emergence of large, integrated firms with massive fixed capital requirements was largely a postbellum phenomenon. While it remains unclear just how well postbellum financial institutions promoted the development of such firms and industries, extant evidence from the antebellum era suggests that manufacturing firms were not starved of bank-supplied credit.

Chapters 4 and 5 turn to a related issue. Although the results presented in Chapters 2 and 3 suggest that banks were mechanisms – maybe even the ghosts in the machine – in economic development, several questions concerning the efficiency with which they performed their critical intermediary function remain. Richard Sylla argued that an important criterion by which to adjudge any banking system is that it demonstrates a "maximum" responsiveness to tech-

54. Ibid., p. ix.

nological and demand-induced changes in the larger economy.[55] In particular, that the speed with which banks alter their intermediary and currency functions in response to changing geographic and sectoral demands keep pace with those changing real sector demands. In short, Sylla's criterion is that capital be, at least reasonably, mobile. Despite Charles Conant's assertion that the "mechanism of modern finance has been devised piece by piece to meet the constantly growing demand for more efficient methods of giving mobility to capital," the recent historiography arising out of the cliometric revolution is radically different.[56]

Studies by Lance Davis, John James, Sylla, and others have suggested that capital was not even reasonably mobile.[57] Davis defined capital immobility such: "Capital can be said to be immobile if savers are unwilling or unable to make their accumulations available to capital users whose activities yield the highest economic returns."[58] Such immobility could result from any number of factors, including the lack of an effective and operative capital market, that savers valued safety above all else, that savers may have been unwilling to invest in enterprises divorced from their personal experience, or if there were substantial noneconomic rewards to investments whose returns were otherwise low (say, marginal farm land). Davis argued that one or more of these factors operated in the early nineteenth century because both ultimate savers and intermediaries were unwilling to move any significant amount of capital across geographic or industrial boundaries. The principal evidence of this presumed lack of mobility was the apparently large differentials in short-term interest rates across regions of the United States in the late nineteenth century. Though not stating the conclusion implicitly, the presumption has been that if late nineteenth-century capital markets failed to engender short-term capital mobility, then early nineteenth-century markets could only have been less effective mobilizers.

While Chapter 3 addresses intersectoral capital movements, Chapters 4 and 5 challenge the traditional conclusion that banks were par-

---

55. Sylla, *American Capital Market*, p. 24.
56. Conant, *Wall Street and the Country*, pp. 3–4.
57. See Davis, "The Investment Market; James, *Money and Capital Markets*; and Sylla, "Federal Policy."
58. Davis, "Capital Immobilities and Finance Capitalism," p. 582.

ticularly ineffective geographic mobilizers of capital. Several series of
state and regional interest rates are developed spanning the antebellum era and suggest that early nineteenth-century financial institutions brought about a reasonable interregional mobility to short-term
capital. Short-term, bank interest rates were nearly equal across a
broad expanse of the country east of the Mississippi River, and when
rates diverged (say, during a financial panic) such divergences were
short-lived, transitory phenomena. Many have suspected that the lack
of federal oversight and a set of consistent rules and regulations for
banks created a dispersed and *dis-integrated* system incapable of
effecting capital transfers. It appears, however, that the opposite was
true. Because they operated under different rules and regulations,
banks could meet the unique needs of their local clientele. The credit
needs of livestock brokers in Indiana differed from those of cotton
factors in Alabama; the needs of grain farmers in the Virginia Pied-
mont differed from those of dairymen in the Berkshires; the demands
of foreign exchange brokers in New Orleans differed from those in
New York. The value of the federalist polity with banking structures
constructed at the state level was that it allowed each state to develop
a set of financial institutions that could cater to these different
demands. Yet, these divergent, state-level systems could communicate
and interact and cooperate. Should short-term capital have become
more valuable in New Orleans than in New York (that is, should
interest rates rise in New Orleans relative to New York), New York
banks stood ready to capitalize on the differentials and could, and
did, transfer funds to profit from them.

Could it have been then that the set of common federal rules and
regulations imposed on national banks during the Civil War era that
created the noted regional divergence in postbellum regional interest rates? What happened in the decade between 1860 and 1870 that
drove regional interest rates apart? The Epilogue provides a preliminary answer and a challenge to the traditional interpretation. While
it deals with an era outside the professed scope of the work, a look
ahead to the twentieth century is useful for two reasons. It overturns
a long-established and widely held stylized fact and offers a much
longer-term look at bank performance in the United States. By
extending regional interest rate series into the mid twentieth century,
it becomes possible to adjudge the performance of the antebellum
period on a comparative basis. Few would reasonably argue that U.S.

financial markets circa 1950 or 1960 operated in pockets of capital immobility. Compared against that standard it becomes apparent that markets of earlier eras, while certainly not as sophisticated, operated efficiently within the technological bounds afforded them.

The result of this study will be to alter the history of early American banking. Instead of being viewed as the root cause of economic instability, banks were in fact a fundamental element in the process of growth and development. It is undoubtedly true that bad bankers existed; at some times and in some places they even throve, more so earlier in U.S. history than later. "Yet from the point of view of the economy," wrote Hammond, "things were not bad enough to check the country's growth. There were more banks that helped than hindered."[59] For some unfortunate reason, historians have been enthralled with the ones that hindered. Here we shall consider by far the largest majority: those that helped.

59. Hammond, *Banks and Politics*, p. 676.

2   Financial Development and Economic Growth in Antebellum America

Our bank officers are invested with a controlling power over the market. They can positively command the ship of commerce, and guide it through the storm, or they can dash it upon the rocks.

J. S. Gibbons (1859)

It is believed to be impossible to account for the rapid augmentation of wealth which is daily witnessed, upon any other hypothesis, than that use which has been made of credit in this country has been exceedingly productive.

New York Bank Commissioners (1835)

Banks are the props of national wealth and industry, not the foundations of them. ... The credit and circulation of bank paper are the effects rather than the causes of a profitable commerce and a well-ordered system of finance.

Logan McKnight (1852)

Now, without intending to underrate the influence of banks ... we have no doubt that their influence upon trade is vastly overrated, and that they are too often looked upon as the leaders rather than the followers of business.

New York Bank Commissioners (1837)

Raymond Goldsmith contended that in most countries a "rough parallelism" could be observed between economic growth and financial development. As real per capita wealth and income increase the financial sector also grows in size, complexity, and sophistication. But Goldsmith was reluctant to assign a causal mechanism because he remained unsure "whether financial factors were responsible for the acceleration of economic development or whether financial develop-

28

ment reflected economic growth whose mainsprings must be sought elsewhere."[1]

The epigraphs at the head of this chapter demonstrate fundamental divisions regarding the importance of banks dating back to the mid-1830s. J. S. Gibbons believed banks affected macroeconomic performance and encouraged economic development. Logan McKnight did not. And, given the reluctance of a scholar of Goldsmith's ability to draw definite conclusions, such disagreements were not unexpected. The New York bank commissioners' about-face, however, is intriguing. In 1835 they held banks and credit in high regard, attributing to them some responsibility for the changes then rippling throughout the economy. Two years later banks had been reduced to a lesser status, that of passive agents pulled along in the sweep of fundamental economic change. The commissioners' changed attitude probably reflected the economic dislocations following the financial panic of 1837 and the banks' inability to right Gibbons's ship of commerce. Regardless of the cause of the commissioners' irresolute opinions, they reflected a difference of opinion concerning the role of financial institutions that remains unresolved to this day.

Traditionally, neoclassical growth models do not place much emphasis on the role of financial institutions in the growth process, particularly their role as intermediaries. Mark Gertler, for one, argued that most macroeconomic theory presumes that whatever financial structure exists operates smoothly, smoothly enough, at least, that theory can abstract out financial considerations.[2] Real business cycle theory, for example, proceeds under the hypothesis that the financial system is irrelevant and, to a first approximation, the same can be said of much of the traditional literature. When financial institutions are dealt with at all, the line of influence moves from their role as suppliers of money to real economic activity not in how well they intermediate between borrowers and savers.

This attitude, while widely held, is less than universal. In a series of studies appearing between 1955 and 1975, John Gurley, Edward Shaw, Raymond Goldsmith, and Ronald McKinnon provided theoretical constructs and empirical studies demonstrating the impor-

1. Goldsmith, *Financial Structure*, p. 48.
2. Gertler, "Financial Structure," p. 559.

tance of financial structure in the process of economic development.[3] But in 1958 the Modigliani-Miller theorem appeared, which derived the formal proposition that real economic decisions were independent of financing choices.[4] In 1980, Eugene Fama extended the Modigliani-Miller theorem to banks.[5] In Fama's construct, "banks hold portfolios on behalf of their depositors because this probably allows them to provide transaction services (the accounting system of exchange) more efficiently, but the portfolio management activities of banks affect nothing, including prices and real activity."[6] Accordingly then, banks assume a very small role in the development process.

Of course, Gurley and Shaw and others envisioned a world far removed from that of the Modigliani-Miller theorem. Those writers emphasizing the importance of banking and other financial intermediaries had in mind a different economic environment than the neoclassical first approximation of perfect competition, perfect information, and perfect foresight. The Gurley-Shaw-McKinnon world was one characterized by imperfect competition (if there was competition at all), by institutional rigidities, by poor information, by unfavorable legal and legislative environments, by high – sometimes prohibitive – transactions costs, by traditional economies where a large proportion of the populace struggled to subsist. Without question, this world is more difficult to model and these scholars had no formal model to offer as an alternative to the compact mathematical Modigliani-Miller theorem. Instead, they could offer only messy and wordy models without simple conclusions. The result has been that, while their work has not been altogether ignored, it has been underappreciated as it did not (and, given the formalistic, mathematical ethos of post-Samuelson economists, could not) provide a serious challenge to neoclassical conclusions.[7]

The remainder of this chapter provides a preliminary test of the

3. Early contributions to the relationship between financial and economic development include, but are limited to, Gurley and Shaw, *Money in a Theory of Finance*; Gurley and Shaw, "Financial Aspects;" Gurley and Shaw, "Financial Intermediaries;" Shaw, *Financial Deepening*; Goldsmith, *Financial Intermediaries*; Goldsmith, *Financial Institutions*; Goldsmith, *Financial Structure*; McKinnon, *Money and Capital*.
4. Modigliani and Miller, "Cost of Capital."
5. Fama, "Banking in a Theory," p. 45.
6. Selgin and White, "How Would the Invisible Hand," p. 1,737.
7. Gertler, "Financial Structure," p. 565.

competing hypotheses of the role of finance in development. Combining newly produced information on state-level incomes and growth rates in the antebellum era with various measures of financial depth, several empirical tests of the link between finance and growth are offered. The results, while sometimes equivocal, suggest that finance led growth during the antebellum period. It did so in two ways: (1) financial institutions monetized economies, and (2) financial institutions intermediated credit. Before the tests are specified and the results presented, however, it is first necessary to take the reader on a short tour of antebellum America's distinct regional banking systems. Each region's system evolved differently, though not in isolation, yet each system shared a common purpose: the advancement of the commonweal through its assistance to economic progress.

AMERICA'S REGIONAL BANKING SYSTEMS

It was noted in the preceding chapter that nineteenth-century America produced a relatively large class of financial entrepreneurs. The social, cultural and economic conditions underlying this willingness to take risk were varied, but Douglass North has credited the adaptability of America's formal rules and informal constraints that rewarded adventurism in both the economic and noneconomic spheres. Underlying this adaptability was the nation's decentralized, federal polity which provided wide enough latitude for each state to experiment and develop a banking system appropriate to its needs. Wide differences in geography, climate, crop production, manufacturing capability, population density and a host of other relevant variables meant that the most preferred or effective banking system in Rhode Island would bear little resemblance to the most preferred or effective system in far away Louisiana or Missouri or, perhaps, even neighboring Connecticut. The result, of course, was that each state's banking system took a unique form. Despite these differences, their purpose was always the same: to provide the state with monetary and intermediary services and to promote the economic welfare of the state's inhabitants. Later sections of this chapter will assess whether this goal was systematically realized.

New England: Stability and the Suffolk

New England's banks probably most closely resemble the common conceptualization of the antebellum bank. They were relatively small, unit banks, their stock was closely held, they granted discounts to local farmers, merchants and artisans with whom the managers had more than a passing familiarity, and the state took little direct interest in their day-to-day operations.

Of the banking systems that arose and evolved in antebellum America, New England's banks have typically been viewed as the most stable and most conservatively run. Milton Friedman and Anna Schwartz attributed this to a typically Old World concern with reputation, familial ties and family legacies.[8] New England was long settled, its society well established, and its business community reasonably mature. Wealthy businessmen and bankers with strong ties to the community – like the Browns of Providence and the Bowdoins of Boston – placed an emphasis on stability not simply for their own reputation but because an unsound banking system was bad for business.

Besides a reputation for soundness, the two other defining characteristics of New England's early banks were their insider nature and their small size. The typical New England bank was small in comparison to banks in other regions. In 1850 the average Massachusetts country bank operated on about two-thirds the paid-in capital of a Pennsylvania country bank.[9] Rhode Island's banks operated on less than one-third.[10]

Several explanations have been offered for the relatively small size of the region's banks. Nathan Appleton attributed it to the states' propensity to tax bank capital which worked to the detriment of large banks.[11] Appleton's thesis, and the one accepted by Fenstermaker, was that banks with large capitals found it difficult to attain the same profit rates as smaller banks because of a disproportionate tax burden on large banks.[12] Data compiled from Massachusetts' bank reports, however, suggest that large banks were not disadvantaged by taxes

8. Friedman and Schwartz, "Has the Government Any Role," pp. 50–1.
9. U.S. House, 32d Congress, 1st Session, *Executive Document No. 122*; Pennsylvania, *Senate Journal*, vol. 2 (1850), pp. 372–9.
10. Rhode Island, General Assembly, *Acts and Resolves* (1850).
11. Appleton, *Examination*, pp. 34–5.
12. Fenstermaker, *Development*, p. 78.

on capital. Large banks realized rates of return on investment as high or higher than small or medium banks.

Naomi Lamoreaux offered a different explanation for the relatively small size of New England's banks.[13] The region's banks were not the impersonal financial intermediaries of neoclassical theory. Instead, they acted as the financial arms of extended kinship business networks. Throughout the antebellum era banks catered to insiders: directors, officers, stockholders, or business partners and family members of directors, officers, and stockholders. This preference toward insiders represented the perpetuation of the eighteenth-century custom of pooling capital to finance family enterprises. In the nineteenth century the practice continued under corporate auspices because the corporate form enabled merchants to raise capital in greater amounts than the family could raise on its own.

Once the familial and kinship orientation of the region's banks was established it perpetuated itself. When outsiders found it impossible to obtain loans in preferred quantities from the existing familial banks, they simply founded their own. In doing so its promoters assured themselves a steady supply of credit and created a "vehicle of mobility."[14] State legislatures accommodated this system with their liberal chartering policies and allowed it to proliferate. By 1860 Rhode Island had 91 banks, Maine had 68, New Hampshire 51, Vermont 44, Connecticut 74, and Massachusetts 178.[15]

Besides their size and their insider nature, perhaps the true defining characteristic of New England's banking system was the region-wide banknote redemption and clearing mechanism established by the Suffolk Bank of Boston. Because country merchants and farmers were typically indebted to Boston merchants, country banknotes tended to flow toward Boston. By 1800, country banknotes had become a constant irritant for city bankers. It was thought that country banknotes displaced Boston banknotes in local exchanges and a group of Boston banks joined together in 1803 to buy up and return country banknotes in an effort to reduce their circulation. The venture encountered so many obstacles, however, that it was quickly

---

13. Lamoreaux, "Banks"; Lamoreaux, *Insider Lending*; Lamoreaux, "Information Problems;" Lamoreaux and Glaisek, "Vehicles of Privilege or Mobility." Vatter, "Industrial Borrowing," anticipated some of Lamoreaux's findings.
14. Lamoreaux and Glaisek, "Vehicles of Privilege or Mobility."
15. U.S. Comptroller of the Currency, *Annual Report* (1876), Appendix.

abandoned. Several other schemes were proposed in the following two decades, but none proved any more successful than the 1803 attempt.

In 1818 the Suffolk Bank was chartered and, by 1819, its directors resolved to deal with the influx of country banknotes. The Suffolk sponsored another consortium of Boston banks in which each member appointed the Suffolk its representative and contributed to a fund used to purchase and redeem country banknotes. At this first, usually uncomfortable, sometimes combative, meeting with the issuing bank's managers the Suffolk's agent presented the country bank with an ultimatum: Join in a regular and organized redemption system or be liable to further unannounced redemption calls. After considerable protestations and several ingenious attempts at delay, most country banks acquiesced and joined the system.

The traditional interpretation of the Suffolk was that it exhibited some of the features of a proto-central bank and probably exerted some control over the money supply by limiting banknote circulation and forcing banks to maintain adequate reserves. Recent interpretations have been less quick to assume that the Suffolk exercised any real or effective control over the region's banking system or money supply. Donald Mullineaux, for example, argued that the Suffolk's redemption system was actually self-defeating.[16] By eliminating the discount on country banknotes, the Suffolk ensured that city and country banknotes became perfect substitutes which effectively increased the demand for country banknotes and made it more, rather than less, difficult for Boston banks to keep their notes in circulation.

J. Van Fenstermaker and John Filer also contested the long-held notion that the Suffolk was capable of controlling banknote issues. They found that the Suffolk had "no visible impact upon the reserve-bank money ratio and no significant impact on the growth of bank money."[17] The end result of the Suffolk, too, was to increase banknotes as a percent of total bank money so that deposit banking was less extensively used in New England than in any other long-settled region. Fenstermaker and Filer's explanation is similar to Mullineaux's. Notes of nearly all banks became acceptable anywhere in New England so that noteholders were less inclined to redeem

16. Mullineaux, "Competitive Monies," p. 890.
17. Fenstermaker and Filer, "Impact of the First and Second Banks," p. 39.

notes. With such wide acceptance of their banknotes, there were few incentives for banks to encourage the use of demand deposits.

New England's system can be summarized as follows: Small unit banks predominated; many banks catered to small groups of capitalists bound together by personal and familial relationships; banking was increasingly becoming an adjunct to other lines of business-like insurance, shipping and, by the 1840s, canals, railroads and manufacturing firms; the state took little direct interest in the daily operations of banks and, in fact, required little more than an annual report of condition; the state rarely took a shareholding stake or required banks to act as its fiscal agent; and the Suffolk developed an interbank clearing arrangement that facilitated the use of money throughout the region, but probably had little effective control over the money supply or bank credit. But, as we shall see later in the chapter, the Suffolk's ineffectiveness in achieving its stated goal of decreasing country banknote issues may have promoted the continued economic development of the region.

The Middle Atlantic: Hotbed of Experimentation

In Rhode Island after 1810 or so, bank charters were rarely granted on the presumption that some *direct* benefit would accrue to the community at large. They were granted for the personal gain of the shareholders and in proportion to the personal, political, or economic influence of the petitioners.[18] Neither Rhode Island nor any other New England state took a significant financial stake in their banks.

In those respects, New England differed from other regions. From the beginning of state-chartered commercial banking in Pennsylvania, the Commonwealth took a direct interest in the operations and profits of its banks. The Bank of North America represented the obvious case, chartered to provide support to the colonial belligerents and the fledgling nation. After the war, however, the bank was dominated by Philadelphia's elite merchants who were loathe to lend to other than their own. Most of the city's inhabitants and many of the state's legislators, perhaps rightly, considered the bank of little practical use. The legislature responded by chartering the Bank of Pennsylvania in 1793, which, as its name implied, became

---

18. Stokes, "Public and Private Finance," p. 282.

a de facto arm of the state. The Commonwealth subscribed $1 million of the bank's capital demanding, in return, that it could appoint six of thirteen directors and that the state be given a $500,000 line of credit at a constant 6 percent interest.[19] The bank became the state's fiscal agent, which meant a constant inflow of deposits as the monies from western land sales flowed into the state treasury and thus into the bank.

By 1803 Philadelphia merchants had again grown dissatisfied with the existing banks. The Bank of North America still catered to an elite few and the Bank of Pennsylvania's resources were tied up with state business. A group of merchants petitioned the state legislature for a charter for the Philadelphia Bank. Strenuous lobbying by the incumbent banks nearly sank the petitioner's hopes until they established a precedent that lasted throughout the antebellum era – they bribed the legislature with a payment of $135,000 in return for a charter.[20] In addition, the state could subscribe for $300,000 (or one-sixth) of the bank's capital with the opportunity to acquire more later. And, like the Bank of Pennsylvania, the Philadelphia Bank opened a line of credit for the state.

Between 1803 and 1814, Pennsylvania chartered only one other bank – the Farmers and Mechanics Bank – the charter of which established a second, much copied precedent. Because existing banks preferred lending to merchants, a growing middle class of artisans and manufacturers found it difficult to attract short-term credit at reasonable rates. The Farmers and Mechanics Bank was chartered to provide credit specifically to this group. Its charter required that a majority of the thirteen directors be farmers, mechanics or manufacturers and that the bank lend the equivalent of 10 percent of its capital to farmers on long-term mortgages at 6 percent annual interest.[21]

In 1813 the Commonwealth held shares in each of its chartered banks – $1,500,000 in the Bank of Pennsylvania, $523,000 in the Philadelphia Bank, and $85,400 in the Farmers and Mechanics Bank – and the dividends represented a significant share of the state's revenues. But in the 1810s and 1820s New York City, Philadelphia, and Baltimore became locked in a pitched battle for

19. Daniels, *Pennsylvania*, p. 62.
20. Wainwright, *History of the Philadelphia National Bank*, pp. 13–15.
21. Daniels, *Pennsylvania*, pp. 91–2.

dominance in the export of western produce. New York's ambitious Erie Canal and Maryland's proposal to connect the Ohio and Potomac rivers with a turnpike scared Pennsylvania's legislature into action.

Competing with its neighbors and embarking upon its own internal improvements program required money – lots of it – and the legislature chose to raise it by exchanging banks charters for cash. In theory, the plan made perfect sense. It was simply a matter of forcing shareholders to relinquish the discounted stream of future monopoly rents to the state. After all, the three existing banks had paid handsome bonuses for their privileges. In 1814 the legislature authorized forty-one new banks with a combined capital of $17 million.[22] The act specified the city or town in which each would open an office, it established the name under which each would operate, determined the total capital and the par value of shares, set maximum interest rates, sct maximum debt-equity ratios, and limited each bank's range of operations. More importantly, it set the terms by which the state would profit from these banks. Dividends were taxed, and the state guaranteed a steady income by providing that charters would be revoked if dividends were not declared in any twelve-month period.[23] Each bank, too, was required to lend to the state at 5 percent interest whenever the state came to call.

Of the 41 banks authorized by the act, 39 opened, but few thrived. By 1822 only 22 continued and many were weak, ineffective intermediaries. By the mid-1830s the tax on dividends was insufficient to defray the costs of the internal improvements program and the state was deeply in debt, mostly to the banks themselves. The financial panics of the late 1830s and the depression of the early 1840s deepcned the state's fiscal woes. To raise funds, the legislature authorized the sale of all bank stocks held by the state treasury, except those of the Bank of Pennsylvania, which was required to loan the state yet another $4 million.[24] After the mid-1840s, then, Pennsylvania held little sway over its banks. But Pennsylvania's banks, many nearly bankrupted by the state itself, sold off or wrote off their internal improvement investments and adopted conscrvative lending strategies. The state, too, grew reluctant to charter new banks, so that by

22. Ibid., pp. 148–9.
23. Fenstermaker, *Development*, pp. 19–20.
24. Daniels, *Pennsylvania*, p. 66.

1860 the birthplace of American commercial banking had the fewest banks per capita of any state in the Mid-Atlantic region.

Unlike Pennsylvania, state-chartered commercial banking in New York began under less auspicious circumstances. The Bank of New York opened in 1784, but operated without a charter in open violation of the law until 1791 when the legislature finally recognized it. The second bank to obtain a New York charter did so only surreptitiously, if not dishonestly. Aaron Burr petitioned the legislature to incorporate a company to supply fresh water to the inhabitants of Manhattan Island. The proposed Manhattan Company was hailed by some as "a delivering angel," but Burr had tucked a clause into the charter granting the company the right to employ any excess capital in "moneyed transactions or operations not inconsistent with the laws and constitution of the State of New York."[25] Once chartered, the company quickly announced that $500,000 of its capital would be employed in banking. Subsequent growth in banking was more rapid in New York than in Philadelphia, so that by 1812 New York had seven banks, all with a paid-in capital in excess of $1 million.[26]

In spite of its dubious start, New York introduced two innovations that influenced American banking policy even into the next century. The Safety Fund system, introduced in 1829, was the country's first bank liability insurance program (similar in intent to the modern Federal Deposit Insurance Corporation). The Act was the first to authorize a board of commissioners charged with regular quarterly inspections of each member bank.[27] An equally novel aspect of the law was that it established a "safety fund" insuring holders of banknotes against loss in the event of a bank's failure. This insurance fund was financed by six annual assessments of one-half of 1 percent on each member bank's capital stock. If the fund was depleted by the failure of one or more banks, additional assessments could be levied until the fund was restored to 3 percent of aggregate bank capital.

As promising an idea as the Safety Fund was, it failed to bring any real stability to New York's banking system. Its first (and only) test came during the panic of 1837 when the failure of just eleven

---

25. Nevins, *History of the Bank of New York*, pp. 30–1.
26. Ibid., p. 32.
27. Chaddock, *Safety Fund Banking*, provides a comprehensive history of the system. Calomiris, "Deposit Insurance," and Bodenhorn, "Zombie Banks," provide modern interpretations.

members effectively bankrupted the system. Reimbursements to creditors of failed banks exceeded $2.5 million, while the fund realized only about $150,000 on assets forfeited by those banks.[28] More importantly, creditor claims were disbursed so slowly that many frustrated creditors, mostly banknote holders, sold their claims at cents on the dollar. Despite its promise, the Safety Fund failed to protect the payments system generally or bank creditors individually.

Although the Safety Fund operated until the late 1850s, no new banks joined the Safety Fund system after the introduction of free banking in 1838.[29] Free banking represented a compromise between those most concerned with the underlying safety and stability of the currency and those most concerned with competition and freeing the country's entrepreneurs from unduly harsh and anticompetitive restraints. Under free banking, a prospective banker could start a bank anywhere he saw fit, provided that he met a handful of regulatory prerequisites. The free bank's capital was invested in state or federal bonds that were lodged with the state's comptroller from whom the bank received the banknotes that it circulated. If a bank failed to redeem its banknotes into specie the Comptroller initiated bankruptcy proceedings and sold the collateral bonds to reimburse noteholders.

New York was not first to pass a free banking act. Michigan enacted free banking in 1837, but its law was a hastily drawn act modeled after a proposal then before the New York Assembly. New York's free banking act, then, proved one of the more important financial innovations of the era, as it was widely copied – even before New York had passed on it. By 1860 eighteen states adopted free banking and three others introduced watered-down variants.[30] And the National Banking Act of 1862 was modeled after and adopted most of the substantive provisions of New York's 1838 act.

Both the Safety Fund system and free banking were attempts to protect society from losses consequent on bank failure and, thereby,

28. Helderman, *National and State Banks*, p. 12.
29. The literature on free banking has grown far too vast to cite in detail here. Readers are referred to Hammond, *Banks and Politics*, and Redlich, *Molding*, for the traditional view. A wave of fresh interpretations have come forth in recent years. Interested readers are referred especially to Rockoff, *Free Banking Era*; Rolnick and Weber, "New Evidence"; and Rolnick and Weber, "Causes of Free Bank Failures."
30. Virginia, Kentucky and Missouri never adopted full-fledged free banking, but they did charter banks with bond-secured note issues. See Rockoff, *Free Banking Era*, p. 3.

to entice people to hold financial assets. Banks and bank-supplied currency were novel developments in the hinterlands of the early nineteenth century and some part of the rural population were unsure, perhaps even skeptical, of the real value of pretty bits of paper and corporate promises to pay. Trust was built slowly and destroyed quickly. The failure of a single bank could, in a single week, destroy the confidence in a system built up over a decade. New York's experiments were designed to mitigate, if not eliminate, the negative consequences of bank failures and elicit confidence in the system. New York's Safety Fund, therefore, differed in its details but not in its intent, from New England's Suffolk System. Bankers and legislators in each region grappled with the difficult issue of protecting a fragile, yet vital, sector of the economy. As different as the solutions to these problems were in New England and the Mid-Atlantic, bankers and legislators in the South and West settled on a different one yet.

The South and West: Branch Banking and the Commonweal

One distinguishing characteristic of southern and western banks were their extensive branch networks. Pennsylvania provided for branch banking in the early nineteenth century, but the experiment failed and was quickly abandoned. Both the Bank of Pennsylvania and the Philadelphia Bank opened branches outside Philadelphia and neither system proved profitable. Indeed, branch losses ate up profits generated at the home office. The Philadelphia Bank, for example, opened four branches in 1809. By 1811 the bank passed on a dividend as a direct result of losses on its branch operations. An internal committee reported to the stockholders that not only had the branches ceased to be profitable, they "have actually been the cause of positive and serious loss and have contributed more than any other circumstance to embarrass and cripple the funds of the bank."[31]

At root, branch losses resulted from a combination of ineffective central office control of branch lending policy and central office policies inconsistent with the realities of hinterland lending. Directors in

31. Quoted in Holdsworth, *Financing an Empire*, p. 179.

Philadelphia instructed branch managers to invest only in high-quality, short-term loans based on shipments bound for eastern ports (so-called real bills). Rural banks, however, found it difficult to build up portfolios of real bills and turned to loans secured by real estate and personal security instead of goods in transit. Before the Philadelphia office developed an effective monitoring scheme, branch managers built up substantial portfolios of non-performing, poorly secured loans. As late as 1830, long after the branch experiment was abandoned, the Philadelphia Bank carried more than $126,000 in unrecovered loans granted at the Washington and Wilkes-Barre branches years before.

In Virginia, as in most other southern and western states, branch banks thrived. The first branch bank – the Bank of Virginia – was chartered in 1804 and until the Civil War branch banking dominated the state's financial markets. Several small, independent banks were chartered in the 1850s, but they never threatened the predominance of the states "Big Six" branch banks. And branches at Virginia's banks, unlike those in Pennsylvania, generated profits and provided geographic loan diversification. In 1821, for example, the net return to capital at the Richmond (home) office of Farmers Bank of Virginia was 5.4 percent. Rates of return at its other branches ranged from a low of 3 percent at Norfolk to 9 percent at Winchester. In 1835, the last year for which branch data were separately reported, net returns to capital ranged between 2.9 and 11.7 percent, with an average of 7.9 percent.[32]

The Norfolk branches of three of the state's large banks consistently generated the lowest (though never negative) returns and political rather than economic considerations kept them open. In the immediate post-Revolutionary years, the value of exports shipped from Virginia's ports (notably Alexandria and Norfolk) slightly exceeded those shipped from Baltimore.[33] By 1800 the numbers had turned sharply in Baltimore's favor and Virginia entered the internal-improvements craze and the battle for western shipments. Banks represented the first stage of the state's internal-improvement efforts as many Virginians believed that Baltimore's banks played a decisive role in the increasing volume of goods flowing out of that port. If

32. Virginia, *House Documents* (1835/36).
33. Starnes, *Sixty Years*, p. 26.

Norfolk, with one of the best natural harbors in the Mid-Atlantic, was to compete as an outlet for western produce, the city needed banks and the state supplied them by requiring three of the Big Six to maintain branches there. Other southern and western states acted similarly, locating branches in a city (like Memphis, Louisville, Natchez, and Mobile) that might, with some encouragement, grow into an important entrepôt.

The second distinguishing characteristic of southern and western banking was sweeping state involvement and intervention. Virginia, for example, interjected the state into the banking system by taking significant stakes in its first chartered banks (subsidizing their initial capitals) and by requiring the banks, in turn, once they established themselves, to subsidize the state's continuing internal-improvements program of the 1820s and 1830s. South Carolina followed a wholly different strategy. Even while it chartered banks in which the state took no financial interest whatsoever, it chartered the Bank of the State of South Carolina, a bank wholly owned by the state-designed to lend to planters and farmers who constantly lamented the existing banks' preference for mercantile lending.[34] The bank ultimately divided its lending between merchants and farmers and dominated South Carolina's financial markets.

The 1820s and 1830s witnessed a deluge of new banks in the South and West and a corresponding increase in state involvement. No state, however, matched Louisiana's breadth of involvement in the 1830s as it chartered three distinct types of banks: commercial banks that catered to merchants and manufacturers; improvement banks that financed various internal improvements; and property banks that extended long-term mortgage credit to planters and other property owners. Louisiana's improvement banks included the New Orleans Canal and Banking Company (1831) whose charter required it to build a canal connecting Lake Ponchartrain to the Mississippi River. The Exchange and Banking Company (1835) and the New Orleans Improvement and Banking Company (1836) were required to build and operate hotels in New Orleans. The New Orleans Gas Light and Banking Company (1835) had to construct and operate gas street-lights in New Orleans and five other towns in which it had branches.

---

34. Lesesne, *Bank of the State*.

Given the astonishing scope of activity forced on its banks, it was not surprising that Louisiana asked its banks to take it into the railroad age. The Carrollton Railroad and Banking Company (1835) and the Atchafalaya Railroad and Banking Company (1836) were rail construction companies with bank subsidiaries designed to subsidize road construction.[35]

Louisiana's property banks received the lion's share of the state's support, however. The state chartered three property banks – the Consolidated Association of Planters (1827), the Union Bank (1832) and the Citizens Bank (1833) – whose capital was raised through the sale of state-guaranteed bonds backed by mortgages drawn against real property. Planters became shareholders by offering their property for mortgage and took a share in proportion to the value of their property and could borrow amounts prorated by a similar formula. No dividends were to be paid from operating profits. Instead, they were placed in a sinking fund to meet interest and principal on the bonds. By 1837 Louisiana raised $20 million by marketing the state-guaranteed bonds in Europe. Another $7 million were sold in New York, Philadelphia, and Boston. With the state's assistance, these property banks "became one of the most important agencies for capital import for about a decade."[36] Additionally, the state's banking system, taken as a whole, "was an effective financial intermediary, mobilizing domestic and foreign savings and channeling them to Louisiana's credit-thirsty agriculture, commerce, and social-overhead projects."[37]

Louisiana's exuberance for banking in the 1830s reflected what some historians have labeled the "commonwealth ideal" of banking – the promotion of the general welfare through the promotion of banks.[38] Legislatures in the South and West, however, never demonstrated a greater commitment to the commonwealth ideal than during the tough times of the early 1820s. With the collapse of the postwar land boom in 1819, a political coalition of debt-strapped landowners lobbied legislatures throughout the region for relief and an especial focus was banking. Relief advocates lobbied for inflation-

---

35. Caldwell, *Banking History*, pp. 51–2; Fenstermaker, *Development*, Appendix A-12.
36. Redlich, *Molding*, p. 206.
37. Green, *Finance and Economic Development*, p. 17.
38. Royalty, "Banking and the Commonwealth Ideal."

ary banking that would reduce the real burden of debts taken on during the prior flush times.

Several western states responded to these calls and chartered a number of state-sponsored, state-subsidized and state-managed banks designed to reinflate their embattled economies. Chartered in 1821, the Bank of the Commonwealth of Kentucky was designed to loan on mortgages at longer periods than had been customary and all Kentucky landowners were eligible for $1,000 in loans.[39] It was hoped that these $1,000 loans would allow landowners to discharge their debts without being forced to liquidate their property at ruinously low, depression-era prices. Though the bank's notes were not redeemable in specie they were given currency in two ways. First, they were accepted by the state treasury for the payment of all taxes and levies. Simultaneously, and second, the state passed a replevy law that forced creditors to accept notes of the Bank of the Commonwealth or forgo collection of the debt for two years.

The commonwealth ideal was not singularly Kentuckian. In the throes of the depression of the early 1820s, Tennessee chartered the State Bank of Tennessee, Illinois chartered the State Bank of Illinois, and Louisiana chartered the Louisiana State Bank and the Louisiana Bank. Though they took slightly different forms, they all had the same intent, to relieve "distressed and embarrassed" farmers and planters.[40] Regardless of the exact form, these banks represented the commonwealth ideal – the notion that the state should promote both the general welfare and economic growth.

Despite sharp differences in the particular form and structure of each region's banking structures, they were all aimed squarely at the same goal, namely, realizing that region's economic potential. They did so in two ways: (1) Financial institutions monetized economies, which reduced the costs of transacting and shifting consumption through time and space; and (2) Financial institutions provided credit, which released entrepreneurial spirits and talents. The remainder of this chapter attempts to measure the relative importance of these two functions, but it is necessary first to discuss the role of banks and expand on the previous chapter's discussion. A simple parable provides the impetus for the subsequent discussion.

39. Ibid., pp. 94–6.
40. Green, *Finance and Economic Development*, pp. 19–20.

THE LINK BETWEEN FINANCIAL AND
ECONOMIC DEVELOPMENT: A PARABLE

A stylized version of the Gurley-Shaw-Goldsmith model of the link between financial development and economic growth can be laid out rather easily in the form of a simple parable.[41] First, imagine a world with no financial intermediaries. The economy consists of three sectors: households, businesses, and government. Money consists of specie (gold, silver, and other metals) and is exogenously determined. All individuals within each sector can be classified as either a surplus or deficit unit. Surplus units are those whose current income exceeds current expenditure; deficit units have incomes less than desired expenditure. Generally, households will be surplus units; businesses, deficit units; and government can be either, though governments tend to run deficits at least as often as surpluses.

Without financial intermediation, investment funds flow from either of two sources: funds provided by the investing unit itself (internal finance) or those originating outside the investing unit (external finance). Regardless of their source, investment results in an increase in the volume of primary securities, both in absolute value and as a percentage of real national income. With internal finance these primary securities consist of equities; that is, more shares are transferred to investing partners or net worth is increased in the capital account. Under conditions of external finance, these primary securities may consist of equities, bonds, mortgages, short-term commercial paper, or uncollateralized trade credit.

Balance sheets of deficit units contain liabilities and equities in the debit column; investment in the form of physical assets or claims on physical assets in the credit column. The balance sheets of surplus units, on the other hand, report a net worth representing their holdings of primary securities issued by deficit units in addition to money and physical assets.[42] In the absence of financial intermediaries, borrowers are required to market their primary securities directly to the ultimate lender, though some brokerage appears even in financially backward economies. Even if brokers or other non-financial middle-

41. This section draws heavily from Goldsmith, *Financial Structure*, Chapter 1; Gurley and Shaw, "Financial Aspects"; and Cameron, "Theoretical Bases," pp. 6–8.
42. Goldsmith, *Financial Institutions*, pp. 10–11.

men have appeared, direct contact between investors and lenders remains limited. Information asymmetries usually exist, as do differences in maturity preferences and in the scale of lending or borrowing between borrowers and savers. The result is that, without financial intermediaries, investment is, with a few exceptions, largely confined to that consistent with internal finance.

Add now a financial sector to this highly stylized, financially undeveloped world. By definition, this sector consists of those institutions whose principal function is to intermediate between borrowers and savers. As such, the bulk of the assets held by financial intermediaries consists of primary securities issued by borrowers. (They also hold commodity money and just enough physical assets to allow them to conduct business, which may include such things as vaults, furnishings, a mailbox, a flagpole, and whatnot.) In acquiring these assets, financial intermediaries issue their own securities that take the form of demand deposits, time deposits, banknotes, equities, and bonds. Some of these indirect securities perform the functions of money and thereby displace some fraction of the circulating commodity money in everyday transactions.

The arrival of financial institutions, therefore, represents a fundamental and important innovation in the saving-investment process. At its most fundamental level, credit money, such as banknotes and deposits, facilitates economic growth by economizing on the stock of idle specie and, by varying liquidity and leverage ratios, makes the supply of money more elastic than it would otherwise be. No longer tied *directly* to inflows and outflows (though to this point international influences have been ignored) the money supply can expand and contract in response to internal macroeconomic circumstances, while the stock of specie can be employed in settling international debts or industrial uses. In addition, depending on the state of a country's coinage, the substitution of bank-issued money for commodity money can facilitate transactions. One feature of most western countries on the verge of developing was the rather sad state of the domestic coinage. It was notoriously bad in England and Scotland, and Rondo Cameron claimed that it was equally bad in Germany, Belgium, and Japan.[43] North America, too, labored under

---

43. Cameron, "Theoretical Bases," p. 13.

the weight of a poor coinage that increased transaction costs at least until the mid-nineteenth century.[44]

Intermediaries, however, play a more important role than simply replacing a poor currency with a better one – though that role should not be minimized as the search for alternatives may lead to imaginative improvisation out of which original credit instruments develop.[45] More importantly, financial institutions permit households and businesses to move resources through time to better meet their temporal consumption preferences. In a world in which each economic unit took in exactly the same amount as its desired expenditures there would be no role for financial intermediaries. No enterprise would require external financing, nor would any unit have a surplus searching for investment. But, it is indeed rare that consumption preferences are perfectly synchronized with income flows. Merchants require funds for inventories prior to sale. Farmers demand funds for seed and fertilizer before the crop is harvested. Manufacturers demand funds to pay for labor and raw materials before production is complete. Households want homes before they have the full purchase price. In the end, meeting these differing temporal consumption preferences gives rise to financial intermediaries.

Why can't surplus and deficit units meet these preferences without the intervention of banks? Why must banks substitute their own debt for the direct debt offered by ultimate borrowers? The short answer is that financial intermediaries bridge the gap between the often incompatible preferences of borrowers and lenders. There are two distinct gaps. The first arises from the high, often prohibitive, costs involved in matching borrowers and lenders. The gap between net returns to lenders and gross costs to borrowers is greater with the absence of than in the presence of banks. Lenders concern themselves with their *net* returns, which represents the *gross* return less search costs, illiquidity costs, and a risk premium reflecting uncertainty about the borrower's credit worthiness. Borrowers, on the other hand, add these costs to the direct interest payment they have to offer in the presence of costless transacting and perfect risk-matching.[46] Simple

44. Redish, "Why Was Specie Scarce."
45. Cameron, "Theoretical Bases," p. 14.
46. Fry, *Money, Interest and Banking*, p. 235.

brokers reduce this gap between gross and net returns by reducing search costs, but full-fledged financial intermediaries reduce these costs still further by exploiting economies of scale in lending, by specializing in gathering information on the credit worthiness of borrowers, and by reducing denomination and maturity mismatches between ultimate borrowers and lenders.

Intermediaries lower these costs by creating nodes where borrowers and lenders of all types meet: those more and less wealthy, more and less risk averse, more and less credit worthy. Financial intermediaries, therefore, overcome differing preferences for liquidity and security that individual borrowers and lenders cannot contractually overcome on their own. Savers may prefer high liquidity and unquestioned security. Borrowers may be unable or unwilling to offer either. Financial intermediaries reconcile these differences by offering a saver liquidity and security while employing the funds in investment projects with various levels of risk and liquidity. By pooling savings they transform the credits taken in into other forms because the risks of the borrowing pool differ from that of its constituent parts. It is simply an application of the law of large numbers – the central limit theorem – in that the probability of default among a large group is easily ascertainable while the default risk of any individual is highly uncertain.[47] Financial intermediaries, then, represent a type of insurance fund for savers. With direct borrowing and lending a single default may devastate the savings of one or more lenders. When pooled through a financial intermediary, that same default, so long as it represents a relatively small proportion of the intermediary's portfolio – a reasonable assumption given substantial diversification – will have little effect on savers and negatively affect the returns received by the intermediary's owners only slightly.

Financial institutions, then, arise when it is preferable to substitute indirect for direct debt, to substitute external for internal finance on an unprecedentedly large scale. Intermediation thus involves a transformation of funds, a transformation akin to more commonly regarded production processes wherein raw materials enter through the back door of an enterprise, are worked upon, and exit through the front door in a different form. The most important transforma-

---

47. Smith, *Money and Financial Intermediation*, p. 124; Patrick, "Financial Development," pp. 182–3.

tion effected by financial institutions is what Goldsmith labeled "debtor substitution"; the substitution of the bank's own debt for that of its borrowers.[48] This substitution of debts is attractive to the ultimate lenders because debt issued by banks is better known, the issuer generally more credit worthy, and is more easily resalable in organized markets than is primary debt issued by the ultimate borrower.

This traditional view of financial intermediaries and their leading role in the economy focus on the divergent preferences of investors and savers. Banks raise real returns to savers and lower real costs to investors by accommodating savers' liquidity preferences, reducing risk through diversification and realizing economies of scale in lending. Recent models of the interaction between financial and real activity, while not dismissing the benefits of intermediaries under this traditional paradigm, focus instead on information asymmetries between borrowers and lenders. Two specific problems arise from these asymmetries: adverse selection, wherein parties have different information prior to contracting; and moral hazard, where the asymmetry arises subsequent to an agreement.

Of course, these problems were recognized long ago. Robert Hare, for instance, writing in 1810 observed that banks "by extensive means of information, are enabled duly to estimate the degree of confidence to which traders may be entitled."[49] Most modern theories of financial intermediation can be traced back to information asymmetries and the treatment of them offered by George Akerloff's "lemons model."[50] Akerloff demonstrated how asymmetric information between buyers and sellers about product quality can cause a market to malfunction. Because the market price of a good reflects its expected *average* quality, sellers of low-quality goods (lemons) receive a higher price than in the presence of perfect information, while sellers of high-quality goods receive a lower price. Such price-quality discrepancies, in turn, affect the volume of market transactions. Some sellers of high-quality goods stay out of the market at the low, quality-adjusted price. Most sellers of low-quality goods, however, enter the market. If buyers perceive the presence of many low-quality sellers and few high-quality sellers, the market may fail to appear as buyers stay away in droves.

48. Goldsmith, *Financial Institutions*, pp. 25–6.
49. Quoted in Miller, *Banking Theories*, p. 60.
50. Akerloff, "Market for Lemons."

Financial markets are particularly susceptible to information asymmetries. Adverse selection arises because, at any posted interest rate, only those entrepreneurial projects offering an expected internal rate of return greater than the effective interest rate (which generally implies higher risks) will apply for credit. Entrepreneurs with projects with lower yields and therefore low risks do not apply. The result is that, without some additional monitoring, intermediaries will be catering to borrowers of higher than average risk.[51] Moral hazard problems also arise because with fixed payoff contracts, once the payment is set, the borrower faces incentives to shirk and deliver fewer goods than initially contracted for. The role of financial intermediaries is to control and mitigate both of these information-based problems inherent in lending.

It is, in fact, when these dual information problems are brought to bear that the role of intermediaries appears. It could be possible that simple information gatherers and disseminators arise, but questions about the quality of the information signal may still arise. Akerlof's lemons model requires that information itself would sell at a price reflecting its average quality so that high-quality information would remain scarce. The second problem with simple information gathering is the public goods nature of information. Once the information has been produced and provided, it can be supplied to others without loss of quality to the original purchaser. Information providers can not then extract the full value of the information from those who consume it and, therefore, provide socially suboptimal quantities.

Information production and financial intermediation are most effective when consolidated in a single enterprise. The firm that generates the information is the same that employs it in its decision making so it will produce information until the marginal value of additional quality just equals the marginal cost of generating it. As the appropriability problem disappears, the lemons problem does as well. Although the information produced by the intermediary can be observed indirectly (that is, to whom the intermediary lends and to whom it does not) the returns to that information cannot be directly appropriated.[52]

51. This is a common theme running throughout the credit rationing literature. See Jaffe and Stiglitz, "Credit Rationing," for a particularly good review of the literature.
52. Leland and Pyle, "Information Asymmetries," pp. 383–4.

This dual information-gathering and intermediating role of banks also explains why individuals pay more for bank loans than for debt obligations placed directly in the open market.[53] Only those individuals or businesses with widely known, easily observed reputations can directly place their debt at profitable rates. Others must reimburse banks for their information-gathering and risk-taking services. Yet the use of an intermediary's services minimizes the total social costs of intermediation. In the absence of banks, borrowers with investment demands in amounts greater than could be supplied by a single lender would force independent monitoring by several lenders which would not be efficient if the total social costs of duplicated monitoring exceeded the social benefits.[54] This costly duplication can be avoided when monitoring is centralized and delegated to credible specialists.

Banks establish their credibility in two ways. The first is that banks develop long-term relationships with borrowers, but they specialize in short-term renewable contracts.[55] As the contracts are renewed and renegotiated, the bank can alter the terms of the agreement to reflect all available, including newly acquired, information about the borrower's expected future performance. The intermediary faces an incentive to continually monitor and gather timely information about its customers. But the bank faces the task of convincing potential savers that their information is good. Second, the bank signals its credibility, like all other firms, by investing in its own enterprise.[56] In the case of a bank, owner-contributed capital placed at risk provides a signal to savers that the bank intends to gather, process and act on information in a cost-effective, profitable manner.

Douglas Diamond provided a model that ties together the traditional and new views of financial intermediaries.[57] In the presence of information asymmetries, lenders cannot costlessly observe the potential returns on entrepreneurial projects. To conserve on scarce resources by decreasing aggregate monitoring costs, financial institutions channel funds between savers and investors. These financial intermediaries perform three tasks. First, intermediaries provide

53. Fama, "Contract Costs," p. S84.
54. Fama, "What's Different," pp. 36–7.
55. Ibid., p. 38; Fama, "Contract Costs," p. S85.
56. Leland and Pyle, "Information Asymmetries," p. 384.
57. Diamond, "Financial Intermediation."

short-term loan contracts to individual borrowers and monitor them for default. Second, the intermediary holds a highly diversified portfolio of loans representing a broad cross-section of entrepreneurial projects. Third, intermediaries transform assets for savers by issuing their own liabilities that have smoother payoff streams than the direct securities offered by ultimate investors. The latter two functions imply that intermediaries eliminate the need to duplicate costly monitoring. But the question arises, who monitors the monitor? Diamond argues that because banks hold highly diversified portfolios, the necessity for monitoring is lessened (not eliminated, but lessened). By holding a highly diversified portfolio, the intermediary's returns are not tied to the risks inherent in a single or even a small number of investment projects. Debt-issuing banks, then, represent a type of mutual fund allowing savers to invest in a bank-issued obligation (say, banknotes or demand deposits or certificates of deposit) with relatively low risk that still meets their liquidity and transactions needs.

The implications of this for economic growth are apparent. As the risks of saving declines, holding everything else constant, the volume of saving should increase both in the aggregate and per capita. This response, in turn, provides entrepreneurs with an increased volume of investment funds and most growth models predict that increased savings and investment rates lead to more rapid rates of economic growth. Thus banks are important because they act as intermediaries, channeling funds from the ultimate saver to the ultimate investor and their performance should have a direct effect on real macroeconomic activity.

Financial intermediation, then, is ultimately motivated by the preferences and objectives of borrowers, which make themselves felt through the demand for funds in primary markets, and by the preferences and objectives of savers, which influence the supply of funds to intermediaries who then meet and contract with borrowers. Although the demand for funds must ultimately be met by surpluses provided by households and businesses, barriers to direct interaction give rise to intermediation. Most of the funds available to borrowers are supplied by financial institutions that have raised funds from individuals with current surpluses. The story of financing, which appears on its face to be a simple activity, turns out to be a complex problem wherein financial intermediaries must meet the preferences of both investors and savers with quite different objectives and expectations. Success or failure by intermediaries in providing these services ultimately affect the level of real aggregate economic activity.

THE PARABLE REVISITED: RECENT FORMULATIONS

While models developed by Diamond and others, following in the tradition of Akerlof's asymmetric information lemons model, have immediate implications for aggregate economic activity, their impetus was not to link financial to economic development. Instead, they were designed either to demonstrate the role of banks in the intermediation process or, very often, to highlight the fragility of the banking system itself. However, following a silence on the issue for nearly two decades, the so-called endogenous growth literature has refocused attention on the linkages between finance and growth.

The implications of the new endogenous growth literature for the subject at hand – the interaction between finance and growth – can be most effectively portrayed with a simple aggregate production function. This characterization is useful as well because it can be used to highlight the differences between the Goldsmith and McKinnon-Shaw hypotheses. It should be remembered, however, that the Goldsmith and McKinnon-Shaw interpretations were not fundamentally different. Both believed that finance influenced growth, yet they stressed different aspects and highlighted different transmission mechanisms.

Begin by assuming that output (y) is a function of capital (k) and everything else (x).[58] The functional relationship can then be written in the form[59]

$$y_t = f(k_t, x_t) \qquad\qquad 2.1$$

By totally differentiating, dividing by y_t, and rearranging terms, equation 2.1 yields:

---

58. This model is adapted from that presented in De Gregario and Guidotti, "Financial Development," p. 434. King and Levine, "Finance and Growth," p. 272 presents a similar formulation.
59. Everything else (x_t) can include such things as human capital, technical advance, or any and all of the multitude of factors thought to influence growth.

$$dy_t = (dk_t/y_t)df(\bullet)/dk_t + (dx_t/y_t)df(\bullet)/(dx_t) \qquad 2.2$$

which can be simplified as

$$dy_t = s_t\,\theta_t + v_t\,\phi_t \qquad 2.3$$

where s_t denotes the savings rate, θ_t the marginal productivity of capital, v_t represents the growth rate in the vector x of everything else that influences growth, and ϕ_t the marginal productivity of everything else. The rate of growth is then determined by two things: (1) the product of the average rate of saving (investment) and the marginal productivity of capital, and (2) the product of the growth rate of everything else including human capital investments, technological advance, and so forth and the marginal productivity of those factors.

Financial development, then, influences economic growth through either of two mechanisms. On one hand, financial markets may enhance the marginal efficiency of additional capital accumulation (increases in θ_t), which was the principal transmission mechanism envisioned by Goldsmith. He argued that indirect financing was more efficient than direct financing because it increased the marginal rate of return on investment that results from a more efficient allocation of saving among potential investments.[60] Furthermore, indirect finance and more efficient allocations flowed directly from the operation of financial institutions.

Hugh Patrick and Ronald McKinnon, too, highlighted this transmission mechanism and related it back to Schumpeter's growth model. The emergence and presence of banks altered temporal allocations which in turn affected the level of entrepreneurial activity. Intertemporal decision making by entrepreneurs depends on three things: the entrepreneur's initial endowment, the entrepreneur's peculiar investment opportunities, and his or her access to external finance.[61] Patrick and McKinnon argued that these three components are badly correlated, particularly in developing countries. The most efficient distribution of investment differs from the distribution of savings because savings depends on income while efficient investment depends on entrepreneurial talents, knowledge, and willingness to accept risk.[62] Savers are not entrepreneurs, and entrepreneurs

60. Goldsmith, *Financial Structure*, p. 395.
61. McKinnon, *Money and Capital*, pp. 10–11.
62. Patrick, "Financial Development," p. 182.

cannot self-finance their investment desires. This low correlation commonly manifests itself in wide dispersions in real marginal rates of return between alternative projects, reflecting a growth-retarding misallocation of resources.

A common thread running throughout Goldsmith's work is that financial intermediaries influence economic growth by overcoming these low correlations between entrepreneurship and savings. The financial superstructure, he wrote, "accelerates economic growth and improves economic performance to the extent that it facilitates the migration of funds to the best user, i.e., to the place in the economic system where funds will yield the highest social return."[63] Intermediaries match savers and investors in a socially optimal manner. By gathering information and monitoring, banks become the arbiters of investment, deciding which enterprises are funded and which are not, and do so at a lower social cost than individual lenders could do independently.

Ronald McKinnon and Edward Shaw, however, focus on the importance of increased savings rates (s_t in equation 2.3). Aggregate volumes of savings and investment are simply greater in the presence of financial intermediaries than without them. "Larger lumps of investment are feasible in the private sector," wrote Shaw, "when savings are pooled in financial markets."[64] Financial institutions do not upset the basic social accounting, they simply increase the size of the accounts. In the absence of banks or other intermediaries, individuals wishing to maintain a deficit condition (expenditure exceeds income) have to do so by issuing direct debt instruments, instruments purchased by the ultimate saver so that savings equals investment.

Even when intermediaries intercede between borrowers and lenders, the accumulation of financial assets by savers must, by definition, equal the accumulation of debt by borrowers. While the intervention of financial intermediaries does not change the essential accounting identity, the total volume of debt increases at a faster pace than when financing projects occurs through direct placement or through internal finance.[65] For the entrepreneur the increased supply of funds can be of considerable importance. For one, the costs of bor-

63. Goldsmith, *Financial Structure*, p. 400.
64. Shaw, *Financial Deepening*, p. 75.
65. Gurley and Shaw, "Financial Aspects," p. 519.

rowing are lowered because intermediation decreases search and marketing costs as borrowers no longer have to tailor their debt to meet the liquidity, risk, and denominational preferences of savers. Total borrowing costs are lowered because large investments (relative to average savings) can be financed through a single (or a few sources) rather than by a large number of small savers.

But Patrick argued that the importance of financial intermediaries extended far beyond their cost-reducing aspect. The availability of funds in large amounts could arouse Lord Keynes's animal spirits.[66] Indeed, awakening or encouraging the expression of these entrepreneurial spirits was the fundamental role of banks and credit in Schumpeter's framework. Though most associate Schumpeter with his notion of "creative destruction," whereby new enterprises through the competitive process drive existing firms from the field, it was credit that was fundamental to this process. "The essential function of credit," wrote Schumpeter, "consists in enabling the entrepreneur to . . . force the economic system into new channels."[67]

Regardless of the actual mechanism – increased efficiency of investment or increased investment proper – the intermediary role of banks outlined in the preceding section becomes manifest in realizing finance-induced growth. Recent research on the linkages between financial development and economic growth has received an impetus from the so-called endogenous growth literature. Theoretical and empirical studies in the spirit of Valerie Bencivenga and Bruce Smith, Jeremy Greenwood and Boyan Jovanovic, and Robert King and Ross Levine have refocused attention to the vital links between finance and growth.[68]

Most of these studies follow Goldsmith's tradition in that financial intermediaries affect growth by channeling funds to their most productive employments and hence affect the marginal efficiency of investment. Greenwood and Jovanovic's characterization, however, is provocative in that they provide a model in which financial intermediaries bring about both an increased savings rate and greater efficiency in investment. Instead of a simple causal mechanism

---

66. Patrick, "Financial Development," p. 185.
67. Schumpeter, *Theory of Economic Development*, p. 106.
68. Bencivenga and Smith, "Financial Intermediation;" Greenwood and Jovanovic, "Financial Development;" King and Levine, "Finance and Growth."

moving from financial development to economic growth, Greenwood and Jovanovic posit a two-way causal relationship characterized by feedback loops. On one hand, economic growth promotes increased participation in financial markets, increasing the size of the sector relative to national income. On the other hand, by collecting and analyzing investment projects from among any number of possibilities, financial intermediaries channel funds into their most productive employments and hence stimulate growth and development.[69]

An alternative perspective of the linkage has been offered by several writers and is one that seems particularly applicable to economies in transition – which, of course, the United States was in the first half of the nineteenth century. These models focus on the growth in the savings rate itself rather than on the marginal efficiency of investment. They recognize that many investors face sharp borrowing constraints; that is, they cannot borrow freely against anticipated future income.[70] Such constraints have implications for the behavior of households and businesses. As profitable investment opportunities become apparent, some – generally young and untested firms – will not be able to borrow sufficient amounts to enter the industry at the minimum optimal scale. Large firms, on the other hand, with a track record and substantial collateral to put at risk, face lesser constraints.[71] An inability to borrow sufficient amounts at current rates will induce potential entrants to save in the short term. When they are unable to borrow, entrepreneurs must build up financial wealth in the current period to finance the next period's investment. The obvious result, of course, is that present period investment opportunities may actually spur current period savings. A widespread recognition of investment possibilities, therefore, spurs savings and, hence, investment, which has immediate implications for growth.

Despite the recent outpouring of work, no consensus has yet been reached about the exact role or the ultimate effect of increased financial participation on growth. Nor have any empirical findings established a clear line of causation. The only thing that seems clear, without further investigation, is that banks and other financial intermediaries were a "social invention of the continuous attempt of

69. Greenwood and Jovanovic, "Financial Development."
70. De Gregario and Guidotti, "Financial Development."
71. Gertler, "Financial Structure," p. 573.

people to take advantage of the potentials of economic growth."[72] That was certainly how early Americans viewed them. In reviewing the history of western Pennsylvania, Albert Gallatin claimed that: "We know of the great difficulties which were encountered by those who first attempted to establish the most necessary manufactures, and that they would have been essentially relieved and some of them saved from ruin by moderate bank loans. . . . the general progress of the country was extremely slow, and might have been hastened by such institutions."[73] Simon Kuznets noted that it can be taken for granted that financial institutions were formed in response to the requirement "of balancing changing volumes and forms of saving on the supply side and changing volumes and forms of investment opportunities on the demand side."[74] How well were these changing demands met? Did antebellum banks funnel the increasing flow of savings into productive, growth-enhancing industries? Did they alter their operations in such a way, under the constraints of law and custom, so as to accommodate a changing economic environment? In short, did banks matter? It is to raise these questions that it becomes immediately apparent how hard it is to answer them. What follows is an attempt to draw some preliminary conclusions.

THE EMPIRICS OF FINANCE AND GROWTH

A common theme running throughout the theoretical literature out-lined above is the classic chicken-and-egg puzzle: which came first? In terms of financial intermediaries, the puzzle is probably better stated as: Which influences what? In the previous chapter the debate was laid out in terms of the classic supply-leading or demand-following paradigms. In the abstract, however, these competing characterizations are not particularly useful in framing empirical investigations. Instead, we are forced to seek guidance from empirical tests introduced in the endogenous growth literature. Two types of tests, first suggested by King and Levine, are offered to resolve the puzzle of whether finance affects subsequent growth or whether finance simply follows on the coat-tails of sweeping economic change.

72. Kuznets, "Foreword," p. xii in Goldsmith, *Financial Intermediaries*.
73. Gallatin, *Writings*, vol. 3, pp. 315–16.
74. Kuznets, "Foreword," p. xiii in Goldsmith, *Financial Intermediaries*.

To determine if Schumpeter was correct – that finance leads growth – it is necessary first to define and measure financial development. To this end four measures of financial development are constructed. Due to data limitations, these measures are not as sophisticated nor as inclusive as measures developed in studies of modern economies, but they should adequately reflect the process of financial development.[75] In particular, the four measures of financial development ultimately reflect what might be better termed *financial depth*. The measures include the volume of bank-supplied money and credit per capita as well as the volume of money and credit to income or output. While these measures have their shortcomings, they are quite useful in that they can also allow for a preliminary exploration of the channel through which financial development is linked to growth in the earliest stages of the development process. Did money or credit or both or neither lead to or influence growth? Or did growth lead to money and credit?

To answer these questions, two sets of results are reported each designed to address a particular viewpoint. As noted previously, one line of thought suggests that broad economic growth influences money and credit. That is, economic growth occurs first which then leads to a supply response on the part of financial intermediaries. A corollary to the argument that finance is of small import is that growth in indicators of both economic aggregates and financial development would follow similar tracks. Exogenous shocks that influence broad economic activity should be reflected in financial activity. To test this proposition of contemporaneous movement, the empirical tests proceed by studying the strength of the partial correlations between economic growth and financial development in the period 1830 to 1860. Additionally, because of the wide swings in economic activity over this interval – most notably, the depression of the late 1830s to early 1840s as well as the recessions of the late 1840s and late 1850s – the correlations are reported by decades. The results suggest a weak contemporaneous relationship between finance and growth in the short term.

The second set of tests focus on the relationship between the initial level of economic development and subsequent economic growth.

---

75. King and Levine, "Finance and Growth"; and De Gregario and Guidotti, "Financial Development," for a description of measures used in modern studies.

This is, in essence, Schumpeter's thesis: that financial institutions and some amount of financial development must predate economic growth so that entrepreneurs have access to accumulations of funds to finance their investment projects. It is found, in fact, that initial levels of financial depth are highly correlated with subsequent economic growth over both the short- and long-term, though the relationship is strongest in the long run. The findings, quite simply, suggest that finance may, as Schumpeter believed, lead economic development.

Contemporaneous Correlations between Finance and Growth

Our analysis of the relationship between finance and growth begins by considering contemporaneous correlations between growth in real per capita income and the rate of growth of financial intermediation at the state level. In particular, the strength of the relationship between per capita income growth and four different measures of the growth in financial depth is considered.

Before we proceed it is necessary to construct various measures of financial depth. There have been nearly as many measures of financial development as there have been studies of the relationship and there are few good reasons for preferring one to another a priori. The most commonly employed measures are expressed as ratios: bank money-to-gross domestic product (GDP); bank credit-to-GDP; money per capita; credit per capita; or bank offices per capita. Other measures of the degree of financial depth or sophistication include the ratio of credit extended by commercial banks to the total volume of external, private credit, or the ratio of commercial bank credit to the sum of commercial bank credit and central bank credit.[76] Besides commercial banks, more developed economies tend to witness the arrival of other more specialized financial intermediaries, such as savings banks, mortgage banks, investment banks, consumer credit companies, insurance companies, dominant central banks, and so forth. True financial maturity, therefore, requires a relative rise in the proportion

---

76. King and Levine, "Finance and Growth"; and De Gregario and Guidotti, "Finance and Development," construct several measures for modern economies. Much of the data underlying their constructs simply does not exist for antebellum America.

of intermediation performed by such specialized intermediaries at the expense of commercial banks. The subsequent analysis, however, considers only the commercial banking sector which undoubtedly underestimates the total volume of intermediation in antebellum America as savings banks, private bankers, commercial paper brokers, private lenders, and insurance companies surely provided intermediary services. That little information on these sources of credit are available, however, should not greatly distort the picture because in antebellum America commercial banks provided the bulk of the circulating media and a majority of commercial, agricultural, and industrial credit.

Four measures of financial depth or development were constructed. Following in the McKinnon-Shaw tradition, the size of the banking sector relative to both population and GDP is used to measure financial depth. These authors have argued that the greater a country or state's financial depth, the greater the volume of services provided by the financial sector. One measure of financial depth, money per capita, equals the ratio of bank money held outside the banking system to total population. Bank money was defined to consist of banknotes in circulation plus deposits less notes held by other banks.

But pure money holdings may not accurately reflect the level of non-monetary financial services provided by banks, services such as risk management, information gathering, and monitoring emphasized in recent theoretical models of bank behavior. In addition, money holding by the public may not accurately reflect the size of the banking sector. A given economy may have had a rather sophisticated financial sector with several different types of financial assets from which the public could choose. In this case, a financially deep economy could demonstrate a low level of money holding per capita. At the same time, an economy with few financial intermediaries could exhibit low money holdings because of high inflation expectations. In this case, the public may have low monetary holdings as people look to minimize money holdings and purchase inflation hedges. For antebellum America neither of these should be of great concern. Most states witnessed similar patterns of financial development and there is little evidence that individual state systems produced rates of inflation significantly different from the national average. Using monetary figures as a proxy for financial development then seems reasonable as the two were closely linked, especially in the early stages of development.

Despite the possibility that money and credit are closely intertwined, a second measure of financial depth, LOANS PER CAPITA, is constructed to more accurately reflect the level of bank intermediation. This proxy is calculated simply as the sum of all bank loans and discounts made by the banks to total population. Government debt held by the banks was eliminated from this measure because it is believed that credit channeled to the private sector was more likely to stimulate economic growth than were loans to governments. Again, this may underestimate the effects of banking as some states drew upon banks to fund infrastructure projects like railroads and canals, but most banks in most states worked diligently to keep these types of loans to a minimum. Antebellum banks simply did not like to extend long-term credit to massive improvement projects whose prospects were uncertain.

Table 2.1 reports money per capita and Table 2.2 reports loans per capita values by state at decadal intervals. It is readily seen that states experienced relatively wide variations in both absolute values and growth rates in each variable. In 1830, for example, the District of Columbia was the most monetized territory with its banks issuing in excess of $44 per capita. Arkansas, Iowa, Minnesota, Texas, and Wisconsin, on the other hand, had no banks and therefore no indigenous bank money per capita. Certainly, money from other states migrated into these regions, but it was unlikely that it migrated in amounts sufficient to fully meet the preferences or demands of these state's inhabitants. By 1860 all states and territories with the exception of Texas had at least experimented with banking to supply its populace with money and credit and all but a handful of states had banks which supplied more than $1 per capita in both money and loans. Most states had money per capita values in excess of $5. Louisiana and Massachusetts had more than $40 per capita. Rhode Island's banks had extended an incredible $153 per capita in credit.

As informative as these measures may be, most studies of the relationship between finance and growth prefer to measure the size of the financial sector relative to economic output or income. Goldsmith, for example, argued that an appropriate measure is the ratio

Table 2.1. Bank money per capita by state at decade intervals, 1830-1860

State	1830	1840	1850	1860
Maine	$2.40	$3.51	$6.33	$10.12
New Hampshire	3.30	5.08	6.59	13.52
Vermont	3.71	4.33	10.43	14.41
Massachusetts	16.56	21.18	24.27	40.21
Rhode Island	17.37	20.71	23.75	35.14
Connecticut	4.93	9.77	18.66	27.89
New York	4.62	9.35	20.73	33.95
New Jersey	0.59	5.27	8.29	14.72
Pennsylvania	9.94	8.23	10.51	12.05
Delaware	14.37	12.19	14.40	17.73
Maryland	6.84	10.95	12.84	16.13
District of Columbia	44.19	42.42	19.98	0.00
Virginia	4.53	7.34	8.97	10.18
North Carolina	2.10	3.38	4.30	6.53
South Carolina	3.48	10.80	16.98	21.60
Georgia	7.52	7.76	12.91	11.78
Florida	0.00	14.15	0.00	2.06
Ohio	0.28	3.74	7.27	4.76
Indiana	1.47	4.65	3.91	4.94
Illinois	5.86	9.09	1.93	5.45
Wisconsin	0.00	3.59	3.24	8.49
Michigan	1.53	2.36	2.10	0.74
Kentucky	0.80	5.66	8.34	15.92
Tennessee	0.33	6.53	4.72	8.44
Mississippi	7.33	59.02	0.27	0.28
Alabama	2.42	12.43	4.81	12.12
Louisiana	4.49	25.48	24.70	44.29
Missouri	8.18	3.37	5.77	8.63

Note: Bank money = circulation + deposits - notes of other banks
Sources: Fenstermaker, *Development*, Appendix B; U.S. Comptroller of the Currency, *Annual Report* (1876); U.S. Census Office, Ninth Census (1870), *Compendium*, Table VIII

Table 2.2. Bank credit per capita by state at decade intervals, 1830-1860

State	1830	1840	1850	1860
Maine	$6.38	$11.76	$10.00	$20.14
New Hampshire	10.13	14.41	12.11	26.97
Vermont	3.48	6.89	14.08	21.42
Massachusetts	45.85	63.05	63.68	96.80
Rhode Island	61.95	115.42	105.00	153.02
Connecticut	17.37	33.64	39.13	66.32
New York	6.61	21.73	30.88	51.63
New Jersey	1.05	13.22	13.03	22.19
Pennsylvania	14.25	20.19	15.11	20.41
Delaware	16.06	21.04	24.73	28.07
Maryland	13.64	28.92	23.61	30.42
District of Columbia	123.17	76.33	29.34	0.00
Virginia	6.15	12.58	12.78	15.65
North Carolina	5.70	6.70	5.95	12.30
South Carolina	4.83	30.87	30.82	39.51
Georgia	12.09	19.94	7.67	15.87
Florida	0.00	86.97	0.00	3.31
Ohio	0.84	8.83	8.23	4.74
Indiana	1.55	6.68	3.96	5.68
Illinois	7.83	12.45	0.69	0.23
Wisconsin	0.00	4.32	3.81	9.79
Michigan	0.97	10.14	2.72	1.19
Kentucky	1.35	13.49	11.85	21.88
Tennessee	0.98	12.09	8.98	10.59
Mississippi	14.70	128.67	0.19	0.50
Alabama	3.38	43.75	2.74	14.07
Louisiana	16.24	139.44	35.93	50.00
Missouri	6.95	5.42	4.79	13.08

Note: Bank credit = loans and discounts + bills of exchange
Sources: See Table 2.1

of the value of all financial assets to national income.[77] It is simply not possible to construct such a measure for antebellum America. In its stead, it is possible to construct indirect measures such as MONEY TO GDP and LOANS TO GDP using newly available state-level income measures.

Recent research by Thomas Weiss has made possible the construction of state-level GDP estimates for the antebellum era. After making several adjustments to labor participation rates, Weiss used an ingenious methodology first employed by Paul David to construct conjectural estimates of per capita economic output.[78] Fortunately, Weiss reported his underlying data in sufficient detail so as to allow for the construction of state-level estimates of GDP at decadal intervals between 1830 and 1860. This information was used to calculate per capita income estimates for each of thirty-two states or territories in the eastern part of the United States. Once these estimates were derived, GDP estimates could be used to determine both state-level estimates of annual average growth in per capita income and the relevant measures of financial depth – money to GDP and loans to GDP.[79]

Most theory predicts that the ratio of money and financial intermediation to income should increase as economic growth progresses. John Gurley and Edward Shaw, in a study of about seventy developed and developing countries, concluded that money-to-income ratios are typically below 0.1 for poor or undeveloped countries, rising to a peak of about 0.3 for more developed countries.[80] Because the link between money supply and credit intermediation were so close in antebellum America, loan-to-income ratios should be of a similar order of magnitude.

Table 2.3 shows that the United States's experience in the antebellum era conform quite closely to the Gurley-Shaw delineations. In 1830 the only states with money/income ratios in excess of 0.2, implying a significant degree of financial maturity were the District of Columbia and Delaware with ratios of 0.49 and 0.24. But these extraordinarily high ratios resulted more from a few moderate-sized banks

---

77. Goldsmith, *Financial Structure*, pp. 26–30.
78. Weiss, "U.S. Labor Force Estimates"; Weiss, "Economic Growth before 1860"; David, "Growth in Real Product."
79. The details of constructing these estimates are provided in the Appendix.
80. Gurley and Shaw, "Financial Intermediaries," p. 261.

Table 2.3. Ratio of bank money to real income by state at decade intervals, 1830-1860

State	1830	1840	1850	1860
Maine	0.04	0.05	0.07	0.09
New Hampshire	0.03	0.07	0.07	0.11
Vermont	0.07	0.07	0.14	0.15
Massachusetts	0.18	0.19	0.19	0.26
Rhode Island	0.19	0.18	0.18	0.21
Connecticut	0.07	0.11	0.17	0.21
New York	0.07	0.12	0.21	0.26
New Jersey	0.01	0.06	0.09	0.12
Pennsylvania	0.14	0.10	0.11	0.10
Delaware	0.24	0.17	0.18	0.16
Maryland	0.08	0.11	0.12	0.13
District of Columbia	0.49	0.46	0.16	0.00
Virginia	0.06	0.08	0.10	0.09
North Carolina	0.03	0.04	0.04	0.06
South Carolina	0.04	0.10	0.15	0.16
Georgia	0.09	0.09	0.14	0.10
Florida	0.00	0.13	0.00	0.02
Ohio	0.01	0.06	0.10	0.05
Indiana	0.04	0.09	0.06	0.06
Illinois	0.13	0.16	0.03	0.06
Wisconsin	0.00	0.03	0.05	0.09
Michigan	0.02	0.04	0.03	0.01
Kentucky	0.01	0.07	0.10	0.16
Tennessee	0.01	0.10	0.07	0.09
Mississippi	0.08	0.61	0.00	0.00
Alabama	0.03	0.13	0.05	0.10
Louisiana	0.04	0.20	0.20	0.30
Missouri	0.00	0.05	0.07	0.09

Note: See Table 2.1 for definitions and Appendix for real income derivations
Sources: See Table 2.1 and Weiss, "U.S. Labor Force Estimates;" Weiss, "Economic Growth Before 1860."

and a low population rather than from legitimate financial maturity. Ratios between 0.1 and 0.2, such as those in Massachusetts, Rhode Island and Pennsylvania, were probably more reasonable and more indicative of economic and financial development. The money/ income ratio in most states, in fact, fell well below 0.1, with about one-half of them with ratios less than 0.05. By 1860, four important commercial and industrial seaboard states had money/income ratios in excess of 0.2. Even the least financially developed states had money/income ratios approaching 0.1 and ten states could be considered moderately developed with ratios between 0.1 and 0.2.

Figures in Table 2.4, which reports loan/income ratios, support the impressions provided by the money/income ratios. In 1830 only five states had loan/income ratios of 0.2 or greater, but again Delaware and the District of Columbia's figures result from small populations and a few banks. By 1860 eleven states had loan/income ratios in excess of 0.2, with ten others with ratios between 0.1 and 0.2. All but three states or territories realized real growth in the ratios between 1830 and 1860. By the standards established by Gurley and Shaw most states had achieved a degree of moderate financial development; several had achieved levels displayed by modern developed economies.

If the Goldsmith-McKinnon-Shaw hypotheses are correct, increases or decreases in financial depth should have exerted an influence on growth. The agnostic premise, on the other hand, suggests that financial and economic development occur at similar rates and are pushed or pulled along by exogenous or endogenous shocks that affected both in broadly similar ways. Tables 2.5 through 2.7 present partial correlation coefficients between the contemporaneous growth in financial depth and real per capita income in an attempt to determine which hypothesis, if either, is closer to the mark. In conducting the tests, states were divided into three categories. Fast growers were defined as the top third of states in terms of growth in real per capita income; moderate growers, the second third; slow growers the lowest third. The final row in each column reports the average annualized growth rates in per capita income for each group and for the entire population of states.

Again, correlations are reported for each decade for which income figures are available in order to more fully capture the effects of short-run aggregate shocks, notably the depression of the late 1830s

Table 2.4. Ratio of bank credit to real income by state at decade intervals, 1830-1860

State	1830	1840	1850	1860
Maine	0.11	0.18	0.11	0.17
New Hampshire	0.10	0.19	0.12	0.21
Vermont	0.07	0.12	0.19	0.22
Massachusetts	0.49	0.55	0.49	0.62
Rhode Island	0.66	1.02	0.79	0.93
Connecticut	0.23	0.38	0.37	0.49
New York	0.10	0.27	0.31	0.39
New Jersey	0.01	0.16	0.14	0.18
Pennsylvania	0.20	0.25	0.16	0.17
Delaware	0.27	0.29	0.31	0.25
Maryland	0.16	0.29	0.23	0.25
District of Columbia	1.37	0.82	0.24	0.00
Virginia	0.08	0.13	0.14	0.14
North Carolina	0.08	0.08	0.05	0.11
South Carolina	0.05	0.29	0.28	0.29
Georgia	0.15	0.22	0.08	0.13
Florida	0.00	0.81	0.00	0.03
Ohio	0.02	0.14	0.11	0.05
Indiana	0.04	0.14	0.07	0.07
Illinois	0.17	0.21	0.01	0.00
Wisconsin	0.00	0.04	0.05	0.11
Michigan	0.01	0.17	0.04	0.01
Kentucky	0.02	0.18	0.15	0.22
Tennessee	0.02	0.18	0.12	0.11
Mississippi	0.17	1.33	0.00	0.00
Alabama	0.04	0.47	0.03	0.11
Louisiana	0.15	1.10	0.29	0.34
Missouri	0.00	0.08	0.06	0.14

Notes: See Tables 2.1 and 2.3
Sources: See Tables 2.1 and 2.3

Table 2.5. Simple correlations between contemporaneous growth in financial depth and real per capita income, 1830-1840

| | States experiencing | | | |
	Fast growth	Medium growth	Slow growth	All states
Money / person	0.29 (0.80)	-0.23 (-0.63)	0.46 (1.47)*	0.09 (0.46)
Credit / person	0.50 (1.53)*	-0.28 (-0.77)	0.31 (0.92)	0.15 (0.77)
Money / income	0.36 (1.02)	-0.25 (-0.68)	0.30 (0.89)	0.00 (0.00)
Credit / income	0.50 (1.53)*	-0.53 (-1.65)*	0.13 (0.37)	0.09 (0.46)
Average GDP growth	2.10	1.47	0.33	1.25

Notes: For definitions and method of calculation see notes to Table 2.3.
Approximately ten states in each category. Student t statistics in parentheses.
* implies significance at 10 percent confidence.
Sources: See sources to Tables 2.3

and the lesser recessions of 1848 and 1857–8. In general the results seem to support Robert Lucas's contention that the relationship between financial development and economic growth has been overemphasized.[81]

In the decade 1830–40, for example, only increases in the volume of loans, both per capita and per dollar of real income, are significantly correlated with increases in real per capita income. The importance of credit growth was strongest among the fastest growing economies. Money growth, on the other hand, appeared to be more

81. Lucas, "On the Mechanics."

Table 2.6. Simple correlations between contemporaneous growth in financial depth and real per capita income, 1840-1850

	States experiencing			
	Fast growth	Medium growth	Slow growth	All states
Money / person	-0.35 (-1.06)	0.30 (0.89)	-0.03 (-0.08)	0.37 (2.11)*
Credit / person	-0.15 (-0.43)	0.49 (1.59)*	-0.09 (-0.26)	0.35 (1.98)*
Money / income	-0.39 (-1.20)	0.25 (0.73)	-0.12 (-0.34)	0.29 (1.60)*
Credit / income	-0.27 (-0.79)	0.45 (1.43)*	-0.14 (-0.40)	0.30 (1.66)*
Average GDP growth	2.38	1.05	-0.38	1.02

Note: See Table 2.5. * implies significance at 10 percent confidence.
Sources: See Table 2.5

important among slow-growing economies than intermediation. One interpretation is that fast-growing economies already had some banking services and were already reasonably monetized and it was increases in credit that fostered growth, at least more so than increased monetization. Given that the fastest growing economies during this decade included such states as Massachusetts, Delaware, Rhode Island, Ohio, New York, and Virginia, this seems an appropriate interpretation. The slowest growing economies included several states that had been recently settled and where monetization would be expected to be low: Michigan, Kentucky, Tennessee, and Mississippi. For moderate-growth economies neither money nor credit growth was highly correlated with income growth.

Table 2.7. Simple correlations between contemporaneous growth in financial depth and real per capita income, 1850-1860

	States experiencing			
	Fast growth	Medium growth	Slow growth	All states
Money / person	0.45 (1.33)	0.42 (1.31)	0.10 (0.30)	0.02 (0.11)
Credit / person	0.15 (0.40)	0.54 (1.81)*	-0.04 (-0.12)	0.05 (0.26)
Money / income	0.32 (0.89)	0.41 (1.27)	-0.03 (-0.09)	0.03 (0.16)
Credit / income	0.26 (0.71)	0.52 (1.72)*	-0.05 (-0.15)	0.00 (0.00)
Average GDP growth	2.87	2.42	1.82	2.33

Notes: See Table 2.5. * implies significance at 10 percent confidence.
Sources: See Table 2.5

In the interval between 1840 and 1850 (possibly the one for which the results are most difficult to interpret given that the trough of the depression occurred during 1841–2) the situation was apparently reversed. Correlations between money growth, credit growth and income growth reported in Table 2.6 were significant across all classes, but the correlation was strongest among moderate-growth states. And, as in the preceding decade, credit growth was more highly correlated with income growth than money growth and, therefore, seemingly more important than money growth. Again when considering the states comprising this group – Massachusetts, Rhode Island, Pennsylvania, Maryland and New Jersey – this conclusion seems sensible as these were already well-monetized economies in which additional credit would have been more important than money.

Correlations for this decade may be somewhat misleading, however, given the financial dislocations taking place during the depression of the early 1840s. Although the correlations do not suggest a strong relationship, the group of slow-growing economies consisted of several whose banking systems partially or completely collapsed. Louisiana, for example, lost about one-half of its banks and banking capital during the depression. The banking systems of Arkansas, Mississippi, and Florida utterly collapsed. Iowa and Wisconsin adopted constitutions prohibiting the chartering of banks. For this decade the low correlations between financial and economic growth suggest that banking did not simply follow on the heels of broad aggregate changes when states are grouped by rates of growth. When considering the sample as a whole, however, the effect of common influences appears to be stronger.

Correlations for the decade 1850–60 (reported in Table 2.7) are largely similar to those of the prior decade. Again, those states experiencing moderate growth rates in per capita income demonstrate the highest correlations between financial development and economic growth, and credit growth was more highly correlated with growth than increased monetization. Among the group of slow growers, correlations between financial development and economic growth are essentially zero, with these states experiencing positive growth rates despite a declining relative size of the financial sector.

On their face, the results of the correlations between contemporaneous growth rates in finance and income suggest that the agnostics are incorrect. There simply does not appear to be any significant coincident movements in both financial development and economic growth. If finance simply followed on the heels of broad aggregate change or was simply subject to the same shocks as the larger economy, finance and income growth should have moved in similar directions at roughly similar rates. The evidence from the three decades before the Civil War, however, suggests that such was not the case. Although money growth or credit growth was significantly correlated with income growth for some states in some decades, the strength of the link was quite low. This implies that economies can experience real economic growth without concurrent growth in financial depth or sophistication. Yet the strength of the correlations in the 1840s – a decade of sharp depression and equally sharp recovery – suggest that there were at least coincident effects. The reality appears to be that banks were of some consequence, particularly when we peer behind the faceless correlations and consider the components individually. The absence or particularly the disappearance of banks materially slowed the pace of economic growth in the 1840s.

Initial Financial Depth and Subsequent Economic Growth

An alternative to the agnostic view that financial and economic development were only modestly linked or, more likely, prone to similar influences is Schumpeter's view that financial development was a necessary prerequisite for economic development. A straightforward test of these competing hypotheses can be easily formulated. If financial development was, in fact, a necessary precondition to economic growth, the initial values of the financial indicators developed above should be highly correlated with subsequent (or future) economic growth. If finance did not matter or passively followed growth, the initial degree of financial development should be uncorrelated with subsequent economic growth.

The empirical analysis follows the lead of studies by Robert Barro, Barro and Xavier Sala-i-Martin, King and Levine, De Gregario and Guidotti, and other empirical investigations inspired by the endogenous growth literature.[82] These studies have found that economic growth depends on such things as the investment rate, school enrollments or literacy, government spending, political stability, the initial level of real per capita income, and financial considerations. Due to data limitations, several of these variables cannot be included in state-level regressions for antebellum America; others would make little sense (assassination of state legislators or governors were few, though canings and fistfights on the floors of various assemblies occurred every so often).

The principal independent variables used in OLS regressions, with economic growth rates as the dependent variable, are the initial level of real per capita income, literacy rates, and two measures of financial

---

82. Barro, "Economic Growth"; Barro and Sala-i-Martin, "Convergence;" Barro and Sala-i-Martin, "Convergence across States and Regions"; King and Levine, "Finance and Growth"; King and Levine, "Finance, Entrepreneurship, and Growth"; De Gregario and Guidotti, "Financial Development." See references therein for advances in endogenous growth theory, particularly Mankiw, Romer and Weil, "Contribution to the Empirics."

depth (money/income and credit/income ratios reported in Tables 2.2 and 2.3). Initial levels of per capita income are included because nearly all studies have found a convergence phenomenon wherein poor countries tend to grow more quickly than rich countries. Barro and Sala-i-Martin, for example, estimate that income gaps tend to narrow at about two percent per year.[83] Similarly, most studies have found that investments in human capital also promote economic growth. While most studies include school (either primary or secondary or both) enrollments as measures of human capital investment, such data is unavailable for antebellum America. In its stead, literacy rates among free people in 1850 were employed.[84]

In addition a sector variable was constructed to include in the regressions. Shocks to particular sectors, say, agriculture or commerce, can affect different economies differently. Yet such shocks can influence economies within a given region similarly; say, declining world cotton or wheat prices. In that case, error terms are no longer independent and random. To correct for this, regional dummy variables were included as well as the SECTOR variable, defined as:

$$\text{SECTOR}_{it} = \sum_{j=1}^{n} w_{ijt} * \log(y_{j,t+T}/y_{j,t}) \qquad 2.4$$

where w_{ijt} is the proportion of sector j in state i's income at time t. The term $y_{j,t}$ is the national average of personal income originating in sector j at time t, expressed in per capita terms. In addition to accounting for changing sectoral shares in economy i, the SECTOR variable equals the growth rate of state i's per capita income between years t and t + T if each of state i's sectors grew (or declined) at the same rate as the national average.[85] The variable also acts as a proxy for common effects related to the sectoral composition of each state's economy. If agriculture, for example, suffers a shock common to all states, the variable's effect will differ across states due to differences in the share of income originating in agriculture across states.

83. Barro and Sala-i-Martin, "Convergence across States and Regions," pp. 112–13.
84. Obviously, literacy rates for each decade would have been more informative than using 1850 literacy rates throughout, but the 1850 census was the first to record literacy and that data is used in all specifications. Secondly, initial regressions using literacy rates for the entire population, including slaves, differed very little from those reported. The only real effect of including slaves was collinearity between the literacy variable and the regional dummy variables.
85. The sector variable was adopted from Barro and Sala-i-Martin, "Convergence," p. 234. They argue that its inclusion ensures that the error terms are independent.

Because movements in prices, particularly agricultural prices, vary from one period to the next, the variable was constructed for each subperiod regression reported below. Finally, given the focus of this study, the initial degree of financial depth was included in each regression.

Table 2.8 reports the results of ordinary least squares (OLS) regressions employing the money/income ratios as the measure of financial depth. Estimates were made for each decadal subperiod as well as the longer-term intervals 1840 to 1860 and 1830 to 1860. The short-term (or single decade) regressions are reported as a basis of comparison for the preceding contemporaneous correlations. These results should also reflect, in a sense, coincident effects of shocks on both finance and growth, while the long-term regressions should capture the effects of initial financial development on subsequent economic growth.

The parameter estimates are largely consistent with previous research on economic growth in a cross-section of developed and developing countries. In particular, the negative coefficient on initial income levels supports Barro's "convergence" hypothesis.[86] That is, poorer economies tend to grow at more rapid rates than richer economies. Using the 1830–60 estimate (Table 2.7) as an example, because the initial income variable is measured in 1840 dollars the −1.34 parameter estimate should be interpreted to mean that as per capita income increased by $1 the subsequent growth rate was diminished by 1.34 percentage points. Convergence was occurring, but it was a painfully slow process. With everything else constant, equalization of income would require the better part of a century.

Literacy (a proxy for human capital investment) is also positively correlated with growth. The literacy coefficient is statistically significant only in the 1850–60 specification, but that probably results from the fact that literacy rates were not collected in the United States until 1850 and those literacy rates were employed in all regressions. If literacy rates had been available at the beginning of each interval, it is likely that they too would have been significant.

The sector variable is generally insignificant, implying that most state economies still revolved around agriculture in the antebellum era. But the variable is positive in most specifications. That is, states

86. Barro, "Economic Growth."

Table 2.8. Economic growth and initial financial depth

	Dependent variable = per capita income growth				
	1830-40	1840-50	1850-60	1840-60	1830-60
Constant	4.92	24.74	3.99	12.13	4.20
	(0.50)	(2.83)**	(0.66)	(3.41)**	(1.70)
Initial	0.06	-6.38	-4.19	-3.58	-1.34
income	(0.03)	(-3.60)**	(-5.88)**	(-4.86)**	(-3.02)**
Literacy	1.84	3.97	16.65	4.76	3.88
	(0.17)	(0.41)	(3.37)**	(1.19)	(1.48)
Sector	-52.60	13.83	4.05	3.41	-1.19
	(-1.83)*	(1.54)	(0.59)	(1.18)	(-0.89)
Mid-	0.22	-0.88	0.59	-0.23	-0.02
Atlantic	(0.31)	(-1.26)	(1.40)	(-0.78)	(-0.11)
South	-0.69	0.20	0.35	-0.10	-0.28
Atlantic	(-0.61)	(0.19)	(0.74)	(-0.22)	(-1.02)
Old	-0.97	-2.25	-0.70	-1.09	-0.39
NW	(-1.19)	(-3.43)**	(-1.41)	(-3.99)**	(-1.95)*
Old	-0.77	-0.87	0.30	-0.54	-0.42
SW	(-0.80)	(-0.95)	(0.67)	(-1.41)	(-1.79)*
Money/	3.21	2.42	4.13	1.87	1.68
gdp	(1.18)	(1.44)	(1.82)*	(2.65)*	(2.55)*
Adj R^2	0.06	0.49	0.60	0.70	0.71
N	28	30	32	30	28

Notes: See text for variable definitions. * implies signifiance at 10%;
** at 1%

in which a significant share of their income originated in sectors that did well at the national level tended to have higher growth rates.[87] That is, if cotton agriculture, for example, did well (as it did in the 1850s), states in which cotton accounted for a significant share of state income grew faster. Similarly, if manufacturing did well in some decade, states in which a relatively large share of income originated in manufacturing did well.

Though the parameter estimates are not significant, monetization appears to have been more important in the short term than the long. Over the decade 1850–60, for example, a 10 percent increase in the money/income ratio resulted in a 40 percent increase in the rate of economic growth. That is, if a state's real income had grown at an average annual rate of 2.00 percent, a 10 percent increase in its money/income ratio would have raised it annual growth rate to 2.80 percent. Using the "rule of 72," a 10 percent increase in money per capita reduced the interval at which state per capita income doubled from thirty-six to twenty-five years.

The longer the interval considered, however, the less important increased monetization became. Over the interval 1830–60, for example, a 10 percent increase in a state's monetization would have produced an increase in per capita income growth of about 16.8 percent. Or, had a state's economy grown at 2 percent per annum, an increase in bank-supplied money of 10 percent would have led to growth at the rate of about 2.14 percent per year. A 10 percent increase in monetization, then, would have reduced the income doubling interval from thirty-six to thirty-three years. Admittedly, this is a modest effect when taken in isolation, but banking and monetization was not acting alone and even modest long-run contributions were still important.

Reasons for these short-run, long-run differences are manifold, but the most important cause is that the money/income figures, as measured here, assume that all money was bank-produced and that all bank-produced money circulated only in the bank's home state. Neither was true, especially in states that severely restricted or even prohibited domestic banking operations. Iowa provides an illustrative case. The state's 1846 constitution prohibited the establishment of commercial banks, or any corporate body with the privilege of

---

87. Barro and Sala-i-Martin, "Convergence," p. 234.

"making, issuing, or putting into circulation any bill, check, ticket, certificate, promissory note, or other paper ... to circulate as money."[88] Despite this prohibition, paper money flowed into and circulated in Iowa. Banks were also prohibited from issuing and circulating notes in the neighboring territory of Nebraska, yet the Nebraska territorial legislature chartered several pseudo-banks whose notes were circulated only in Iowa. In addition, notes that circulated as currency were issued by townships, cities, merchants, stagecoach companies, produce buyers, and insurance companies.

By 1856, then, notes of more than three hundred institutions, both domestic and foreign, circulated in the capital of Iowa City. Clearly, a strict prohibition of banking did not proscribe the circulation of paper money. Such prohibitions, however, probably affected the quality of the circulating medium as paper notes issued by such diverse, nonbank enterprises were not as widely accepted as bank-issued money. The effect of bank-supplied money was, therefore, more important in the short run because few substitutes for it were available. In the long run, money from other states flowed in or local entrepreneurs created and circulated their own close substitutes to facilitate exchange and savings. Despite the measurement errors inherent in the parameter estimates, money apparently mattered as much in antebellum America as it does in modern developing countries.[89]

Table 2.9 presents parameter estimates when loan/income ratios are substituted in the regression for money/income ratios. Coefficient estimates for the control variables remain largely unchanged. The negative coefficient on the level of initial income supports the convergence hypothesis. Literacy remains important as does sectoral composition, though neither are significant in all specifications. The Old Northwest, too, grew at a significantly slower pace than did the New England region, possibly as a result of its continued reliance on agriculture and the highly variable prices of farm products between 1830 and 1860.[90] And like money, the initial level of credit and intermediation appears to have had a greater influence in the short run than the long. In the 1850s, for example, a 10 percent increase in

88. Hammond, *Banks and Politics*, pp. 9–10.
89. See King and Levine, "Finance and Growth," pp. 730–4 for a discussion of the role of money and intermediation in developing countries.
90. See Warren and Pearson, *Prices*, table 3 for farm product prices.

Table 2.9. Economic growth and initial financial depth

| | Dependent variable = per capita income | | | | |
	1830-40	1840-50	1850-60	1840-60	1830-60
Constant	4.08	29.21	4.89	14.81	3.78
	(0.43)	(3.40)**	(0.85)	(4.41)**	(1.76)*
Initial	-0.20	-7.74	-4.63	-4.43	-1.47
Income	(-0.11)	(-4.16)**	(-6.41)**	(-5.93)**	(-3.73)**
Literacy	4.61	4.94	17.59	5.25	5.11
	(0.43)	(0.54)	(3.77)**	(1.44)	(2.15)*
Sector	-60.30	16.08	3.88	4.55	-1.89
	(-2.10)*	(1.88)*	(0.60)	(1.70)*	(-1.54)
Mid-	0.46	-0.66	0.91	-0.07	0.10
Atlantic	(0.65)	(-0.99)	(2.21)*	(-0.27)	(0.62)
South	-0.56	0.62	0.71	0.16	-0.22
Atlantic	(-0.51)	(0.61)	(1.44)	(0.39)	(-0.90)
Old	-1.01	-2.12	-0.52	-1.01	-0.41
NW	(-1.27)	(-3.40)**	(-1.07)	(-4.02)**	(-2.32)*
Old	-0.65	-0.73	0.57	-0.43	-0.36
SW	(-0.69)	(-0.84)	(1.23)	(-1.23)	(-1.72)*
Credit/	1.70	1.55	2.34	1.02	0.85
GDP	(1.63)	(2.16)*	(2.50)*	(3.55)**	(3.67)**
Adj R^2	0.12	0.54	0.64	0.75	0.77
N	28	30	32	30	28

Notes: See Table 2.8

credit/income led to a 23.4 percent increase in per capita income. That is, if an economy was experiencing real income growth at the rate of 2.00 percent per year, a ten percent increase in the state-wide loan-to-income ratio would have increased the income growth rate to 2.47 percent. Again, using the "rule of 72" this implied a shortening of the income-doubling interval from thirty-six to twenty-nine years.

Over the long period of 1830 to 1860 the effect increased inter-mediation had on economic growth rates was more modest. A 10 percent increase in the loan/income ratio, for instance, would have generated a sustained increase of the rate of income growth of 8.5 percent. Or, a 2 percent rate of growth would have increased to 2.17 percent. Again, even modest contributions of finance to growth were important because they were not acting in isolation. While they represented only one component of growth, it was a vital component.

Underlying these short- and long-run differences in the importance of credit are causes likely to have been similar to those for money. If a state's banking policies led to suboptimal loan-to-income ratios, alternative sources of credit arose. Private banking, brokerage, and banking operations disguised under other auspices were substituted for domestically produced commercial bank credit and intermediation services. Such services could also flow in from outside the state. When, in the 1840s, Louisiana became reluctant to charter new banks and increase the volume of intermediation, banks outside its borders established agencies in New Orleans and captured for themselves some of the profits to be had.[91] It seems likely, as well, that the longer a given state remained intransigent in its policies, the more likely it was to witness the arrival of various substitutes. Like money, intermediation and the initial loan/income ratio positively and significantly influenced the subsequent pace of economic growth.

CONCLUDING COMMENTS

Bringing the argument full circle, data from antebellum America (imperfect though it be) lends more support to a broadly defined "supply-leading" or Schumpeter's hypothesis than to the "demand-

91. See Green, "Louisiana," and Lesesne, *Bank of the State*, for descriptions of Louisiana's banking policies in the 1840s and their effects on bank intermediation and the incentives they created for banks in other states to enter the New Orleans market.

following" or passive hypotheses of banking and growth. Correlations between the contemporaneous growth in a wide variety of financial indicators and economic growth are weak and seem to have been greatest among economies experiencing moderate growth rates rather than either fast or slow growers. But that, in itself, may not be particularly surprising. Economies experiencing fast or slow growth may have been responding to stimuli far removed from influences that would have directly affected the financial system. Favorable growing weather, or possibly droughts or floods or locusts, were simply beyond the control of even the most progressive banking system. Maybe it was for those economies treading along at a normal pace that banking mattered most.

Regression analysis supported by some institutional details, on the other hand, strongly supports the contention that the initial level of financial depth had ramifications for subsequent rates of economic growth. These findings are consistent with recent research and with both the Goldsmith and McKinnon-Shaw hypotheses that financial services stimulate growth by increasing the rate of accumulation and by channeling funds into more productive investments. Unfortunately, the data do not allow for separating out the relative importance of these two effects, but it is likely that both were important. In the earliest stages of development, it is likely that accumulation (money) mattered more. In the early stages, growth tends to arise from Smithian causes. Growth results from the replacement of subsistence agriculture with commercial agriculture, with the replacement of barter with monetary exchange, and from the simple division of labor. Money facilitates that transition because it allows for increased specialization. The farmer is no longer forced to fill his own root cellar. He can fill his barn with cotton and then stock his root cellar with the proceeds of the sale. Once the economy is adequately monetized (a money/income ratio of about 0.1 to 0.2 according to Gurley and Shaw), credit becomes more important. Now that the farmer can specialize and hold his assets in nonperishable form, his attention can turn to new processes, new hybrids, or simply more land or more capital-intensive production. Credit, to borrow Keynes's term, may awaken men's animal spirits, broaden their economic visions, and promote economic development.

From the evidence presented above, it may be fairly concluded that Schumpeter was correct about the important link between finance and growth. As King and Levine noted, this link is not the mechanism most closely associated with Schumpeter. Instead, his name is most often invoked when discussing the process of "creative destruction" wherein innovation and invention lay waste to old production processes and products with the creation of newer and more efficient processes. But an integral, and often overlooked, component of Schumpeter's story is that financial intermediation makes possible innovation and growth. Credit, in his scheme, "accommodates itself to the purposes of the entrepreneur . . . [and] this function constitutes the keystone of the modern credit structure."[92]

Certainly, without articulating and, perhaps, without fully comprehending the complexities and subtleties of Schumpeter's theory, contemporary Americans nevertheless understood the link between finance and entrepreneurship, between entrepreneurship and growth and, therefore, between finance and growth. Writing in 1831, Nathan Appleton provided a prescient summary of the hypothesis that credit interrupts the circular flow and directs resources into new channels. "Bank capital," wrote Appleton, "consists of money, which the proprietors do not choose to employ themselves, but have established a fund, to be employed by the active and enterprising classes of society. It is thus placed where those classes can command it, at their pleasure. Abundance of such capital is, in the highest degree, favorable to public prosperity, by exciting industry and extending trade."[93] Recognizing this relationship, most states encouraged the development of banking and other financial intermediaries. And the "most persuasive evidence of the crucial role of banks in promoting [growth]," wrote Cameron, "would seem to be the close correspondence in timing between the essentially political decision to permit the growth of a banking network and the beginnings of rapid . . . growth."[94]

This is not to say that banking and financial intermediation was the wellspring of any country's or any region's economic growth. A well-functioning financial sector may contribute to economic growth, but its effects could be masked by unfavorable resource endowments, a low rate of human capital accumulation, a suboptimal rate of population or labor force growth, or inefficient or counterproductive gov-

92. Schumpeter, *Theory*, p. 107.
93. Appleton, *Examination*, p. 29.
94. Cameron, "Theoretical Bases," p. 14.

ernmental policies. Alternatively, even a poorly designed, inefficient financial sector may not positively retard economic growth if all other factors were favorable. "What can be asserted without fear of contradiction," wrote Cameron, "is that any given banking system might, with different policies, have been made more or less effective in its contribution to economic development."[95] The antebellum American experience, indeed, suggests that those states that promoted financial development most, either through liberal chartering, free banking, or broad-based branch banking – Massachusetts, New York, and Virginia are but three examples – consistently experienced moderate to high rates of economic growth.[96] While the exact causal mechanism remains clouded, the evidence supports a connection between the two.

95. Cameron, *Banking and Economic Development*, p. 7 (emphasis deleted).
96. Without wishing to push the interpretation too far, it seems something more than a coincidence that financially repressive policies coincided with relative commercial and financial decline in both Philadelphia and New Orleans. Philadelphia's banking system could not accommodate a growing demand for credit as could New York's and commercial supremacy in the Middle Atlantic region passed hands. Similarly, New Orleans' restrictive policies in the 1840s are sometimes cited as the cause of decline in the growth of the share of Mississippi and Ohio river basin produce moving through the city and financed by the city's banks. See Green, "Louisiana," and Green, *Finance and Economic Development*, for analyses of Louisiana's post-depression financial policies and their consequences.

3   Financing Entrepreneurship: Banks, Merchants, and Manufacturers

The possessor of wealth, even if it is the greatest combine, must resort to credit if he wishes to carry out a new combination, which cannot like an established business be financed by returns from previous production.

Joseph Schumpeter (1934)

Here again the main question to be answered by the statistical material is: Who finances whom?

Raymond Goldsmith (1969)

After an extensive tour of the United States in the 1830s, the French economist Michel Chevalier wrote that banks had "served the Americans as a lever . . . to cover their country with roads, canals, factories . . . with everything that goes to make up a civilization."[1] Contemporary Americans were no less enamored than their French visitor with the benefits arising from the proliferation of banks. As early as 1786, Peletiah Webster wrote that banks were already providing a "great favor to individuals, and increasing trade, manufactures, and husbandry of the State."[2] In the midst of the bank mania of the 1830s, the usually cautious and tempered New York bank commissioners informed the General Assembly that their banks had supported "that system of credit which to a great extent has served as capital to build up our magnificent cities and towns – to despatch 300,000 tons of tonnage abroad – to rear our numerous and flourishing manufacto-

---

1. Chevalier, *Society, Manners and Politics*, p. 36, quoted in Klebaner, *American Commercial Banking*, p. 52.
2. Webster, *Essay on Credit*, p. 224.

84

ries – to give activity to our immense internal trade."[3] In 1837 Ohio's governor attributed no less remarkable feats to his state's banks. "Credit," he reminded the legislature, "has bought our land, built our cities, cleared our fields, founded our churches, erected our colleges and schools."[4] Their luster had not been dulled nor their promises unkept despite the commercial reversals and the suspension or failure of so many banks in the wake of the financial revulsion of 1837. Banks, finance and credit were simply of too great a long-term benefit to abandon them in the midst of a short-term crisis. Not everyone, of course, saw banks as an unmitigated good – as the rhetoric and acrimony of the Bank War well remind us – but more people supported than opposed them.

Despite deeply held convictions among contemporaries about the link between financial and economic development, economists and economic historians have, perhaps rightly so, remained skeptical. Studies of the postbellum American experience suggest that American banks either failed to or were slow to mobilize funds and direct them toward socially optimal employments.[5] Yet the mid- to late-nineteenth century witnessed several technological innovations that should have facilitated the movement of funds. Railroads and steamboat packet lines sped the movement of goods. An emerging financial press increased the dissemination of market information and improvements in transportation increased the speed with which this information, via these newspapers, travelled between markets. The development and spread of the telegraph, too, sped the pace at which financial information moved between commercial centers. In addition to the technological advances occurring in transportation and communication – making it easier to invest in distant geographic markets – new institutions were arising to provide much-needed information to potential lenders, the most important of which were credit reporting agencies like R. G. Dun & Company.[6] Such innovations may have altered distributive techniques in credit through the provision of

3. New York General Assembly, *Assembly Document No. 74* (1835), p. 11.
4. *Ohio Executive Documents* (1837/38), quoted in Golembe, *State Banks and Economic Development*, p. 196.
5. The principal studies drawing these conclusions include Davis, "Investment Market," and Sylla, "Federal Policy." Much more will be said about these and other similar studies in Chapters 4 and 5 and the Epilogue.
6. See Norris, *R. G. Dun & Co.* for a study of the development of credit reporting. Atherton, "Problem of Credit Rating," provides a study of the industry in the agricultural regions of the antebellum South.

more and better information about the credit worthiness of potential borrowers.

If intermediaries were as efficient at utilizing information as modern economic theory suggests, they should have made use of these resources to set in motion new, nontraditional allocations of credit, directing it to incipient but promising sectors. The effect of these technological advances was, as Richard Sylla noted, to increase the volume of funds available to credit users and "to break down their sectoral and geographic compartmentalization."[7] Credit market imperfections loomed large when developing economies were witnessing the emergence of new industries with widely varying rates of growth. "In such situations," Sylla continued, "the compartmentalization of capital markets [could] inhibit growth in the most promising sectors if these sectors [could not] draw funds for expansion from other sectors."[8]

Simultaneous with the westward and southward expansion of agriculture and commerce was an embryonic manufacturing sector growing at a brisk pace and clamoring for funds. Changes like these certainly placed severe stresses on financial intermediaries forced to deal with the challenges of financing geographic mobility and industrial development. New industries, like new territories, were relative unknowns to the financial community. Risks were calculated imprecisely, if at all, as Frank Knight's line between risk and uncertainty was crossed. Much was known, for example, about the risks of wheat farming in Pennsylvania, considerably less about corn farming in Iowa. Similarly, the risks of flour milling in Virginia were calculable; those of a large-scale, integrated iron furnace in western Pennsylvania were not and were dependent, to a great degree, on subjective probabilities. Despite the overwhelming difficulties and overarching uncertainties facing antebellum bankers and other lenders, the evidence suggests that they forged ahead, took risks and provided funds to incipient industrial enterprises.

Whereas the previous chapter employed a *macroeconomic* methodology in that it focused on broad aggregates, this chapter is decidedly *microeconomic* in approach. Instead of determining whether banks as a group influenced the state-level rate of economic growth, this chapter looks at the portfolios, the banking philosophies

7. Sylla, *American Capital Markets*, p. 146.
8. Ibid.

and the lending practices at a handful of antebellum banks. While the small sample provides only tentative results, the results suggest that banks directed capital to manufacturing firms, transportation enterprises and service providers – three growth centers in the First Industrial Revolution. The results, then, reinforce the conclusions of the previous chapter in that banks contributed to economic growth in myriad ways.

In summarizing antebellum America's banking experience, Jeremy Atack and Peter Passell posed the ultimate question: "Did banks really matter to economic growth?" Their answer: "Banks undoubtedly mobilized savings, but as for their value as market makers – efficient allocators of capital to those who could used it most productively – we know relatively little."[9] The remainder of this chapter offers some new insights and some preliminary answers.

BANKS AND THE WORKING CAPITAL–FIXED CAPITAL DEBATE

Whereas economic *growth* implies an increase in per capita output (or income), economic *development* implies an increase in per capita output *and* a changing sectoral composition of output. That is, economic growth can occur in even the most rudimentary, largely agrarian economy through, say, the development of more efficient agricultural techniques (manuring, crop rotation, irrigation, and so forth) with no change in the sectoral composition of output. Economic development, on the other hand, occurs when commerce, transportation, and manufacturing grow in importance while agriculture's position as the dominant employer is gradually eroded.

Nineteenth-century America experienced both growth and development. Thomas Weiss estimated that between 1800 and 1820 real per capita output increased by about 0.4 percent, between 1820 and 1840, by 1.2 percent; and by 1.6 percent between 1840 and 1860.[10] Only a small fraction of this accelerating economic growth resulted from productivity growth in agriculture, however. Paul David estimated an 8.3 percent rise in agricultural output per worker between 1800 and 1840, largely a result of the spatial redistribution of the farm

9. Atack and Passell, *A New Economic View*, p. 107.
10. Weiss, "Economic Growth before 1860," p. 27.

labor force. Agricultural productivity increased as farmers abandoned marginal land in the East for more productive, infra-marginal lands in the West.

Most of the growth in real per capita income resulted from the changing sectoral composition of the labor force.[11] In 1800 about 76 percent of the labor force was engaged in agricultural pursuits. By 1860 the percentage so employed had fallen to less than 53 percent. This shifting pattern of employment radically changed the relative importance of industrial sectors. In 1839 agriculture accounted for 42 percent of value added in GNP, while commerce, transportation, and manufacturing accounted for about 37 percent. By 1859 the situation was nearly reversed; agriculture contributed 35 percent of GNP while the commercial and manufacturing sectors contributed 46 percent.[12] While use of the term "Industrial Revolution" has fallen into disfavor among some in recent years, changes occurring during the first half of the nineteenth century suggest that "something was stirring, important transformations were under way."[13]

Information from the 1850 and 1860 censuses of manufacturing, while representative only of short-term change, is indicative of the sweeping transformation taking place in America. Table 3.1 reports the number of manufacturing establishments by region and demonstrates that all regions, except New England, witnessed an increase in the number of manufacturing establishments. For the United States as a whole, the number of manufacturing concerns increased by about 14 percent, from about 123,000 in 1850 to nearly 141,000 in 1860.[14] More important from the standpoint of economic development, perhaps, was the increased use of capital in manufacturing. Between 1850 and 1860, capital per establishment increased at an average annual rate of 5.2 percent. Even the manufacturing-impaired South Atlantic states experienced real growth.

Not only did the capital stock grow in absolute terms in the 1850s, it grew relative to the labor force. During the decade capital per

---

11. David, "Growth of Real Product," pp. 183, 185, 195.
12. Weiss, "Revised Estimates," pp. 646, 649 and tables 12.1 and 12.3. Richard Easterlin's estimates suggest changes of a similar order of magnitude. He estimated that between 60 and 70 percent of personal income was generated in agriculture in 1840. By 1880 only about 46 percent of personal income originated in agriculture. See Easterlin, "Interregional Differences in Per Capita Income," pp. 97–9.
13. Weiss, "U.S. Labor Force Estimates," p. 23.
14. U.S. Census Office, Ninth Census (1870), *Compendium*, pp. 798–9.

Table 3.1. Indicators of growth in manufacturing by region, 1850-1860

	Establishments		Capital/establishment		Capital/worker	
	1850	1860	1850	1860	1850	1860
New England	22,487	20,671	$7,368	$12,456	$530	$657
Mid-Atlantic	30,068	30,234	4,479	8,575	616	828
Old Northwest	21,471	27,226	2,465	5,250	570	902
South Atlantic	10,458	12,379	3,598	4,550	627	789
Old Southwest	12,400	13,358	3,001	5,641	585	1,006
U.S.	123,025	140,433	4,334	7,191	557	770

Notes: New England includes Maine, New Hampshire, Vermont, Massachusetts, Rhode Island, and Connecticut. Mid-Atlantic includes New York, New Jersey, Pennsylvania, Delaware, Maryland, and District of Columbia. Old Northwest includes Ohio, Indiana, Illinois, Michigan, and Wisconsin. South Atlantic includes Virginia, North Carolina, South Carolina, Georgia, and Florida. Old Southwest includes Kentucky, Tennessee, Mississippi, Alabama, Louisiana, and Missouri
Source: U.S. Census Office, Ninth Census (1870), *Compendium*, pp. 798-99

worker grew by 3.3 percent per annum. Economic theory predicts that such increases in the capital/labor ratio should have increased the marginal product of labor, everything else equal. Everything did not, of course, remain equal, yet output per manufacturing worker increased from $1,064 in 1850 to $1,438 in 1860, implying an annual growth rate of nearly 3.1 percent. The shift from agriculture to manufacturing and the increasing use of capital within the manufacturing sector then, as both David and Weiss noted, accounted for a large part of the growth in American incomes during the antebellum era.[15]

Manufacturing, too, was altering the consumption possibilities of America's consumers. One contemporary observer noted that "the

15. David, "Growth of Real Product"; Weiss, "Economic Growth before 1860."

attention and labor of many have been diverted from other pursuits, especially agricultural, to various manufacturing pursuits, which have rendered them more dependent for the necessities of life upon others. The people formerly wore homespun, now they wear factory and imported cloths and silks; formerly they subsisted chiefly upon provisions of their own raising, now they rely much more upon foreign produce."[16] Changing consumption patterns, then, fed back into productivity. Because farmers, for example, no longer had to rely on home-produced cloth, they could channel more of their energies into market-oriented production. If specialization and the division of labor had even the most modest effects predicted by theory, the economic pie surely grew.

What evidence is there that banks participated in this industrial transformation of the United States, that they promoted or, at least, facilitated the adoption of more capital-intensive processes? The traditional answer when considering both British and American banks is not promising. Unlike their German counterparts, at roughly the same stage of development, British and American banks are widely viewed as having played a passive role. Instead of providing manufacturers with long- and short-term credit (both equity and working capital), American banks, like their British forebears, provided short-term credit almost exclusively. Budding manufacturing enterprises were expected to provide their own fixed capital.

The rhetoric of nineteenth-century bank regulators and monetary theorists generally supports the historiography of Anglo-bank passivity. Fritz Redlich, for example, noted that the dominant theory of banking – the real-bills doctrine – held that a bank should "furnish a medium of trade and not capital."[17] Liquidity, particularly in an economy with a history of business cycles of relatively short cycle and rather sharp downturns, was paramount and required that bank credit remain short-term. In their reports to the General Assembly in 1833 New York's bank commissioners "pointed out that the legitimate function of banks is not the loaning of capital, but to furnish a sound currency. Capital for industry should be borrowed from individuals or corporations not associated with the business of circulation, for the bank of issue, in order to sustain its circulation, must

16. Anonymous, "Banks of Massachusetts," p. 152.
17. Redlich, *Molding*, p. 46.

make loans for short periods."[18] Although bankers themselves were less than religious adherents to the real-bills doctrine, they nevertheless focused on the provision of short-term credit, implying that banks were of limited utility to manufacturers for whom, it appeared obvious, long-term credit was critical. "Commercial banks," wrote Robert Puth, "[were] imperfect devices for meeting some of the financial needs of new industries."[19]

Indeed, in his study of capital formation in the early stages of the industrial revolution in Britain, T. S. Ashton stressed the importance of internally generated long-term capital required for expansion. Though he cites a handful of examples of prominent manufacturers who received long-term credits from various bankers, Ashton argued that it was "doubtful whether the banking system was a principle source of the capital by which the new technique was applied to manufacture."[20] Most manufacturing concerns were new, untested and unknown enterprises, and banks had too little experience with them to risk long-term, large-scale commitments. They were willing to develop long-term relationships, but ones involving only short-term contracts that were renewable at regular recontracting intervals. In that way bankers could periodically reevaluate the borrowers' standings and determine how much credit the bank was willing to offer a fledgling enterprise.

Such attitudes among bankers manifested themselves, according to several scholars, in the bankers' preference for dealing predominantly with merchants. Founded by merchants, banks catered to merchants to the exclusion of promising, but cash-strapped manufacturers. N. S. B. Gras, in his history of the Massachusetts Bank, was critical of that bank's conservative policies and its unwillingness to aid the development of industry and manufacturing in New England. "The Bank responded to opportunities for gain from sea traffic and from purely local trade," wrote Gras, "but it failed . . . to participate in the development of New England as a whole."[21] Herman Krooss argued that this conservatism arose from the insider nature of most banks. Banks founded and controlled by merchants preferred to serve their own, principally those drawn from the same social and

18. Cited in Chaddock, *Safety Fund*, pp. 275–6.
19. Puth, *American Economic History*, p. 248.
20. Ashton, *Industrial Revolution*, pp. 66–75, quote from p. 73.
21. Gras, *Massachusetts First National*, p. 41.

commercial circles. "In the sociable, small-town atmosphere that pre-vailed in the major cities of the day," wrote Krooss, "everyone who was anybody knew everyone else who was anybody."[22] And bank accommodations were kept within this relatively narrow circle to the detriment of entrepreneurial upstarts. Older, established bankers were risk averse and emphasized safety and solvency.[23]

It was for these and other reasons that many economists and eco-nomic historians have minimized the role of banking in development. Because banks financed only a small share, at most, of fixed-capital investment in the first half of the nineteenth century, they could not have been terribly important. Yet a great deal of research has sug-gested that fixed capital played a relatively minor role in the earliest stages of development. P. Colquhoun's estimates from the early nine-teenth century suggest that working capital – or circulating capital in Adam Smith's taxonomy – was of far greater importance to manu-facturers than fixed capital, which may have been why Smith gave cir-culating capital such a prominent role in his work.[24] Considering only reproducible capital (excluding land), working capital accounted for nearly 38 percent of Britain's total capital stock. Machinery and equipment accounted for less than 14 percent; the remaining 48 percent was invested in buildings (some of which were undoubtedly employed in manufacturing), mines and social infrastructure. Phyllis Deane accepted Colquhoun's estimates as rough approximations, at best, but believed that they were probably indicative of relative investment proportions. If so, she wrote, it was not obvious "that the nation's economic activity was appreciably more capital inten-sive" midway through the Industrial Revolution than it had been previously.[25]

Nor had manufacturing become significantly more capital intensive

22. Krooss, "Financial Institutions," p. 115.
23. Lamoreaux and Glaisek's interpretation is somewhat different. They argued that a combination of liberal chartering and the insider nature of banks actually expanded the range of opportunities for young entrepreneurs. Unable to obtain credit from established (insider) banks, those with demands for funds established their own banks, drawing equity capital from small circles and exploiting the note issue privilege to leverage their projects. Krooss, however, also recognized that this was sometimes the case and became more important in the Jacksonian era. See Lamoreaux and Glaisek, "Vehicles of Privilege"; and Krooss, "Financial Institutions," p. 118.
24. Smith, Adam, *Wealth of Nations*, Book II, Chapter I.
25. P. Colquhoun, *Treatise on Wealth, Power and Resources of the British Empire* (1815), cited in Deane, "Role of Capital," pp. 355–6.

by the late stages of the First Industrial Revolution. As late as the 1830s, possibly even the 1850s, investments in the types of fixed capital closely associated with industrial modernity absorbed a relatively small share of most firms' total capital investment. Sidney Pollard's findings for Britain in the early nineteenth century suggest that the ratio of fixed to working capital changed very little, even in large-scale enterprises. In the metallurgical industries (iron and copper furnaces), for example, the ratio of fixed to total capital averaged about 11 percent; in textiles between 8 and 17 percent; in brewing, 10 percent or less.[26] The emergent factory system of the late eighteenth century witnessed increased fixed investment ratios, but even here the importance or predominance of fixed capital was often exaggerated. In a state-of-the-art cotton textile mill, circa 1780 to 1830, fixed capital represented about one-half of invested capital. For other textile concerns – woolens and linens – the proportion was far less. In industries outside textiles, it was smaller still.

The dominant position afforded fixed capital, wrote Pollard, resulted from early preoccupations with new industries and new techniques. But as Pollard pointed out, even the most technologically advanced textile mills and furnaces employed relatively unsophisticated and inexpensive fixed capital. Moreover, few industries were as advanced as textiles and metals and few whose growth defined the industrial revolution achieved growth through the installation of much machinery.[27] Although economic development was (and is) typically associated with a high and increasing usage of machinery and equipment – those kinds of capital conducive to continuous technological advances – "the British economy had not gone far along this path by the first decade of the nineteenth century."[28] There were, wrote Deane, "no signs of a dramatic leap" in the capital formation ratio or a sharp discontinuity in the nature of capital itself.[29]

What of the United States employing its more capital-intensive "American system" of manufacturers? Using information contained in the *McLane Report* of 1832 (a survey of manufactures in the northeastern United States), Kenneth Sokoloff concluded that working

26. Pollard, "Fixed Capital," pp. 301–2.
27. Ibid., p. 301.
28. Deane, "Role of Capital," p. 357.
29. Ibid., p. 358.

capital absorbed a much greater percentage of most manufacturers' investment than fixed capital. Defining working capital to include accounts receivable, the working capital share of total capital varied across industries, but ranged between 40 and 90 percent. Yet this figure, too, may overstate the fixed capital requirements of most manufacturers. With the exception of textiles, machinery and tools accounted for a very small percentage of total capital. For most industries, the ratio of machinery and tools to total capital ranged from about 1 to 12 percent. The lion's share of fixed capital was tied up in land and buildings.[30] If renting was a legitimate option, as it apparently was in Britain, fixed capital requirements facing a typical manufacturer could, indeed, have been quite small and posed no significant barrier to entry or expansion. As G. S. Callender noted, the "amount of capital necessary to establish a manufacturing industry was not large, and could easily be supplied by a few men."[31]

With working capital weighing so heavily in the financing decisions of early industrial firms, the principal concern of manufacturers was that of financing circulating or working capital. Fixed capital investments could be satisfied with a modest initial investment supplemented with regularly plowed-back profits. Obtaining short-term credit to finance their inventories and work in progress, as well as rents, wages and accounts receivable was of paramount concern for manufacturers. These items, noted Pollard, were "so large in relation to fixed [capital] . . . that normal variation in them . . . could easily be of an order of magnitude equivalent to the total capital that was tied up in a firm as a productive unit."[32] Manufacturers then faced financing decisions and problems not unlike those facing merchants whose fixed capital requirements might involve as little as a small structure and a few fixtures or as much as a warehouse and a few sea-going or coastal vessels. Regardless of their scale of operation, financing inventory and goods in transit was the merchant's principal concern. Apparently, it was little different for early nineteenth-century manufacturers whose most critical needs centered around financing inventory and work in progress.[33]

Finding that working capital weighed much more heavily than fixed

---

30. Sokoloff, "Investment in Fixed and Working Capital," pp. 548–50.
31. Callender, "Early Transportation and Banking," p. 150.
32. Pollard, "Fixed Capital," p. 306.
33. Sokoloff, "Invention, Innovation, and Manufacturing," p. 361.

capital in the financing problems of early industrial firms opens up a whole new field of inquiry and one apt to reinterpret both the industrial transformation occurring in the eighteenth and nineteenth centuries and the role of Anglo-American banks in supporting that transformation. Under the established view, like that offered by William Court and others, even here banks were of limited usefulness because they were overly reluctant to offer even short-term credit to enterprising, risk-taking entrepreneurs "in the new, fast-moving and unstable economy which had begun to develop."[34] In this interpretation "is the clear implication that this selectivity of banks, and their lending patterns as a whole, were developed by them according to their [the banks'] own needs."[35] Bank lending policies, therefore, failed to meet the needs of an emerging industrial sector.

Mounting evidence from both Britain and the United States that working capital and the financing of trade credit far outweighed fixed capital requirements suggests that the traditional interpretation is incorrect. American banks did not fail to satisfy demands for long-term credit because little long-term credit was asked for – at least among merchants and manufacturers. (Farmers were the ones notorious for demanding long-term credit and those most vocal when their preferences went unmet.) "What was needed," wrote Pollard, "was a sufficient injection of short-term credit into the system to allow the mutual extension of credit to be developed. For the rest, banks merely had to provide a smooth transfer mechanism."[36] That is, banks had to intermediate *and* provide widely accepted media of exchange (money). Both activities facilitated exchange and credit. Furthermore, noted H. J. Habakkuk: "Financial institutions adapt themselves to meet the principal economic needs of their period and that English [and American] banks concentrated on the provision of working-capital because that was what industry needed; if there had been a large unsatisfied demand from industry to finance fixed capital, financial institutions would, with relative ease, have adapted themselves to meet this need, or new institutions would have arisen for that purpose."[37] That few fundamental institutional or lending policy changes occurred in the face of increasing industrialization

---

34. Court, *Concise Economic History*, p. 92.
35. Pollard, "Fixed Capital," p. 308.
36. Ibid.
37. Habakkuk, *American and British Technology*, p. 175.

implies that few changes were required. Banks, as they were constituted in the mid-nineteenth century could meet the demands of
emerging industries. The question remains: Did they?

THE INDUSTRIAL DISTRIBUTION OF BANK-SUPPLIED CREDIT IN THE LATE ANTEBELLUM ERA

Writing in 1968, Raymond Goldsmith lamented that, even for the
modern era, there was "no comprehensive . . . information of the size
distribution of bank loans, classified by either the amount of the loan
or the size of the borrower;" or, for that matter, the business of the
borrower.[38] If the lack of good information in the 1960s posed an
acute problem for Goldsmith, it presents an even greater hurdle for
those interested in banking practices in the 1850s and before. The
little information that has previously come to light, however, suggests
that antebellum banks did not ignore the credit needs of manufacturers. In his study of eight prominent Massachusetts textile mills,
Lance Davis found that all were "voracious borrowers, consuming
almost every available penny of credit, and borrowing from almost
every existing type of lender."[39] Yet commercial banks – those institutions most closely associated with the financing of mercantile and
agricultural pursuits in traditional accounts – supplied about 90
percent of those textile mills' short-term credit needs. Clearly, then,
at least some of those banks operating in New England were an
important source of working-capital finance for the industry most
commonly associated with incipient industrialization.

In his study of antebellum Rhode Island banking, Howard Kemble
Stokes found that economic considerations effectively reversed the
relationship between manufacturers and bankers inherent in the
German universal banking system.[40] Where the historiography of
American and British banking has criticized those banks for not
supplying significant amounts of share or equity capital to manufacturers, Stokes found that several manufacturers supplied significant

38. Goldsmith, *Financial Institutions*, p. 81.
39. Davis, "New England Textile Mills," p. 2.
40. Stokes, *Chartered Banking*.

amounts of some banks' equity capital. Why would the German universal banking scheme be effectively reversed in antebellum Rhode Island? Two potential explanations present themselves. One is that because fixed capital requirements in manufacturing were not particularly large, profits, instead of being plowed back internally, were invested in another sector to effectively diversify portfolios. A second, and equally plausible, explanation is that while fixed capital requirements were modest working-capital needs loomed large and bank ownership guaranteed a continuous source of short-term credit to finance stocks of raw materials, wages, and trade credit. This seems particularly likely given Lamoreaux's findings that many New England banks were insider affairs, whereby stockholders dominated the banks and absorbed the lion's share of their available credit.[41]

And yet again, it is important not to separate, too far, the dual money creation and intermediation function of antebellum banks. Knowing that the state of America's coinage throughout most of the antebellum era was inadequate in both quantity and quality, effective control over a bank assured that it would issue banknotes in the small denominations most useful to manufacturers, rather than large denominations preferred by merchants. Throughout the antebellum era, Rhode Island's banks issued large volumes of small denomination banknotes employed by manufacturers to meet their payrolls.[42] Banks, therefore, were useful to manufacturers across a broad front.

Information about the actual distribution of bank loans by sector is sorely lacking, however. In his study of Stephen Girard's Philadelphia private banking house, Donald Adams found that about 40 percent of Girard's depositors were merchants, 15 percent were artisans or mechanics, another 11 percent were professionals (probably doctors, lawyers and the like), with the remaining 34 percent employed in miscellaneous or unidentified professions. Twenty years later the occupations of Girard's depositors had changed very little. In 1832, 42 percent of his depositors were merchants, 9 percent were artisans, and 13 percent were professionals.[43] Normally the distribution of depositors may not provide much information about a bank's

41. Lamoreaux, *Insider Lending*.
42. Stokes, *Chartered Banking*, p. 48.
43. Adams, *Finance and Enterprise*, table 27, p. 129.

borrowers, but Girard was adamant that his borrowers maintain compensating balances, and he insisted that his cashier apportion the bank's loans in rough proportion to a depositor's average balance. Although the cashier objected to this policy, Girard's view ultimately prevailed and he stayed the course of "graduating discounts upon deposits."[44]

Although Girard's was a private bank, Adams argued that Girard made every attempt to mimic the policies of Philadelphia's incorporated commercial banks. His bank issued banknotes, accepted deposits, engaged in limited clearing operations with local banks (when they were willing to cooperate with him), discounted commercial bills of exchange and promissory notes, purchased government bonds, and nurtured correspondent relationships with banks in other cities. Until a detailed study of the lending policies of one or more of Philadelphia's commercial banks appears it is impossible to determine if Girard's sectoral lending patterns were, in fact, representative of banking in Philadelphia, but absent such evidence it is not unreasonable to assume that they were. If so, merchants absorbed most of the banks' accommodations, but the short-term credit needs of artisans or manufacturers were not completely disregarded in the early nineteenth century as something like 10 to 15 percent of Girard's loans were granted to artisans and mechanics.

Table 3.2 reports the sectoral composition of loans granted by four banks operating in the late antebellum era located in such disparate locations as Watertown in far northern New York State; Memphis, Tennessee; Charleston, South Carolina; and Petersburg, Virginia. No claim is made that these banks were representative of banking generally or even of banking within their respective states; they are simply four banks for which detailed information on their lending could be gathered from various archives.[45]

The Black River Bank of Watertown was organized in 1845 under

44. Ibid., pp. 104–5.
45. This caveat should be kept in mind throughout the discussion that follows. Four banks, admittedly, represent a very small sample from a universe of about 700 banks and all conclusions are drawn with that fact in mind. In a sense, this chapter represents much more a call to arms to other financial historians than it does a conclusive exposition. More-complete answers to fundamental questions can be had only by delving more deeply into the microeconomics of early American banking than financial historians have heretofore been willing to do.

Table 3.2. Sectoral composition of loans and discounts by value, selected years

	Ag	Con	Mer	Mfg	Ser	Tran	Misc	Unkown
a. Black River Bank of Watertown, New York								
1855	0.2%	0.2%	33.9%	3.7%	20.7%	0.0%	0.3%	39.1%
1856	0.2	0.2	23.1	13.0	4.5	0.0	0.1	58.8
1857	0.3	0.2	22.0	10.4	5.8	0.0	0.1	61.1
1858	0.1	0.1	37.4	13.4	5.8	0.5	0.0	42.7
1859	5.8	4.3	15.8	19.2	12.1	0.0	12.1	30.7
b. Bank of Tennessee branch at Memphis								
1858	1.1	1.0	23.1	7.6	26.8	0.4	10.9	29.0
1859	1.5	4.7	28.7	8.3	27.2	4.2	4.3	21.2
1860	0.0	2.1	37.2	5.6	16.8	15.3	5.3	17.6
1861	0.3	2.5	44.8	2.9	16.5	2.3	3.8	26.9
c. Branch & Company of Petersburg, Virginia								
1850	10.9	0.0	12.7	46.0	8.0	0.9	1.3	20.2
1851	14.4	0.0	21.6	20.6	9.1	1.0	0.4	33.0
1852	12.3	0.0	25.1	38.3	4.8	1.5	0.5	17.5
1853	11.1	0.0	13.2	39.2	13.3	0.8	0.0	22.4
1854	6.6	0.0	31.6	17.9	13.7	1.5	0.0	28.1
1855	11.7	0.0	18.3	13.6	22.4	0.8	0.3	32.9
d. Bank of Charleston of Charleston, South Carolina								
1863	0.2	0.6	49.2	6.3	6.0	1.1	1.1	35.6

Notes: For sectoral definitions, see footnote 22, Chapter 3.
Sources: Black River Bank: JCHS, *Black River Bank Records*; *Watertown Directory for 1856-57*; Eighth Census (1860), Population manuscript; New York 1855 Census, manuscript. Bank of Tennessee: Tennessee State Library and Archives, *Bank of Tennessee, 1838-1865*; *Williams Memphis Directory*; Branch & Company: VHS, *Branch & Company Records*; *First Annual Directory*; *Richmond, Petersburg Directory*; Eighth Census (1860), Population manuscript. Bank of Charleston: Robert Scott Small Library, College of Charleston, *Records of the Bank of Charleston*; *Directory of the City of Charleston*.

New York's free banking law and operated as a state-chartered bank under the direction of the Paddock family until it was voluntarily liquidated in the 1880s. The Bank of Tennessee (based in Nashville) opened the Memphis branch in 1858. It remained in operation until 1862 when its directors and officers were forced to flee with its assets to Athens, Georgia, when Union troops advanced on Memphis. The Bank of Charleston was chartered in 1836 and opened for business in the building previously occupied by the Charleston branch of the Second Bank of the United States. It, too, was forced to close and secrete its books and assets out of the city under fire and was one of the few southern banks to reopen in the postwar era. Branch & Company was a private banking house built upon Thomas Branch's commission merchant business during the late 1840s. Though a private bank, its operations are likely to reflect Virginia banking practice as Branch's cashier was trained at the Petersburg branch of the Farmers' Bank of Virginia and because Branch & Company rediscounted a large percentage of its notes at branches of Virginia's three principal banks.

Drawers of notes and bills discounted at each of these banks were matched to either a city directory, a manuscript census, or both to determine the principal occupation of drawers who were then classed into six principal categories: agriculture, construction, mercantile, manufacturing, service/professional and transportation. Two caveats about this matching procedure should be kept in mind, however. First, a substantial number of borrowing individuals and firms were not matched to either source, so we can not be sure that the results of the matches accurately portray the occupations of borrowers; but if those that were matched represent a random sample, there is reason to believe that the distribution of those not matched would be similar. The second is that many nineteenth-century entrepreneurs simultaneously had their hands in several enterprises. A commission merchant, for example, may have been engaged in wholesale and retail trade, warehousing, and insurance agency. He could, as well, have been engaged in some limited banking operations and might have supplied some equity capital to a manufacturing firm. Similarly, he could just as well have been on the board of directors of a bank, a railroad, a canal, or some other corporation. Nevertheless, it is assumed that the occupation listed was each individual's principal occupation, the one that absorbed the majority of his or her time and entrepreneurial energies.[46]

The results illustrated in Figure 3.1 suggest that merchants absorbed the better part of most banks' lending, generally between about one-third and one-half of all lending. Professionals absorbed another one-eighth to one-fifth. With the exception of the private banking house of Branch & Company, manufacturers received about one-tenth or less of a bank's loans.[47] The significance of Branch's apparently divergent behavior is difficult to interpret. On the one hand, it may have been that Petersburg was a thriving industrial center (by southern standards, at least), as it ranked fifth among southern cities (forty-ninth nationwide) in terms of manufacturing output. On the other hand, private bankers may have thrived in the 1840s and 1850s because they catered to groups unserved by commercial banks.[48] Private banks may have been, as Habakkuk sug-

46. This appears to be a reasonable assumption because many of the people matched to both a city directory and a manuscript census identified themselves similarly. The few exceptions were in the South, where some borrowers were listed as a merchant in a city directory and a farmer or planter in the manuscript census. In most of these cases, it seems that while they may have owned a plantation or farm, most of their business energies were directed toward their mercantile, professional or manufacturing enterprise. A simple case would be a lawyer with a city office and a residence who also owned a plantation, often left to the charge of an overseer. In such cases, it was not always easy to determine whether the money was borrowed to finance the farm or the law office. If the use of the funds was ambiguous, the loan was assigned to the "Unknown" category. If the loan seemed more likely to be directed toward one or the other it was categorized appropriately. A representative case may have been of the form of a loan granted to John Smith of the firm Smith & Dunn with two endorsers. If John Smith were both planter and lawyer, this loan was assigned to his legal practice. If, on the other hand, there was a loan to John Smith of a relatively large amount during the planting season for six months with no endorsers, the loan was assigned to the "Agriculture" category.
47. *Agriculture* included those listed as planters and farmers. *Construction* included architects, bricklayers, carpenters, joiners, masons, painters, wallpaperers, etc. *Merchants* included clothiers, commission merchants, grocers, hardware dealers, jewelers, junk dealers, shoe dealers, etc. *Manufacturers* included blacksmiths, boot and shoe makers, cabinet makers, carriage makers, coopers, distillers, founders, millers, machinists, sawmills, etc. *Service/Professional* included attorneys, clerks, dentists, doctors, hostlers, insurance agents, liveries, tavern keepers, teachers, etc. Attorneys dominated this group, though doctors and dentists borrowed regularly from all four banks. *Transportation* included railroads, steamship lines, and express companies. *Miscellaneous* occupations were those employed by governments, such as sheriffs, county clerks, commissioners of the poor, and the like. These were not reported as government loans because it was not always clear whether the borrowing was done on behalf of the government agency or for the individual.
48. See Bodenhorn, "Private Banking in Antebellum Virginia," for a more detailed study of Branch & Company's banking operations.

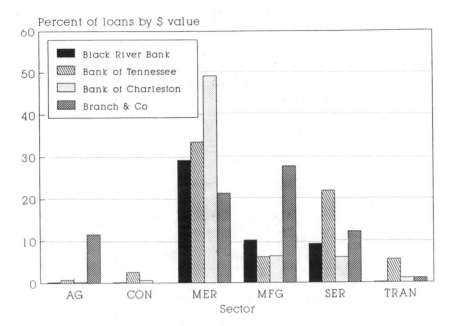

Figure 3.1. Loans by industrial sector of borrowers at four banks

gested, an endogenous market response to fill a market niche. Only additional research can answer the question satisfactorily and while both factors were probably operative, the former was more likely. Branch & Company, as previously noted, rediscounted between one-quarter and one-third of their notes and bills at local offices of Virginia's commercial banks and those banks were as likely to rediscount notes of manufacturers as those of merchants.

Comparisons of the sectoral breakdown of lending at the Black River Bank and Branch & Company with business directories from those cities strengthens the interpretation that manufacturers received discounts in roughly the same proportion as their numbers. Figures 3.2 and 3.3 plot the proportion of loans by sector with the sectoral distribution of businesses listed in each city's directory. Both figures demonstrate that each sector received loans in about the same proportion as its representation among the local business community. Manufacturing concerns in Watertown accounted for about 16 percent of the city's businesses; and about 19 percent of the Black

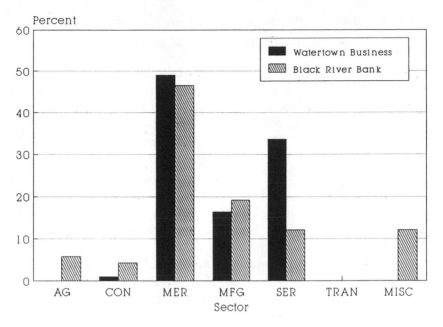

Figure 3.2. Loans by sector at the Black River Bank and percentage of Watertown's firms by sector

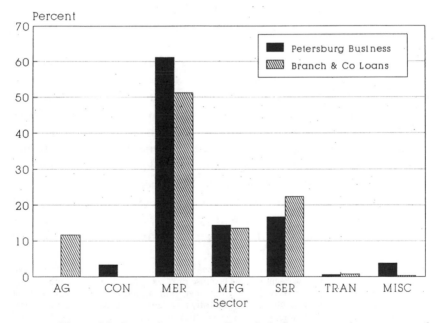

Figure 3.3. Loans by sector at Branch & Company and percentage of Petersburg's firms by sector

River Bank's loans in 1859 went to manufacturers. Much the same pattern was evident in Petersburg, Virginia. Merchants constituted about 61 percent of that city's businesses in 1859; manufacturers about 14 percent. In 1855 about 51 percent of Branch & Company's loans were extended to merchants (assuming that most unidentified borrowers were merchants); about 14 percent to manufacturers.[49] This suggests that manufacturers were neither ignored nor discriminated against by contemporary bankers. If anything, they received credit in roughly the same proportion as their representation in the larger business community. This does not, of course, imply that they received loans in proportion to their preferences, simply in rough proportion to their numbers.

Moreover, the credit manufacturers received was not substantially different in amount or type from that received by merchants and others. As Figure 3.4 shows, agriculture – as has been long suspected – received the longest-term loans, but even agricultural loans were only about 20 percent longer than average. Borrowers engaged in construction, mercantile pursuits, manufacturing and services received loans of approximately similar duration; about 65 days at the Bank of Charleston; 70 days a the Black River Bank, and 80 days at the Bank of Tennessee. Nor were manufacturers charged different interest rates (Figure 3.5). If anything, they paid slightly lower rates. The Black River Bank charged farmers an average of 7.3 percent, merchants 7.2 percent; professionals 7.1 percent; and manufacturers 6.7 percent. A similar pattern is evident at the Bank of Charleston, with manufacturers paying slightly lower interest rates than businesses in other sectors.

These findings suggest two conclusions. One, that manufacturing was not viewed by bankers as inherently riskier than merchanting, otherwise manufacturers would have been asked to pay a risk premium. Second, that manufacturing enterprises were probably not credit strapped operations. Had they suffered from chronic short-term credit shortages, manufacturers would have bid up the effective

49. In the case of Branch & Company, it seems appropriate to assume that most unidentified borrowers were merchants because most were listed in the discount books as partnerships (e.g., Smith & Jones) and most unidentified discounts were bills of exchange payable in distant locations, generally large cities such as Boston, New York, Philadelphia, and Baltimore, which suggests that they were drawn by agents of city commission merchants who were buying livestock, agricultural produce, timber, etc., having it transported to a distant market.

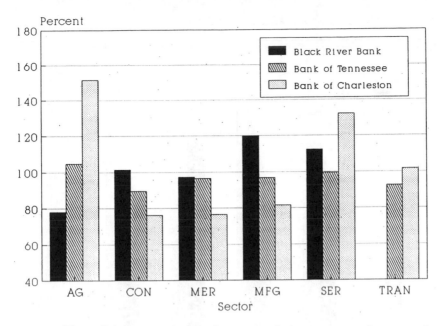

Figure 3.4. Loan maturities by sector relative to average loan maturities at three banks

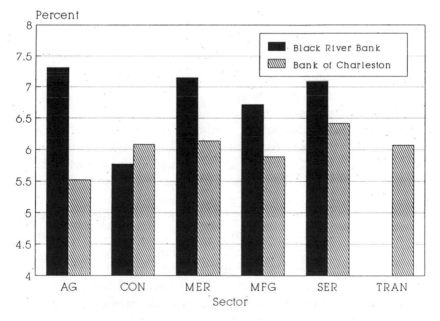

Figure 3.5. Loan interest rates by sector relative to average interest rates at three banks

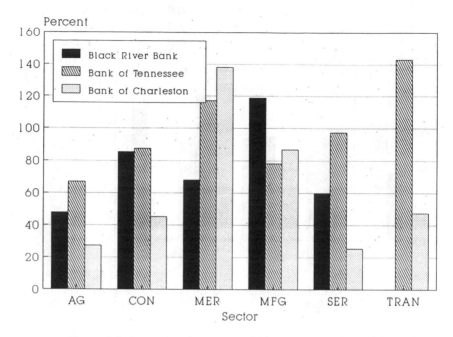

Figure 3.6. Loan sizes by sector relative to average loan sizes at three banks

price they were willing to pay for credit relative to prices paid in other sectors. That they did not, suggests that they had access to bank-supplied credit similar to that received by merchants.

Neither is there compelling evidence that manufacturers were credit rationed (Figure 3.6). At the Black River Bank, manufacturers received loans about 20 percent larger than average, even while being allowed to borrow for slightly longer than average and paying about five basis points less than average for it. Among southern banks, merchants and railroads were afforded the longest maturities, but manufacturers did not face significantly shorter terms than others. On the whole then, it appears that antebellum commercial banks supported manufacturing and the emerging industrial transformation. True, they never adopted the practices of German universal banks that supported and steered firms from cradle to grave, providing share and commercial credit as well as entrepreneurial and managerial advice and direction. But their failure to do so does not imply – as some have concluded – that banks provided little help to leading industrial enterprises. That manufacturing enterprises remained small, relative at least to their postbellum successors, meant that their credit needs were also small relative to those arising after the war.

Bank credit also influenced the pace of industrialization in ways beyond the mere sectoral division of accommodation. Indirectly, the discounting of promissory notes and bills of exchange, whether offered to merchants, manufacturers or farmers, freed mercantile and industrial capital for fixed investment. "If businessmen," wrote Peter Mathias, "had had to finance the expansion of their trade as well as their plant – with most of the capital coming out of profits – that rate of expansion would have been cut down."[50] The relatively wide availability of short-term trade credit, consequent upon the rapid expansion in the number of banks in the 1820s, 1830s, and 1840s, meant that manufacturers had only to raise their modest fixed-capital investments from kith and kin.

And banks, of course, were but one source of short-term credit for manufacturers. Merchants themselves supplied large volumes of credit to industrialists. Merchants who supplied raw materials to manufacturers surely took up notes or bills drawn by the manufacturer payable at a future date. If these notes had been subsequently discounted at a bank, the bank became the ultimate credit provider. Had the merchant, on the other hand, opted to hold the note or bill to maturity, the merchant became the credit provider, supplementing but not supplanting the work of financial intermediaries.

Credit networks, too, supplied manufacturers with credit from the other side of the ledger. If a wholesaling merchant or jobber who took up the manufacturer's finished product remitted a bill or note in payment, the manufacturer did not have to carry the receivable to maturity and supply downstream sectors with credit. Anytime the manufacturer was in need of funds, the merchant's note could be rediscounted at a bank. For this reason, the figures reported in Table 3.2 may underrepresent the volume of credit supplied either directly or indirectly to manufacturers because in this latter case, the bank's books would report a bill or note owed by a merchant (the ultimate drawer) rather than by a manufacturer (the rediscounter). It was, as Pollard noted, a case where merchants "supplied a large part of the

50. Mathias, *First Industrial Nation*, p. 175.

circulating capital to industry. But while the existence of this source of capital is generally recognized, its importance is sometimes underrated, simply because capital appearing as 'bills' or 'creditors' is not easily recognized as such, as a shareholding or bank credit overdraft."[51]

While conclusions should be drawn with caution, the limited evidence also suggests that southern banks should not be taken to task for the "deplorable scarcity" of manufacturing in the antebellum South. "In its most extreme form," wrote Fred Bateman and Thomas Weiss, "the traditional interpretation depicts the South, even during the late antebellum era, an agrarian-commercial export economy almost totally devoid of any manufacturing."[52] The South was not devoid of manufacturing, but it was laggard, even when compared to the largely agrarian Old Northwest. "The American Industrial Revolution, already apparent in the Northeast and emerging in the Old Northwest, is seen as bypassing the southern states."[53] Bateman and Weiss lay most of the blame at the feet of southern planters – those with the greatest wealth and entrepreneurial talents – for forsaking the high returns in manufacturing for low-return, but high-prestige, plantation agriculture.[54] Southern manufacturing, they believed, was forced to cope with a deadly duo: a general unwillingness to transfer resources out of agriculture; and sluggish and insufficient investment by those who were willing.

While Bateman and Weiss faulted planters directly and only indirectly implicated bankers for the South's failure to industrialize, Lance Davis effectively reversed those sentiments, faulting bankers directly and planters only indirectly. In the South wrote Davis, "commercial banks contributed much less to the mobilization of capital" than their northern counterparts.[55] In the South Atlantic particularly, existing capital accumulations were overwhelmingly invested in agriculture and showed little inclination to migrate into more lucrative

51. Pollard, "Fixed Capital," p. 310.
52. Bateman and Weiss, "Manufacturing in the Antebellum South," p. 1. See also Bateman and Weiss, *Deplorable Scarcity*; and Bateman, Foust and Weiss, "Participation of Planters."
53. Bateman and Weiss, *Deplorable Scarcity*, p. 1.
54. Atack and Passell, *New Economic View*, pp. 206, 267 report comparative rates of return to manufacturing and agriculture by region. Manufacturing returns substantially outweighed agricultural returns in all regions, but the gap may have been greatest in the South.
55. Davis, "Capital Immobilities," p. 593.

employments. Drawing conclusions about the role of antebellum banks from laments by William Gregg, a Charleston, South Carolina textile mill owner, who complained incessantly about the unwillingness of Charleston's banks to provide him with sufficient amounts of short-term credit, Davis condemned the region's banks, which he felt were too beholden to the landed gentry and their preferences for plantation agriculture. In such an environment it was "not surprising that they [the banks] tended to discriminate against industrial loans."[56]

Both the evidence presented above and banking histories of the South suggest that Davis's characterization of antebellum southern banks may require reinterpretation. First, southern planters complained louder and longer than any other group about the lack of credit, even short-term credit, available for agricultural investment. Thus Gregg's complaints about the unwillingness of banks to invest in industry cannot be taken to imply that bank lending to manufacturing was wholly inadequate. If the number or the intensity of complaints were directly proportional to credit/investment shortfalls, the level of southern agricultural investment was woeful – a proposition no historian could defend. Second, Charleston's banks were notoriously commercial and mercantile. According to most accounts, they ignored the state's agricultural interests, focusing instead on financing the shipment of staples to northern and European port cities. The incorporated commercial banks favored this sector to such an extent that the state was forced to charter its own bank – the Bank of the State of South Carolina – to provide planters with credit.[57] The reality of the situation was probably somewhere in between. Evidence presented earlier suggests that banks distributed their credit across sectors in proportions representative of the sectoral composition of the city's businesses. While banks in the Cotton South extended less credit to manufacturers than those in other regions, the blame may not lay with bankers. If there were few substantial manufacturers in a bank's locale, there were correspondingly few opportunities to promote industry through the provision of short-term, industrial credit. It simply was not within the realm of nineteenth-century Anglo-American banking theory or practice to establish, fund, and

56. Ibid., p. 593.
57. See Lesesne, *Bank of the State*; and Clark, *History of Banking Institutions* for histories of banking in South Carolina.

promote industrial concerns in the mode of the Credit Mobilier. The best that banks could do was work with and promote whatever and whomever was there.[58]

CHARACTERISTICS OF BANK BORROWERS

Having now some notion of the sectoral composition of loans, who were these people borrowing from the banks? We know little about whether banks financed old or young, established merchants and manufacturers or commercial and industrial neophytes or lent to those with substantial wealth or upstarts with little collateral. If banks catered to established merchants with substantial amounts of accumulated wealth, they may have contributed little to development. If, on the other hand, they loaned meaningful amounts to commercially aggressive arrivistes hell-bent to make their fortune and leave their mark in the wake of the Jacksonian-era commercial revolution, banks may have mattered, may have directly and indirectly promoted entrepreneurship and, hence, development.

Herman Krooss, without much evidence, accepted the latter interpretation. "The older merchant bankers," wrote Krooss, "emphasized safety and solvency; the younger ones growth and enterprise."[59] The Jacksonian era was characterized, he believed, "as the age of the hustler, of the entrepreneur on the make." The old social and economic order was giving way under the weight of the radical laissez-faire philosophy and practice embraced by young, adventurous entrepreneurs. In his travels through the United States, Alexis de Tocqueville found that Americans accepted risk taking as a matter of

58. This does not imply that southern banks were "demand following." This characterization fits the modified supply-leading hypothesis laid out in Chapter 1. The point is that the shortage of manufacturing in the South should not be attributed to banks as Davis contended. Rather, social values, as Bateman and Weiss contend, were probably of greater importance. The South simply failed to produce as many entrepreneurs interested in manufacturing as the North.

   Neither is the reasoning circular. It is not meant to imply that there were no manufacturers for banks to assist, so it's not the fault of banks that there were no manufacturers. Just as banks cannot be seen as the wellspring of growth, they cannot be seen as the instrument of stagnation and retardation. Banks provided assistance to existing manufacturers, but they were not promoters in the same way that German universal banks were.

59. Krooss, "Financial Institutions," p. 118.

course, hustling was an inevitable but valued part of the process. One whom Tocqueville interviewed informed him that businessmen "may plunge into the most hazardous enterprises, begin without capital, risk in every way the money of his backers without materially damaging his reputation. . . . Almost all our tradesmen play for double or quits."[60] Charles Dickens, too, uncovered the same business ethic, but Dickens found it much more troubling than Tocqueville. Dickens dubbed it "smart dealing" and thought it smacked more of swindle and dishonesty than of shrewdness and acumen.[61]

While the public may have accepted those playing for double or quits without any of their own capital at stake, bankers would have offered them little encouragement and less financing. That is not to say that bankers were unwilling to support adventurous upstarts itching to jump headlong into new endeavors. Nicholas Brown, for example, whose family controlled the Providence Bank of Rhode Island, was well-known for discounting, on his own account, notes of young men just starting out.[62] Stephen Girard, too, preferred small notes to large and he informed his cashier that the bank's object was "to accommodate small dealers, promote the industry of young beginners in trade, and divide the risks for the security of the banker."[63] To contemporary bankers, then, catering to upstarts was not anathema. Because a beginner's credit needs would be small, many more youngsters than experienced men with extensive trading networks could be supported with a given amount of bank capital and the risks better diversified.

Information reported in Table 3.3 shows generalizations about bank borrowers are not easily drawn. The only thing that seems clear is that teenagers were generally denied access to bank credit. Twenty-year-olds received relatively little credit from the Black River Bank, but represented nearly one-fifth of all borrowers at Branch & Company. The Black River Bank, in fact, appears to have catered to men in their thirties, forties and fifties, with the average age of borrowers being nearly 47 years. Branch & Company, on the other hand, seems to have preferred younger men, most of them in their twen-

60. Pierson, *Tocqueville in America*, p. 414.
61. Dickens, *American Notes*, p. 279.
62. Lamoreaux, *Insider Lending*, pp. 54–5.
63. Simpson, *Biography of Stephen Girard*, pp. 114–15, quoted in Adams, "Portfolio Management," p. 75.

Table 3.3. Borrower characteristics at the Black River Bank and Branch & Company

	Black River Bank	Branch & Company
	a. Age of borrowers	
<20	0.0%	0.0%
20-29	4.1	22.3
30-39	29.6	43.8
40-49	24.5	17.7
50-59	23.5	12.3
>60	18.4	3.9
Average (yrs)	46.9	37.4
	b. Wealth of borrowers	
<$2,500	16.1	25.8
$2,500-4,999	20.4	9.1
$5,000-9,999	21.5	12.1
$10K-20K	21.5	19.7
$20K-50K	15.1	21.9
>$50K	4.3	11.4
Average	$12,539	$11,492

Note: Wealth represents reported holdings of real and personal property.
Sources: Black River Bank: JCHS, *Black River Bank Records*; Eighth Census (1860), population manuscripts for Jefferson County, New York. Branch & Company: VHS, *Branch & Company Records*; Eighth Census (1860), population manuscripts for Dinwiddie, Henrico, Chesterfield and several surrounding counties

ties and thirties, and the average age of borrowers at Thomas Branch's bank was nearly nine years younger than that of borrowers at the Black River Bank. What remains unclear is whether Branch's choice of customer represented a conscious, voluntary preference for younger men or whether, as a private banker in a city supporting three commercial banks and two savings banks, he was left to skim whatever cream was left after Virginia's big three banks had taken up all the commercial paper they considered acceptable.

The reason, however, probably mattered less than the result. What mattered was that there was a banker who was willing to take up high-quality paper, even if it was offered by men of lesser experience. Branch, in fact, appears to have been either a remarkably good judge of character or remarkably lucky or both. Of the 1,666 notes Branch discounted between 1847 and 1855, only three were protested (sued upon) for nonpayment at maturity. Thus, it seems unlikely that Branch was forced to dredge from the bottom of the barrel for clients. The presence of three commercial banks, two savings associations, and a handful of private money lenders servicing a city of 18,000 suggests instead a competitive marketplace. If this was the case, Branch's activities, for this and other reasons, may be indicative of urban Virginia banking generally.

Little information exists about the age at which men entered business on their own account in the antebellum era, so we are forced to look for clues about whether these two banks' borrowers were typical. In her study of women in antebellum Petersburg, Suzanne Lebsock found that young, middle-class women were advised not to marry until their betrothed had settled himself into reliable employment.[64] Petersburg's young women apparently took that advice because, late in life, women often lamented that their choices were driven more by economic prospects than by emotional compatibility. Merchants and professional men, too, typically did not marry until their late twenties, the average age at marriage being 28.

While anecdotal evidence is suggestive, it is not conclusive. Comparing the ages of Branch's customers to the ages at which farmers bought their first farm supports the belief that many of Branch's customers were just beginning their commercial careers. Among southern farmers, Atack found that tenancy rates demonstrated their

---

64. Lebsock, *Free Women of Petersburg*, pp. 28–30, 33.

greatest decrease between the age cohorts of 25–34 and 35–44, and it was likely that most of that decrease in tenancy represented a movement to ownership.[65] Branch, then, was lending to young men whose mercantile and manufacturing adventures were beginning at about the same time that their counterparts were buying their first farms. It must have been for these young men that capital, whether mercantile, industrial or agricultural, was most dear, come by only with some difficulty.

Management at the Black River Bank in New York, on the other hand, appear to have preferred men of greater experience. The vast majority of the Black River Bank's borrowers were more than 30 years old, with more than 66 percent being 40 or older. Again, because there is no way to determine how long these men had been in business on their own account, we must turn to agricultural data and make the assumption that business formation in each sector was occurring at similar ages. Atack found that, in the North, farm ownership rates exhibited the greatest increase between the age cohorts of 25–29 and 30–34.[66] The second greatest increase occurred between cohorts aged 30–34 and 35–39. The majority of northern farmers who eventually owned their own farms, therefore, had typically acquired it by age 40. If businessmen were opening their own businesses at about the same ages, the Black River Bank served men who had been in business for some time and who had presumably gained some experience and respect for their business acumen.

The personal wealth of borrowers at the two banks also shows that Branch & Company and the Black River Bank followed somewhat different policies. While 16 percent of all notes and bills discounted at the Black River Bank in 1859 were discounted for those reporting less than $2,500 in real and personal property, nearly 26 percent of notes and bills at Branch & Company were discounted for men of more modest means. On the other hand, managers at the Black River Bank divided their loans relatively equally across all wealth classes, whereas Branch & Company apparently divided its business between two groups: those with less than $2,500 and those with more than $10,000 in accumulated personal wealth.

65. Atack, "Agricultural Ladder Revisited," p. 19.
66. Ibid.

Personal wealth does not, of course, imply a great deal about the amount of capital invested nor the profitability of a borrower's enterprise, but it is probably suggestive. Young enterprises were likely to plow back a much greater percentage of their profits, while older, more established operations were likely to divide and distribute some profits to afford their owners greater consumption possibilities. Another cause of the differences between the two banks was Branch's long-standing relationship with several planters who owned large farms and dozens of slaves. Three of Branch's five wealthiest borrowers in 1855 were planters, the other two being a tobacco manufacturer and a druggist. Interestingly enough, three of the five wealthiest discounters at the Black River Bank in 1859 were private bankers, the other two being millers. So while Loveland Paddock – principal shareholder and president of the Black River Bank – spread his risks among older men distributed nearly equally across all wealth classes, Thomas Branch divided his discounts between young businessmen of more modest wealth and older farmers with substantial plantations.

While, at first blush, Branch's policy may seem odd, it was not contradictory that a banker financed both upstarts and established businesses. "For any given bank," wrote Rondo Cameron, "the majority of its customers must be both established and profitable, otherwise both the bank and its customers would soon go out of business."[67] Branch's experience appears to fit Cameron's characterization quite well. Branch looked to established merchants, manufacturers and farmers as an outlet for the bulk of his loanable capital, but he was not afraid to take a chance and finance a beginner. Still, his lending philosophy remained conservative, witnessed by the remarkably low default rate. Paddock's philosophy was not all that different. Though preferring older men, he still financed men of relatively modest means, as 16 percent of his borrowers held less than $2,500 in personal wealth and fully 58 percent had accumulated less than $10,000 when they borrowed from his bank. It would, therefore, be difficult to argue that they catered to the already well-to-do and ignored enterprising entrepreneurs trying to redirect the existing flow of economic activity.

67. Cameron, *Banking in the Early Stages*, pp. 12–13.

CONCLUDING REMARKS

To reiterate, the interpretations offered in this chapter should be taken with caution. A sample of four banks drawn from a population of 1,000 or more is probably not representative, though it may be. The real purpose of the foregoing discussion was twofold: to shed a ray of light into a dark corner of our understanding; and to suggest to others an agenda for future research. At the outset, it was noted that most studies of antebellum banking have been preoccupied with monetary concerns while forsaking, in large part, issues of inter-mediation. So too, most studies have adopted a decidedly macroeconomic approach, relegating the banks themselves to the status of "black boxes." It has been said more than once that while there are macroeconomic questions, there are only microeconomic answers. There is no need to belabor or defend that opinion here, but what should be noted is that a better understanding of bank behavior and macroeconomic performance requires that we know something about what banks were doing. This chapter was designed to provide a *very* preliminary effort in that direction. Bank records, while difficult to come by and time-consuming to analyze, do exist and there is much to be learned from them about the ultimate role of banks in the earliest stages of economic development.

Given these caveats, what interpretations do the records of these banks afford us? These bankers displayed a preference for lending to merchants, probably because: (1) they had started as merchants themselves and felt comfortable assessing the prospects of other merchants, and (2) because mercantile enterprises loomed larger in the urban economy than other types of businesses. Banks located in the hinterlands probably catered to farmers for much the same reason. Their inherent preferences and possibilities notwithstanding, these bankers did not overlook the profits to be earned by lending to manufacturers, transportation companies and professionals. It is a commonplace that economic development demands growth in man-ufacturing and services relative to agriculture. These banks' pattern of lending, despite the predominance of agricultural pursuits in the antebellum South – or far northern New York, for that matter – demonstrates that not all bankers ignored growth sectors and may, in fact, have played an essential role in their development.

Joseph Schumpeter regarded financial intermediation as one of the two indispensable elements of economic growth and development – entrepreneurial spirit being the other.[68] John Gurley, on the other hand, wrote that banking was not "highly essential" to growth.[69] The reality probably lies somewhere in between. It would be foolhardy to dismiss banking as irrelevant. But it would be equally foolhardy to endow it with magical properties. Banks simply played a part. Albert Gallatin noted about the Jacksonian economy that there was "a general spirit of enterprise in the United States, to which they are greatly indebted for their rapid growth, and it is difficult to ascertain in all cases when it should be encouraged and when it should be checked."[70] By and large, banks encouraged enterprise, especially in newly settled regions of the country – places, Gallatin was forced to admit, where "even the most generally admitted [contemporary] principles of political economy" did not always apply.[71] Even Fritz Redlich, who rarely failed to exploit any opportunity to roundly criticize nineteenth-century banking, admitted that banking contributed to economic development.[72] Redlich's conclusion, though couched in his usual admonitory tone, recognized that banks stimulated industry by affording credit to men of enterprise, an important role regardless of the specific enterprise in which they were engaged.

The question arises whether bankers directed funds to those who could employ them in socially optimal ways. For that to have happened, banks would have had to exercise their intermediary functions responsibly and with something of the same optimism displayed by the era's entrepreneurs. Although Charles Dunbar claimed that banks "directed existing resources to the enterprises and industries most in need of support," traditional accounts have remained considerably more skeptical of that claim.[73] Antebellum banks, by and large, were founded by and for the benefit of merchants, and in some regions of the country remained under the control of a relatively small group who used their banks to their own advantage. Certainly, such banks existed – and probably provided useful services to those fortunate enough to get a foot in the door – but the mercantile/insider character of many of these banks diminished through time.

68. Schumpeter, *Theory*.
69. Cited in Cameron, *Banking and Economic Development*, p. 6.
70. Gallatin, *Writings*, vol. 3, p. 314.
71. Ibid., p. 277.
72. Redlich, *Molding*, p. 66.
73. Dunbar, *Theory and History of Banking*, p. 6.

Though banks were "put in place to solve one set of problems during a particular historical epoch, once they exist they may be used to solve different, unforeseen contingencies," wrote Simon Kuznets.[74] One unforeseen contingency in the 1790s, when the mercantile character of banks was first defined, was the growing importance of and the growing credit needs of manufacturing, whether it took the form of a large-scale integrated cotton textile mill employing hundreds of hands or the artisanal shop employing a half-dozen or fewer journeymen enjoying some of the economies captured in Adam Smith's paradigmatic pin factory. While it remains true that antebellum American banks were built upon merchanting, it also "remains true that the existence of this credit system allowed smaller [manufacturing] firms, in particular, to enter the production circle with only a small fraction of the capital it ultimately used and in this way to accumulate enough to enlarge its operations."[75] It was the postbellum era that witnessed an explosion in the number of extensive, integrated firms whose financing needs could not be met through the agency of commercial banks. In the antebellum era, however, such firms were few and far between, and manufacturing – the progenitor of development – could arise, and thrive with the assistance of the prototypical Anglo-American bank.

74. Kuznets, "Foreword," in Goldsmith, *Financial Intermediaries*, p. xiii.
75. Pollard, "Fixed Capital," p. 309.

4 The Integration of Short-Term Capital Markets in Antebellum America

By 1860 American banking was still regional, if not local, but on the point of taking a more national aspect.

Fritz Redlich (1947)

A perfect capital market would have equalized interest rates throughout the country, so that a person could borrow money on the same terms anywhere in the country. This manifestly was not the case in the nineteenth century.

Peter Temin (1975)

Capital does not recognize the territorial divisions of the common country ... it destroys them.

Charles Francis Adams (1871)

If the financial sector was to play a notable role in the development of the American economy, it would have had to direct capital to where it was most needed – that is, where the marginal product of capital was highest. One part of this role would be directing capital into growth-inducing industries. Another would be directing it geographically. As the epigraphs at the head of the chapter demonstrate there is an apparent disconnect between theoretical expectations and the reality of geographic capital allocation in nineteenth-century America. Being highly liquid and easily directed, short-term capital in antebellum America should, as Walter Bagehot contended, have run "as surely and instantly where it is most wanted, and where there is most to be made of it, as water runs to find its level."[1] Yet Redlich's

---

1. Bagehot, *Lombard Street*, p. 13.

and Temin's interpretations suggest that this was manifestly not the case. Early banks were believed to have operated in isolation. The result was that the United States' local markets remained disorganized and disintegrated, unable to mobilize capital and direct it to where it was most in demand. If this were, in fact, the case, interest rates would not have been equalized across the country and early American capital markets deserve some measure of approbation. Evidence presented below, however, challenges the conventional interpretation and suggests that antebellum capital markets mobilized and directed capital with reasonable efficiency.

In a renowned paper, Lance Davis found that, in the early postbellum period, short-term bank lending rates varied widely across the United States and converged slowly.[2] It was not until the early twentieth century that short term interest rates were nearly equal throughout the United States. Davis's paper stirred enormous interest because it challenged the conventional economic wisdom that markets quickly and efficiently dissipate price differentials on roughly similar goods. The law of one price holds much theoretical appeal among neoclassical economists. Arbitrage possibilities and profit seeking within markets, especially within those markets operating under a unified polity and within a contiguous geography, are supposed to quickly and efficiently eliminate significant price discrepancies. Moreover, capital's mobility and fungibility suggests that markets should eliminate significant price differences more rapidly than for most other goods.

To date, relatively little work has investigated whether a geographic pattern like that observed after the Civil War held before the war. Such an effort is important for several reasons, the most important of which is that the postbellum experience may be misleading if extrapolated to the whole of the nineteenth century. If the dispersed pattern of interest rates observed in the postbellum era resulted from disruptions and dislocations caused by the war itself, then the postbellum pattern may not be indicative of American capital market performance in the first half of the nineteenth century. This is most likely to be true for the South – the major contributor to the impression that regional interest rates diverged until the early twentieth century. War finance, especially the federal government's issue of inconvert-

2. Davis, "Investment Market," pp. 355–99.

ible greenbacks, also created a different monetary standard for the Mountain States and the Pacific Coast until specie payments were resumed in 1879.

If this conjecture proves correct, it sheds new light on the controversy surrounding patterns and changes in postbellum interest rates. If postwar interest rate differentials resulted from irrational prejudices against investing in underdeveloped, capital-poor regions, it seems likely that the antebellum era would demonstrate an interest rate profile similar to that found for the early postbellum period. But if the postbellum experience was the consequence of war-related dislocations, antebellum short-term capital markets may have exhibited greater integration or, perhaps, a different pattern of dispersion. In either case, it is likely that the war disrupted the normal functioning of the capital market. An investigation into the regional pattern of antebellum interest rates, therefore, provides a new benchmark against which to judge the postbellum experience.

For these and other reasons information from a variety of sources has been brought together to generate a portrait of regional interest rates in the United States for the forty years preceding the firing on Fort Sumter. It is found that antebellum markets, indeed, displayed a different geographic pattern of interest rates than that observed in the postbellum era. In short, interest rates were nearly equal across a broad expanse of the Union by at least mid-century and probably well before. Antebellum capital markets were, then, considerably more integrated than postbellum markets. Despite the near equalization of regional interest rates, the plural "markets" is retained throughout. It would be a gross misrepresentation to argue that the United States east of the Mississippi River was served by a single, unified capital market. It was not. But regional markets were drawn together through a complex of institutions and trading patterns that tended to eliminate regional differences.

Before proceeding into a discussion of capital market integration, we must first define the term *integration*. Some writers use the term to describe a process whereby two or more distinct economic regions are unified, either in terms of prices or product flows or whatever. Others, either implicitly or explicitly, use the term to denote a state of affairs ultimately achieved through a process; that is, the state in which factor prices are equalized or product flows are sufficient, in some sense, to believe that the geographically separated regions are economically unified.[3] Davis's study of the postbellum era, for example, is cast as both a process and a state of affairs. He argued that initial regional interest rate differentials were a natural consequence of dispersed and disintegrated regional capital markets. Product flows – in this case, short-term financial instruments – between regions were insufficient to integrate these markets and equalize factor prices in the immediate postbellum economy. Integration was, then, both a sequence of institutional and organizational developments that gradually overcame disintegrating forces and the ultimate state of the world achieved as a consequence of these changes. To Davis, it was the development and spread of the commercial paper house that facilitated interregional short-term capital flows which, ultimately, brought about the unification of several distinct capital markets. For the purposes at hand, integration will be treated as a state of affairs. Several series of interest rates are presented which suggest that antebellum credit markets were integrated quite early. The next chapter deals with integration as a process and highlights those institutions and organizations that contributed to bringing about this state of affairs.

CALCULATING ANTEBELLUM INTEREST RATES

Studies of postbellum capital markets profit from the National Banking Acts, which required that the United States Comptroller of the Currency annually collect and publish bank income statements and balance sheets. Deriving interest rates from these data is a relatively straightforward process of calculating the appropriate ratios – loan income divided by the average volume of loans outstanding. While this ratio may not yield a value identical to the average interest rate charged by banks, it generates, with a few simple corrections, a reasonably good proxy. In fact, net earnings-to-earning asset ratios may be a more appropriate measure because financial institutions would be more concerned with this than raw interest rates in determining where best to allocate capital. Net earnings take into account bank costs and loan losses, where raw interest rates do so only indirectly, and banks were likely to consider the costs and potential

3. Machlup, *History of Thought on Economic Integration*, p. 13.

default risk inherent with a loan or series of loans on the institution's profitability. The net earnings ratio, in short, is the correct variable to employ in an investigation of capital market integration.

As all students of American banking history are aware, bank data for the antebellum period are scarce and scattered. Unlike the national banking system, state banks in the antebellum period were answerable only to the state legislature or some other state authority (like New York's Bank Commissioners), and each state imposed its own set of regulations and requirements. One nearly universal requirement was that each bank forward an annual statement of condition to some oversight bureaucracy or legislative committee. These statements were usually reprinted in state legislative documents or journals and often found their way into contemporary newspapers and journals. *Bankers' Magazine* regularly reprinted balance sheets, particularly those of prominent urban banks, as did Hunt's *Merchants' Magazine and Commercial Review*. Even local newspapers, like New York's *Albany Argus*, which published a special issue in each quarter between 1840 and 1853 that reprinted balance sheets for every New York bank, made this information widely available. Most of the data employed here, however, are from the original sources – state legislative reports and documents. In some cases, it was necessary to use the Reports of the United States Secretary of the Treasury as printed in the United States *House Executive Documents*, but these were used only as a final resort as the reports are spotty for the 1830s, and no reports were collected during the Polk administration (27th and 28th Congresses).

Given their scarce, scattered and limited nature, it is necessary to consider in detail how surviving records can be used to generate interest rate proxies similar to those developed for the postbellum era. To provide concreteness, Panel A of Table 4.1 presents a balance sheet for the Bank of Charleston, South Carolina for 30 June 1840. The principal short-term earning assets of the bank consisted of "Bills Discounted," "Domestic Exchange" (bills of exchange drawn on other North American cities), and "Foreign Exchange" (bills drawn on European cities). But these were not the only earning assets held by the bank. It also held mortgages, stocks of other corporations (such as Louisville, Cincinnati, and Charleston Railroad), and state and federal debt. These assets, too, generated dividend and interest income, but since the principal concern of this study is the short-term

Table 4.1. Balance sheet and profit statement for the Bank of Charleston, 30 June 1840

a. State of the bank on 30 June 1840

Assets		Liabilities	
Bills discounted	$2,186,784	Circulation	$233,885
Domestic exchange	234,416	Deposits	404,803
Foreign exchange	911,330	Due other banks	298,383
Mortgages	135,475	Due agents	704,915
Suspended debt	213,741	Due state	22,034
Due by banks	332,384	Unpaid dividends	4,420
Due by agents	25,936	Dividend #9	126,432
Notes of other banks	669,000		
Real estate	34,761	Equity	
Stocks	58,167		
State bonds	55,610	Capital	3,160,800
U.S. bonds	57,100	Contingent fund	255,708
Specie	150,549		
Bonus due state	84,062		
Miscellaneous	62,061		
Total assets	$5,211,379	Total liabilities	$5,211,379

b. Profit and loss account, year ending 30 June 1840

Debits		Credits	
To bonus	$5,625	By sundries	$7,952
To expenses	33,862	By discounts	140,780
To dividends	246,432	By exchange	122,636
To contingent fund	23,342	By interest	37,893
Total debits	$309,261	Total credits	$309,261

Note: Individual accounts may not sum to column total due to rounding.
Source: Bank of Charleston, Proceedings, (1840), pp. 12-14.

capital market, income from these sources is factored out of the calculations.

What is unusual about the Bank of Charleston's annual report is that the bank included a simplified and highly stylized profit and loss statement, which is reproduced in Panel B, showing how the bank's earnings were distributed. The Bank of Charleston amortized in equal annual installments its initial bonus payment made to South Carolina in 1835 in return for its charter. Its expenses – principally officer salaries and legal fees – amounted to a little less than $34,000. Nearly 80 percent of its operating income was distributed to share-holders as dividends, while about 7.5 percent was retained in a "Con-tingent Fund" to cover past and future loan losses. The bank's earnings, on the other hand, arose from four principal sources – sun-dries (such as rent on or sales of repossessed property), discounts and exchange on notes and bills, and interest on notes, bills, mortgages, stocks, and government debt.

A quick rate-of-return calculation can be had by simply dividing the bank's total income ($309,261) by its total earning assets ($3,638,882), which yields an 8.38 percent return. The underlying concern here, however, is returns to short-term financial instruments and this 8.38 percent measure is contaminated by earnings from long-term debt and real property. To correct for this, income from sundries can be eliminated as can some part of the "Interest" earnings that resulted from the bank's mortgage, stock and bond holdings. To obtain an accurate proxy of short-term rates would require a knowl-edge of the average mortgage rate as well as the types of stocks and bonds held, the price paid for them and their nominal rate of return. Rarely, however, is such detailed information available.

Correcting for these other sources of income was accomplished using the simplest, most straight-forward method possible given the lack of detailed information on bank debt and equity holdings. In the antebellum era, most city, state, and federal, as well as private, bonds were issued with 4 to 6 percent coupons. Actual yields varied with prices paid, terms to maturity, and so forth, but lacking sufficient data, 5 percent of the value of such holdings was subtracted from the bank's earnings.[4] This generates a corrected income from holdings of short-term financial instruments for the year of $285,991. Dividing

4. Homer, *History of Interest Rates*, pp. 274–326.

this by the bank's holdings of short-term assets yields a short-term rate of return of 8.58 percent.[5]

Bank reports as complete as the Bank of Charleston's, however, were exceptionally rare. Most were simple, sometimes, highly aggregated, balance sheets that sometimes also reported dividend disbursements. It was possible, even from these cryptic reports, to generate reasonably accurate short-term interest rate proxies. If dividends were reported, the bulk of a bank's earnings could be calculated by adding dividends to the annual change in its contingent fund. Taking the ratio of this value to short-term earning assets yields a short-term interest rate proxy, after making a few minor adjustments. Although South Carolina imposed no taxes on its banks, many states did. Taxes paid by banks were added to the sum of dividends and changes in contingent fund accounts to develop a pre-tax net rate-of-return proxy.

Tax rates and tax schemes varied from state to state, but some general statements can be made. States typically adopted one of two methods or some combination thereof. Most states placed a direct tax on bank capital. Some, like Pennsylvania and Ohio, taxed dividends. Once tax responsibilities were calculated, it was possible to generate interest rate proxies using the following equation:

$$\text{Rate of Return on Earning Assets} = \text{Net Earnings/Earning Assets} \tag{4.1}$$

where

---

5. Not all "Interest" income is eliminated because, while discounts were the predominant form of extending credit, some loans (especially call loans to brokers) were made and short-term overdraft privileges were sometimes granted to preferred customers.
  The calculation is made in the following manner:

  Rate of Return = [Discounts + Exchange + Interest − 0.05(Mortgages + Stocks + State Bonds + U.S. Bonds)] / [Bills Discounted + Domestic Exchange + Foreign Exchange].

  The calculation assumes a 5 percent yield on mortgages, stocks and bonds, Homer, *History of Interest Rates*, pp. 274–326 collected massive amounts of data on bonds, most of which yielded about 5 percent. Considerably less information about stocks and mortgages is available. Companies, especially financial firms, usually paid dividends of 6 to 8 percent of par value, but many of these stocks traded at well above par. Payment of a 6 percent dividend, a par value of $100 and a market value of $120 (all reasonable assumptions) provided a yield (ignoring capital gains) of 5 percent. In addition, the law in many states restricted mortgage rates to 6 or 7 percent. But a casual reading of several bank letterbooks and directors' minutebooks suggest that defaults and late payment were not uncommon. It is not unreasonable, then, to assume a 5 percent yield on mortgages. Underlying these adjustments is an assumption that risk-adjusted returns on alternative investments were equalized.

Net Earnings = Dividends + Δ Contingent Fund − Securities
Earnings + Taxes (4.2)

and

Earning Assets = Bills Discounted + Bills of Exchange (4.3)

Certainly, this measure is not without its shortcomings, but the biases introduced are small and should be consistent across states so that the resulting interest rate proxies fairly well represent actual early American capital market conditions. Using information on the Bank of Charleston provided in Table 4.1, the rate of return calculated by this procedure is 8.10 percent compared to the more accurate but, in most instances, incalculable full-information rate of 8.58 percent found above. The bias, therefore, is relatively slight, and if it is consistent across states and time periods should not hamper our understanding of early American capital markets. In the end, as well, our concern is as much with movements in rates as it is with the actual rates themselves.[6]

A multitude of refinements could be made to this measure. Experiments with data from the 1850s, however, show that such refinements do not significantly alter the results. It could be argued, for example, that deposit interest could be added to the net earnings figure because it was part of the *gross* earnings of the bank. It was possible to do this for Massachusetts banks, which separately reported interest-earning and other deposits, but this adjustment had little effect. It was unclear, as well, whether a significant proportion of deposits in other states paid interest.

In all cases, balance sheets closest to year-end were used in making the rate-of-return calculations, but some states occasionally changed reporting dates so that some calculations were based on slightly less than or slightly more than one-year intervals. Again, correcting for these changes by interpolating balance sheet figures to a common date, made little difference.

Finally, all securities were assumed to pay a constant 5 percent. This

---

6. An exception was made in the calculation of net earnings for New York. Tax rates on the state's banks were never found, but it is known that free banks had to contribute to a fund that met the expenses of the Office of the Superintendent of the Banks. For this reason, the tax component was not added. To correct for this, securities earnings were not factored out. This may introduce some bias, but experiments with data from other states suggest that the two terms were generally about equal.

was the long-term average rate received on federal and eastern state bonds, but it is conceivable that some securities – railroad bonds, canal bonds, western and southern state bonds – paid somewhat higher rates. This would most likely be the case in the West and South, so, if true, our assumption imparts an upward bias to southern and western rates and, therefore, biases the results against finding equalization of regional interest rates. In any case, the typical bank's holdings of corporate and government securities, with the exception of New York's free banks, were too small (in comparison with holdings of notes and bills) to have generated significant income. They, consequently, had little effect on the interest rate estimates.

THE REGIONAL PATTERN OF EARLY AMERICAN INTEREST RATES

Table 4.2 reports the results of the calculations outlined above for each of thirteen states or cities for which sufficient data were available over a reasonably long period. For each state, an unweighted simple average of all banks is given in Columns (1); a weighted average (weighted by earning assets) is reported in Columns (2). Figures 4.1 and 4.2 plot three-year, centered moving averages of the weighted statistics found in Table 4.3. Interest rates in most regions were close to, and varied around, the rate calculated for New York City, the nation's emerging financial center. The pattern holds from at least the mid-1830s, when the bulk of the series begin. Moreover, the pattern seems consistent as far back as the 1820s in those cases for which information is available. These results imply that the business of banking was similar within the frontier and that short-term capital was reallocated until returns across a broad expanse of the country were roughly equalized.[7]

Some of the results are, perhaps, to be expected. Boston, Philadelphia, Baltimore, and New York City were all thriving financial and commercial centers. Merchants and bankers in these cities would have been well informed of market conditions and could have readily moved funds from one city to another. The evidence supports Davis's contention that "the [antebellum] short-term [credit] market appears

---

7. Large parts of this section and the next are drawn from Bodenhorn and Rockoff, "Regional Interest Rates."

Table 4.2 (a). Net rates of return on short-term earning assets, selected state and cities, 1820-1859

Year	Massachusetts		Rhode Island		Pennsylvania	
	(1)	(2)	(1)	(2)	(1)	(2)
1820	5.46	5.65	--	--	4.24	4.39
1821	4.89	5.27	--	--	4.13	4.43
1822	4.55	4.62	--	--	4.73	4.97
1823	4.69	4.70	--	--	4.25	4.31
1824	5.24	5.32	--	--	4.03	4.83
1825	--	--	--	--	4.42	4.53
1826	--	--	--	--	4.58	5.20
1827	5.08	4.42	--	--	4.52	4.42
1828	5.18	4.80	--	--	4.88	5.75
1829	5.03	4.91	--	--	4.46	4.30
1830	--	--	--	--	5.64	5.55
1831	--	--	--	--	5.18	4.77
1832	--	--	--	--	5.25	4.85
1833	5.14	4.98	--	--	6.19	5.86
1834	4.88	4.62	--	--	3.74	3.57
1835	4.95	4.81	6.24	7.07	5.46	5.94
1836	5.08	4.89	5.78	6.16	6.23	6.38
1837	5.41	5.34	4.88	4.87	4.64	6.22
1838	5.27	5.34	5.27	5.39	4.70	5.09
1839	5.18	5.69	5.46	5.39	4.34	4.22
1840	4.97	5.14	4.43	4.37	5.10	5.59
1841	5.46	5.38	5.44	5.66	4.63	4.81
1842	5.51	5.41	5.31	5.47	2.50	1.96
1843	--	--	5.04	4.91	3.47	3.51
1844	--	--	4.31	3.81	5.21	5.47
1845	4.33	4.38	4.91	4.90	4.76	4.90
1846	5.06	5.18	5.52	5.76	5.18	5.66
1847	4.82	4.80	5.61	5.67	4.39	5.02
1848	5.29	5.61	5.54	5.43	5.27	5.42
1849	5.61	5.94	5.52	5.97	5.30	6.78
1850	5.16	5.11	5.18	5.60	5.55	6.28
1851	5.21	5.33	5.07	5.38	5.11	4.81
1852	5.35	5.35	5.77	5.63	4.72	5.26
1853	5.87	5.70	4.87	5.37	5.36	5.36
1854	5.50	5.66	5.00	5.46	5.85	5.62
1855	5.82	5.95	5.26	5.42	6.20	5.49
1856	5.92	5.94	5.36	5.42	6.12	5.56
1857	5.67	5.75	6.04	6.15	4.82	4.80
1858	5.40	5.04	5.66	5.52	5.27	5.07
1859	5.08	4.78	5.23	5.22	5.57	5.18

Table 4.2 (b).

Year	Virginia		South Carolina		Kentucky	
	(1)	(2)	(1)	(2)	(1)	(2)
1820	--	--	4.36	4.36	--	--
1821	--	--	4.34	4.34	--	--
1822	4.31	4.25	5.78	5.78	6.33	6.33
1823	3.78	3.89	4.86	4.86	4.42	4.42
1824	4.17	4.30	4.62	4.62	4.01	4.01
1825	4.45	4.76	4.15	4.15	3.93	3.93
1826	3.79	4.07	2.53	2.53	3.00	3.00
1827	4.79	4.61	7.82	7.82	3.12	3.12
1828	3.51	3.83	12.90	12.90	3.83	3.83
1829	3.98	4.31	4.10	4.10	3.51	3.51
1830	4.20	4.45	4.15	4.15	5.02	5.02
1831	4.56	4.98	4.49	4.49	3.48	3.48
1832	4.79	5.01	4.24	4.24	3.35	3.35
1833	5.49	5.56	4.38	4.38	2.85	2.85
1834	3.69	3.82	3.54	3.54	--	--
1835	5.07	5.44	4.13	4.13	5.90	4.94
1836	6.24	6.26	4.37	4.37	7.98	7.86
1837	4.42	4.28	6.11	6.11	6.03	6.03
1838	4.16	4.26	6.00	6.00	5.93	6.04
1839	6.79	7.11	5.11	5.11	4.38	4.38
1840	4.35	3.32	5.86	5.79	3.31	3.31
1841	4.21	3.65	5.78	5.78	4.91	4.91
1842	4.20	3.85	5.65	5.61	4.13	5.93
1843	4.12	3.98	6.40	6.34	6.77	6.23
1844	4.15	3.96	5.94	5.74	6.37	6.00
1845	4.32	3.99	5.40	5.23	6.29	6.27
1846	3.95	3.85	5.12	4.99	5.72	5.84
1847	4.99	4.77	6.28	5.98	5.45	5.51
1848	3.70	3.89	5.45	5.37	7.57	6.80
1849	4.19	4.03	5.23	5.12	5.02	5.21
1850	4.52	4.50	5.53	5.29	6.22	6.00
1851	4.71	4.62	7.11	7.11	7.92	6.87
1852	5.53	5.10	6.42	6.38	11.29	11.81
1853	4.46	4.21	8.50	8.95	6.59	5.68
1854	5.04	4.74	6.45	6.62	5.40	6.36
1855	5.17	4.94	6.58	6.45	9.28	9.69
1856	5.09	5.29	5.40	5.45	4.81	5.29
1857	3.88	4.16	5.86	5.95	5.77	5.61
1858	5.90	6.09	5.63	5.81	4.64	4.77
1859	5.96	5.82	4.96	4.91	5.95	5.79

Table 4.2 (c).

Year	Tennessee (2)	Missouri (2)	Ohio (2)	Indiana (2)	New Orleans (1)	New Orleans (2)
1835	--	--	5.56	7.97	5.25	5.24
1836	--	--	8.77	13.37	6.99	6.92
1837	--	--	6.67	8.50	7.17	7.19
1838	--	--	6.22	8.35	4.37	4.30
1839	--	--	7.52	--	5.54	5.52
1840	6.85	--	4.82	--	6.82	6.90
1841	5.48	--	6.73	7.65	6.77	6.84
1842	7.41	--	--	5.05	6.20	6.41
1843	4.85	--	5.83	2.85	6.95	7.12
1844	6.99	--	--	5.74	8.34	8.50
1845	4.24	3.10	--	7.86	6.42	6.63
1846	5.66	5.21	--	5.95	4.40	4.65
1847	4.92	4.97	--	6.32	5.09	5.30
1848	5.62	4.19	--	8.36	6.10	6.10
1849	5.50	4.07	--	7.77	7.32	7.32
1850	4.01	--	6.14	9.45	7.93	7.93
1851	6.08	--	5.48	5.95	8.03	8.03
1852	4.77	6.21	6.36	6.81	5.99	6.12
1853	4.38	3.73	--	6.37	6.79	7.23
1854	5.19	5.30	--	7.70	7.91	9.00
1855	4.65	3.87	--	10.89	9.66	9.93
1856	7.35	4.98	--	9.25	--	--
1857	7.46	8.58	--	--	--	--
1858	6.79	8.97	--	--	--	--
1859	4.48	8.86	--	--	7.90	7.90

Table 4.2 (d).

Year	Boston		Providence		New York City	
	(1)	(2)	(1)	(2)	(1)	(2)
1820	6.13	6.00	--	--	--	--
1821	5.61	5.64	--	--	--	--
1822	4.28	4.50	--	--	--	--
1823	4.71	4.71	--	--	--	--
1824	5.24	5.32	--	--	--	--
1825	--	--	--	--	--	--
1826	--	--	--	--	--	--
1827	4.05	4.07	--	--	--	--
1828	4.64	4.56	--	--	--	--
1829	4.93	4.94	--	--	--	--
1830	--	--	--	--	--	--
1831	--	--	--	--	--	--
1832	--	--	--	--	--	--
1833	4.94	4.85	--	--	5.03	4.85
1834	4.31	4.36	--	--	5.69	5.96
1835	4.52	4.64	7.10	7.65	5.13	5.46
1836	4.56	4.61	6.21	6.37	6.83	6.64
1837	5.11	5.18	4.83	4.79	5.91	6.71
1838	5.21	5.32	5.42	5.46	5.33	6.09
1839	6.09	6.33	5.89	5.50	4.24	4.45
1840	5.46	5.40	4.52	4.35	5.60	5.25
1841	5.46	5.38	5.95	5.83	5.27	5.72
1842	5.51	5.41	5.56	5.55	3.96	4.15
1843	--	--	4.63	4.80	5.37	5.58
1844	--	--	4.48	3.75	5.81	6.43
1845	4.31	4.42	4.78	4.78	5.21	4.91
1846	5.25	5.28	5.92	5.96	4.69	4.68
1847	4.51	4.71	5.61	5.63	5.04	5.27
1848	5.87	5.93	5.27	5.28	5.32	5.05
1849	6.02	6.26	6.44	6.67	7.17	7.08
1850	5.15	5.04	5.33	5.75	5.62	5.90
1851	5.14	5.29	5.12	5.50	5.09	4.84
1852	5.13	5.20	5.65	5.68	7.27	6.65
1853	5.73	5.65	4.74	5.52	4.99	4.40
1854	5.57	5.75	5.12	5.65	4.98	5.24
1855	6.05	6.11	5.54	5.62	5.83	6.24
1856	5.97	6.00	5.62	5.69	6.09	5.88
1857	5.97	5.98	6.36	6.35	5.45	6.13
1858	4.74	4.62	5.83	5.49	4.95	5.03
1859	4.67	4.42	5.57	5.31	4.62	4.25

Table 4.2 (e).

Year	Trenton, N.J.		Philadelphia		Baltimore	
	(1)	(2)	(1)	(2)	(1)	(2)
1820	--	--	5.61	5.58	--	--
1821	--	--	4.79	4.70	--	--
1822	--	--	5.65	5.46	--	--
1823	--	--	3.42	3.41	--	--
1824	--	--	5.43	5.64	--	--
1825	--	--	4.24	4.42	--	--
1826	--	--	5.86	5.91	--	--
1827	--	--	5.39	4.64	--	--
1828	--	--	5.31	6.33	--	--
1829	--	--	4.58	4.33	--	--
1830	--	--	5.22	5.58	--	--
1831	--	--	5.15	4.65	--	--
1832	--	--	4.48	4.61	--	--
1833	--	--	6.54	6.06	--	--
1834	--	--	3.41	3.25	--	--
1835	--	--	6.12	5.95	--	--
1836	--	--	5.74	6.23	--	--
1837	--	--	4.74	6.13	--	--
1838	--	--	5.47	5.32	--	--
1839	--	--	3.44	3.54	--	--
1840	3.52	3.43	5.73	5.94	7.68	7.47
1841	3.52	3.43	4.42	4.75	9.60	9.45
1842	2.24	2.46	2.50	1.96	4.36	4.73
1843	4.11	3.99	3.72	3.00	6.75	6.80
1844	4.37	4.38	5.18	5.38	6.01	6.38
1845	4.23	4.28	4.20	4.39	5.95	5.17
1846	3.77	3.84	6.40	6.49	5.93	6.25
1847	4.35	4.39	5.21	5.80	6.95	7.05
1848	4.19	4.09	4.84	5.25	6.40	6.67
1849	4.58	4.61	6.35	7.65	6.20	6.51
1850	5.12	5.67	6.47	6.90	6.15	5.85
1851	5.58	5.82	4.69	4.53	7.22	7.26
1852	4.13	4.27	5.56	5.73	5.70	6.03
1853	5.18	5.27	5.10	4.94	6.15	6.29
1854	4.40	4.22	5.31	5.45	7.14	7.43
1855	4.57	4.53	6.55	5.13	6.72	6.78
1856	5.50	5.54	4.45	4.62	6.59	6.70
1857	4.92	4.96	3.17	3.32	5.36	5.47
1858	5.18	5.15	4.68	4.45	5.86	5.91
1859	5.05	5.05	4.32	4.46	6.64	6.73

Notes and Sources for Table 4.2:

Notes: City rates reported in Panels (c) through (e) are included in state averages reported in Panels (a) through (c). Columns (1) are simple averages of of all banks for which sufficient data was available to make the calculation. Columns (2) are weighted averages of individual bank rates, weighted by loans and discounts. -- implies insufficient data available to calculate bank rates.

Sources: Federal Documents. United States House, *Executive Documents*: 23d Congress, 1st Session, Doc. No. 498; 23d Congress, 2d Session, Doc. No. 190; 24th Congress, 1st Session, Doc. No. 42; 24th Congress, 2d Session, Doc. No. 65; 25th Congress, 2d Session, Doc. No. 79; 25th Congress, 2d Session, Doc. No. 471; 25th Congress, 3d Session, Doc. No. 227; 26th Congress, 1st Session, Doc. No. 172; 26th Congress, 2d Session, Doc. No. 111; 29th Congress, 1st Session, Doc. No. 226; 29th Congress, 2d Session, Doc. No. 120; 30th Congress, 1st Session, Doc. No. 77; 31st Congress, 1st Session, Doc. No. 68; 32d Congress, 1st Session, Doc. No. 122; 32d Congress, 2d Session, Doc. No. 66; 33d Congress, 1st Session, Doc. No. 102; 33d Congress, 2d Session, Doc. No. 82; 34th Congress, 1st Session, Doc. No. 102; 34th Congress, 3d Session, Doc. No. 87; 35th Congress, 1st Session, Doc. No. 107; 35th Congress, 2d Session, Doc. No. 112; 36th Congress, 1st Session, Doc. No. 49; 36th Congress, 2d Session, Doc. No. 77.

State Documents: Massachusetts, General Court, "True Abstract," 1819-1820, 1822-1823, 1827-1829; Rhode Island, General Assembly, "Abstract of the Returns of the Several Banks," *Acts and Resolves*, 1834, 1837-1845, 1848; New York, General Assembly, "Annual Report of the Bank Commissioners," *Assembly Documents*, 1840-1843; New York, General Assembly, "Annual Report of the Superintendent," *Assembly Documents*, 1856-1861; Pennsylvania, *House Journal*, 1818, 1832, 1839-1840; Pennsylvania, *Senate Journal*, 1819-1831, 1833-1838, 1841-1852; Pennsylvania, *Legislative Documents*, 1853-1860; Virginia, *House Journal*, 1822-1824, 1827-1831; Virginia, *House Documents*, 1825-1826, 1832-1860; South Carolina, *Compilation of all the Acts*; South Carolina, *Reports and Resolutions*, 1844, 1852-1854, 1860; Kentucky, *House Journal*, 1822, 1825, 1832-1833, 1860; Kentucky, *Senate Journal*, 1823-1824, 1826-1832, 1834-1838, 1840; Kentucky, *Legislative Documents*, 1841-1851, 1856, 1858; Tennessee, *House Journal*, 1845, 1848-1849, 1851, 1853-1855, 1859; Tennessee, *Senate Journal*, 1842-1843, 1849; Ohio, *Senate Journal*, 1834-1836; Ohio, *Executive Documents*, 1836-1845.

Other Sources: Gras, *Massachusetts National*, pp. 711-40; Lesesne, *Bank of the State*, pp. 185-186; Martin, *Twenty-One Years*; Wainwright, *Phildelphia National*, pp. 244-45; Lewis, *Bank of North America*, pp. 152-53; Harding, "State Bank of Indiana," pp. 1-36 and Appendix; Huntington, *History of Banking*, pp. 174, 212-13, 176-82; Krooss, "Financial Institutions," p. 120; Bryan, *History of State Banking*, p. 102; Western National Bank, *Brief History*, p. 26; *Albany Argus*, 1840-1852; *Bicknell's*, 1830-1857; *Philadelphia Price Current*, 1827-1830; *Commercial and Shipping List*, 1830-1859; *New Orleans Price Current*, 1835-1839; *Daily Picayune*, 1834-1860; *New York*

Table 4.3 (a). Net rates of return on short-term earning assets by region, 1820-1859

Year	New England		Mid-Atlantic		South Atlantic	
	(1)	(2)	(1)	(2)	(1)	(2)
1820	5.46	5.65	4.24	4.39	4.36	4.36
1821	4.89	5.27	4.13	4.43	4.34	4.34
1822	4.55	4.62	4.73	4.97	4.43	4.64
1823	4.69	4.70	4.25	4.31	3.87	4.15
1824	5.24	5.32	4.03	4.83	4.21	4.40
1825	--	--	4.42	4.58	4.43	4.60
1826	--	--	4.58	5.20	3.69	3.88
1827	5.08	4.42	4.52	4.42	5.01	4.93
1828	5.18	4.80	4.88	5.75	4.18	6.20
1829	5.03	4.91	4.46	4.30	3.99	4.25
1830	--	--	5.64	5.55	4.19	4.37
1831	--	--	5.18	4.77	4.55	4.85
1832	--	--	5.25	4.85	4.75	4.86
1833	5.14	4.98	5.85	5.40	5.42	5.35
1834	4.88	4.62	4.29	4.80	3.68	3.77
1835	5.39	5.22	5.08	5.30	5.01	5.23
1836	5.33	5.12	5.60	6.01	6.14	5.99
1837	5.23	5.25	4.00	5.65	4.51	4.56
1838	5.27	5.34	6.06	5.96	4.33	4.61
1839	5.27	5.62	5.25	4.77	6.45	6.72
1840	4.78	4.98	5.65	5.75	4.78	4.18
1841	5.44	5.53	5.66	6.15	4.60	4.27
1842	5.33	5.44	3.72	4.05	4.68	4.64
1843	5.04	4.91	4.73	5.26	4.77	4.72
1844	4.31	3.81	5.49	6.14	4.60	4.53
1845	4.54	4.50	5.05	4.94	4.59	4.38
1846	5.24	5.31	5.10	5.26	4.24	4.22
1847	5.12	5.00	4.93	5.42	5.31	5.15
1848	5.38	5.57	5.42	5.40	4.20	4.40
1849	5.58	5.95	5.96	6.90	4.53	4.46
1850	5.17	5.22	5.64	6.02	4.81	4.80
1851	5.16	5.34	5.38	5.12	5.31	5.43
1852	5.50	5.40	5.78	6.14	5.75	5.46
1853	5.50	5.63	5.29	4.94	6.99	6.37
1854	5.31	5.62	5.54	5.53	5.96	5.67
1855	5.61	5.84	6.06	6.04	6.22	5.68
1856	5.72	5.83	6.14	5.86	5.32	5.37
1857	5.79	5.84	5.14	5.69	5.39	5.13
1858	5.49	5.13	5.18	5.11	5.66	5.90
1859	5.13	4.86	5.26	4.66	5.22	5.32

Table 4.3 (b).

Year	Old Southwest		Old Northwest	
	(1)	(2)	(1)	(2)
1820	--	--	--	--
1821	--	--	--	--
1822	6.33	6.33	--	--
1823	4.42	4.42	--	--
1824	4.01	4.01	--	--
1825	3.93	3.93	--	--
1826	3.00	3.00	--	--
1827	3.12	3.12	--	--
1828	3.83	3.83	--	--
1829	3.51	3.51	--	--
1830	5.02	5.02	--	--
1831	3.48	3.48	--	--
1832	3.35	3.35	--	--
1833	2.85	2.85	--	--
1834	--	--	--	--
1835	5.46	5.17	6.77	5.94
1836	7.32	7.30	11.07	9.49
1837	6.94	6.83	7.59	6.95
1838	4.89	5.07	7.29	6.66
1839	5.31	5.20	7.52	7.52
1840	6.24	6.21	4.82	4.82
1841	6.24	6.30	7.19	6.96
1842	5.71	6.43	5.05	5.05
1843	6.57	6.36	4.34	5.17
1844	7.30	7.07	5.74	5.74
1845	5.68	5.80	7.86	7.86
1846	5.15	5.26	5.95	5.95
1847	5.19	5.30	6.32	6.32
1848	6.44	6.13	8.36	8.36
1849	5.32	5.36	7.77	7.77
1850	6.12	5.78	6.71	6.81
1851	7.63	6.92	5.24	5.57
1852	7.59	8.61	6.81	6.81
1853	6.14	5.73	6.80	6.37
1854	6.12	6.79	7.70	7.70
1855	8.25	8.18	--	--
1856	5.49	5.64	--	--
1857	6.52	6.59	--	--
1858	5.57	5.66	--	--
1859	6.51	6.38	--	--

Notes and Sources: See Table 4.2

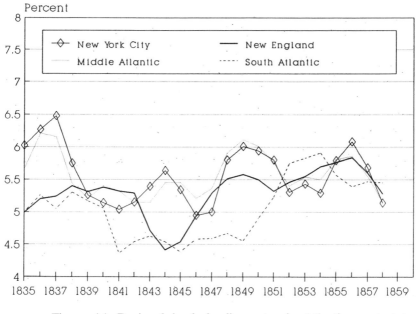

Figure 4.1. Regional bank lending rates in Atlantic coast states, 1835–1859

to have encompassed the entire Northeast ... and probably worked to equalize short-term rates ... in the northeastern cities."[8] It is not surprising, then, that rates within New England were roughly the same as those in New York City. A strong case can be made that if any region constituted a unified capital market before the Civil War, it was New England. By the 1830s, banking had a long history and the majority of its banks operated under the watchful eye of the Suffolk Bank. Banking regulations varied little between states because few bankers took advantage of free banking laws enacted in the 1850s, probably because the region's legislatures granted charters liberally.[9] Even accounting frameworks were similar. More important, perhaps, was that New England was a long-settled region with limited variation in its legal, political, and cultural institutions. Surely networks of businessmen and bankers existed – Lamoreaux's extended kinship networks – through which capital could flow from

8. Davis, "New England Textile Mills," p. 4.
9. Sylla, "Early American Banking," pp. 108, 111.

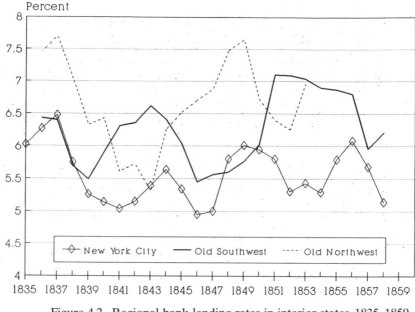

Figure 4.2. Regional bank lending rates in interior states, 1835–1859

one part of New England to another.[10] Localized differences in the region's interest rates were, in other words, as low as the risks, available technology and business environment would allow.[11]

Given Davis's findings for the postbellum era, results for the South Atlantic region were unexpected. As shown in Tables 4.2 and 4.3 and Figure 4.1, short-term bank lending rates appear to have been closely tied to those in New York City in the late 1850s. Before that, southern rates were actually somewhat lower than northeastern rates. It was initially thought that the lower South-Atlantic rates (averaging about 1 percentage point) evident from the mid-1830s through the mid-1850s resulted from the dates of balance sheets employed. As noted above, when a choice of dates was possible, balance sheets nearest year-end were chosen. Virginia's legislature collected balance

10. Lamoreaux, "Banks, Kinship"; Lamoreaux, *Insider Lending.*
11. Schwartz, "Beginning of Competitive Banking," shows that competition can take hold quickly even under traditional chartering regimes.

sheets as of 31 December of each year. Virginia bank lending peaked in December, and it is possible that the low rates found here were not indicative of rates that might have been found had an annual average loan denominator been used in Equation (4.1) above. Such a correction would, of course, have raised the calculated bank lending rates, but so, too, New York's. Bank reports dated December were also used for New York City, and New York bank lending also peaked in the fourth quarter of each year. Even though the use of year-end balance sheets generates a bias, it is consistent across states and regions.

Regardless of the common biases introduced in generating the interest rate proxies, the point is that differences in interest rates between the South-Atlantic region and the nation's emerging financial center were not great. Differences of this magnitude appear long after 1900, when there is reason to believe that regional capital markets were substantially integrated. By 1900, even with the costs of acquiring information much reduced by improved communication networks and with National Banks operating under common regulatory constraints, regional rate differentials of 75 to 100 basis points were still common. Between 1908 and 1914, for example, net rates of return for non-reserve-city banks in the South Atlantic region averaged about 70 basis points more than those in New York City.[12]

Finding that the Old South was financially integrated with the Northeast is surprising only if it is assumed that capital markets were fragmented before the Civil War and that the South constituted a separate region, poor in capital, and lacking energetic, profit-seeking entrepreneurs. The results are not nearly as surprising if we start from the more recent view that the antebellum South was built upon a rational, profit-seeking, albeit morally abhorrent, economic structure.[13]

Turning to the West (Figure 4.2), the results are similar though less clear-cut. Rates in the Old Southwest tracked with New York City rates until the early 1850s, after which time rates there exceeded New

12. Davis, "Investment Market," p. 365; Bodenhorn, "A More Perfect Union."
13. Calomiris and Schweikart, "Panic of 1857," come to a largely similar conclusion based on balance sheet data and the performance of southern banking systems in the face of financial crises.

York rates by about one and one-half to two percentage points. That the rates diverged for about five years and then reconverged also lends credence to the integration hypothesis. Had the markets been truly separate, economic forces may not have brought the disparate rates back into line.[14]

Considering states within the Old Southwest individually (Table 4.2) also provides some useful insights. In the quinquennium 1845–9, for example, bank lending rates in New Orleans exceeded New York rates by an average 60 basis points. Kentucky rates exceeded New York rates by only 53 basis points; while Tennessee rates were marginally lower than rates in New York. In the subsequent quinquennium (1850–4) rates within this region moved further away from those in the Northeast. New Orleans' rates exceeded New York's by an average 224 basis points; Kentucky by 194. A diligent search of the records of these banks failed to provide any clues that shed any insight into this rate behavior.

The most likely candidate is that the demand for banking services outstripped the region's supply of them. The value of goods received at New Orleans from the interior increased rapidly in the 1840s. In 1845–6, New Orleans received in excess of $77 million in produce. By 1850–1, the value of such shipments had increased to nearly $197 million.[15] Assuming that the shipment of this farm produce was financed by bills of exchange drawn on merchants, brokers, and bankers in the region's major commercial ports – namely, Memphis, St. Louis, Louisville, and New Orleans – such a marked increase in demand for credit was bound to drive up interest rates until the financial sector could fully respond to the rapidly changing economic environment. The response manifested itself as a rapid increase in the number of banks. Kentucky had 16 banks in 1850. It had 34 by 1855. In Tennessee, the number of banks increased from 22 to 32 over the same interval.[16] Once the supply of financial services increased to meet the increased demand, regional rates reconverged to the northeastern norm.

The Kentucky rates for the 1820s (Table 4.2), on the other hand, are unusually low and probably should not be taken as indicative of southwestern credit market conditions. The panic of 1819 was partic-

14. Those institutions and forces are considered in the next chapter.
15. North, *Economic Growth*, p. 250.
16. U.S. Comptroller of the Currency, *Annual Report* (1876).

ularly devastating for the region's farmers, particularly those who had bought land on credit. The legislatures of Illinois, Kentucky and Tennessee responded by chartering and subsidizing banks whose express purpose was to relieve the "distresses of the community" by offering low-interest loans to farmers and others on the verge of bankruptcy.[17] The Bank of the Commonwealth of Kentucky, for example, was required by charter to extend low-interest loans to farmers and planters. That the banks successfully met their charge is seen in the low rates in Kentucky.

The Old Northwest's experience presents the greatest challenge to the integration hypothesis. Rates in the Old Northwest exceeded those in New York throughout the 1830s and 1840s, but generally tracked New York City rates. Rates were converging toward the New York benchmark by the early 1840s at which time they moved sharply higher. By the early 1850s, they were again converging toward northern rates when the series ends. To some extent, these regional rate differentials may have resulted from the State Bank of Indiana's monopoly position. The possibility of a frontier premium cannot be ruled out, but substantially lower rates in Ohio in the interval 1835 to 1841 lend credence to the monopoly explanation. In either case, it appears that rates in the Old Northwest were tending toward the northeastern norm.

Having seen the results of the interest rate proxy calculations, the question that naturally follows is how well these rates reflect actual commercial bank rates and financial sector realities. It is not necessary to reiterate the point made above that net returns should mimic regional lending rates and provide information about the integration of antebellum financial markets. But for many purposes, actual rates paid by borrowers may be at issue. A few bits of data exist, and they generally support the claim that the net rates of return reported above accurately reflect actual market conditions. In a study of Stephen Girard's private banking house operated in Philadelphia between 1815 and 1831, Donald Adams produced a quarterly series of interest rates.[18] Comparisons of the rates calculated here for Philadelphia and Adams's series reveal a near equality in most years. Results this close were somewhat unexpected, however, as the Girard

---

17. Fenstermaker, *Development*, pp. 25–6.
18. Adams, *Finance and Enterprise*, p. 107.

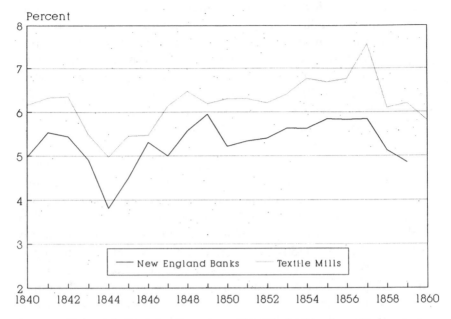

Figure 4.3. Bank lending rates at New England banks and interest rates
paid by New England textile mills, 1840–1859

Bank figures are gross rates whereas those reported in Table 4.2 are
net. But Stephen Girard was quite conservative, investing the bulk of
his funds in United States debt and "prime, double-name" paper.
Chartered Philadelphia banks, on the other hand, could not be or
were not as selective. Charter clauses often mandated that a certain
percentage of each bank's credit be directed toward farmers and
mechanics who, undoubtedly, represented higher risks and were
charged higher rates. If default rates were low, the holding of higher
yield assets would have equalized these net rates with gross rates on
lower yield paper.

In a study of borrowing among eight prominent New England
textile mills, Lance Davis also developed a series of interest rates
spanning the period 1840 to 1860. Since these mills received about 90
percent of their short-term credit from regional banks, his series provides a useful benchmark against which to compare the series constructed above. Figure 4.3 plots annual averages of Davis's monthly
series and the New England series from Table 4.3. The figure reveals
a close correspondence between the two series. The bank rate series,

representing net rates, remains below Davis's series by a nearly constant one percentage point. Net rates calculated above, then, do provide fairly accurate representations of actual borrowing rates. Additionally, the derived bank rate series also accurately represent changes in borrowing rates. A simple correlation coefficient between the annual average of Davis's monthly series and the New England rates reported above is 0.80 and the null hypothesis of no correlation can be rejected at the 99 percent confidence level. It should be clear, then, that the interest rate series developed above are useful for several purposes. They provide reasonably reliable proxies for actual regional interest rates and, more to the point, they provide strong evidence that early American capital markets were considerably more integrated than is generally believed.

While "eyeballing" the evidence suggests that antebellum financial markets were integrated, such a casual practice when dealing with long series of data is always a treacherous procedure. An appropriate statistical technique for determining the existence or extent of financial integration, however, is far from agreed upon. Modern studies rely on so-called cointegration tests, but as La Croix and Grandy noted, cointegration tests are not appropriate to a study of antebellum financial markets.[19] Donald McCloskey, however, offered an interesting alternative – a test he dubbed the Genberg-Zecher test.[20] The essence of the test is that we can a priori identify an integrated market; a distinct geographic subdivision in which, we suspect, prices or interest rates or whatever move in similar directions over some relevant interval. Once such a market is identified, we can calculate a correlation coefficient of prices or interest rates within that market and then compare that correlation to other markets for which we wish to determine the degree of integration.

Applying the Genberg-Zecher test to the antebellum experience would appear to be a straightforward proposition. Identifying an integrated market, however, presents innumerable possibilities for objection and debate. For the sake of argument, let us assume that

19. La Croix and Grandy, "Financial Integration in Antebellum America." Cointegration tests are especially problematic when there are few data points because the test requires first differencing of the dependent variables and the tests have relatively low power even with large data sets.
20. McCloskey, *Rhetoric of Economics*, p. 145. The use of this test is further defended in McCloskey and Zecher, "How the Gold Standard Worked"; and McCloskey and Zecher, "Success of Purchasing Power Parity."

financial intermediaries in Trenton, New Jersey; Philadelphia, Pennsylvania; and Baltimore, Maryland operated in a reasonably integrated market – a not unreasonable assumption given their geographic proximity. Panel A of Table 4.4 provides simple (Pearson) correlation coefficients for several city pairs as well as several state pairs. It is readily seen that the correlations between annual interest rates in our three cities are a relatively modest 0.25. It is also readily seen that antebellum America was characterized not by a single market but by a number of markets in which interest rates moved together. Philadelphia and New York were more closely tied together than, say, Philadelphia and Providence, but the latter pair still demonstrate co-movement in interest rates. And one should not be too quick to conclude that New Orleans constituted a distinct and nonintegrated market. While rates in Philadelphia and New Orleans were uncorrelated and seemingly nonintegrated, so, too, were those in Philadelphia and Boston. Historians would be hard-pressed to argue that markets in Boston and Philadelphia were geographically and financially distinct and separate. Even Lance Davis, as previously noted, suggested that we can think of the northeastern United States as an integrated antebellum market.

Panel B, too, suggests that interest rates throughout the country were subject to similar influences and moved together as least as much as rates within the geographically compact Delaware River valley. Correlations between the Middle Atlantic region (which includes New York City and Philadelphia) and New England were 0.25. Similarly, correlations between most other regions ranged between 0.23 and 0.31. The only regions to show significant differences were the Old Southwest (0.45) and the South Atlantic (0.15). The former is particularly intriguing given the apparent lack of correlation between Philadelphia and New Orleans. It suggests that correspondent and other relations developed between financial intermediaries in the Northeast and the Mississippi River valley brought about an unexpected degree of financial integration between those two regions.[21] Interest rates derived from bank statements, then, suggest that the characterization of financial markets drawn from the late nineteenth century do not well describe the first half of the century.

---

21. These relationships will be discussed in the next chapter.

Table 4.4. Correlations of bank rates for selected cities and regions

Panel A. City pairs

	Correlation	t-stat	N
Philadelphia-New York	0.43	2.39	27
Philadelphia-Boston	0.03	0.17	33
Philadelphia-Trenton	0.25	1.09	20
Philadelphia-Providence	0.22	1.10	25
Philadelphia-Baltimore	0.25	1.09	20
Philadelphia-New Orleans	0.00	0.00	22

Panel B. Region pairs

Mid Atlantic-New England	0.25	1.47	35
Mid Atlantic-South Atlantic	0.15	0.94	40
Mid Atlantic-Old Northwest	0.31	1.41	20
Mid Atlantic-Old Southwest	0.45	3.00	37
South Atlantic-Old Northwest	0.28	1.27	20
South Atlantic-Old Southwest	0.23	1.44	37
Old Northwest-Old Southwest	0.07	0.29	20

Sources: Correlations of rates reported in Tables 4.2 and 4.3

USURY LAWS AND BANK COSTS:
ALTERNATIVES TO INTEGRATION?

An alternative explanation for the observed pattern of regional interest rates might be that usury laws placed a binding ceiling on the rates banks could charge. The regional pattern of interest rates seen in Figures 4.1 and 4.2, in other words, might be the result of lending rates bouncing up against a binding usury ceiling. Even a cursory glance at Table 4.5, which shows legal interest rates and usury penalties in 1841, would appear to confirm the contention that usury laws explain the pattern of antebellum interest rates. Most states had legal rates of 6 or 7 percent. That these laws proved effective, it might be argued, is demonstrated in the net rates, reported in Tables 4.2 and 4.3, which are concentrated around 5 to 6 percent.

Before a causal role can be attributed to usury laws in generating the pattern of regional interest rates, however, it is necessary to consider the real effectiveness of these laws. As Table 4.5 shows, usury laws in several frontier states had escape clauses reflecting, perhaps, capital market pressures in these areas. In Louisiana, for example, the law dictated a 5 percent limit. Banks, however, could charge as much as 6 percent. Several other states allowed significantly higher rates if they were explicitly specified in a contract and agreed upon by both parties. Indiana and Arkansas had 6 percent limits, but, if both parties agreed, 10 percent could be charged. In Wisconsin and Iowa, contracts could specify rates as much as 5 percentage points greater than the legal rate.[22]

The real problem in determining the effectiveness of usury laws is that they were self-policing. That is, government officials or officers of the court did not continually monitor bank rates. Instead, it was left to the aggrieved to file a suit against an offending bank or other lender. Given that banking was characterized by long-term relationships between borrowers and lenders, bankers may well have been able to charge higher than legal rates without fear of suit. A borrower charged a usurious rate might obtain a short-run benefit by suing and recovering the usury (sometimes with penalties), but in doing so may have made an enemy of the bank and destroyed his or her relation-

---

22. In some states, however, banks were not subject to these escape clauses. They were restrained by the 6 or 7 percent rate specified in Table 4.5.

Table 4.5. Legal interest rates and usury penalties in selected states in 1841

State	Legal rate	Usury penalties/Special rates
Maine	6%	Forfeiture of principal
New Hampshire	6	Three times usury
Vermont	6	Recovery of usury with costs
Massachusetts	6	Three times usury
Rhode Island	6	Forfeiture of interest
Connecticut	6	Forfeiture of principal and interest
New York	7	Contract unenforceable
New Jersey	6	Forfeiture of principal and interest
Pennsylvania	6	Forfeiture of principal and interest
Delaware	6	Forfeiture of principal and interest
Maryland	6	Contract void
Virginia	6	Two times usury
North Carolina	6	Two times usury
South Carolina	7	Forfeiture of interest with costs
Georgia	8	Three times usury
Alabama	8	Forfeiture of principal and interest
Mississippi	8	Forfeiture of usury, 10% legal
Louisiana	6	Contract void, 5% nonbank maximum
Tennessee	6	Contract void
Kentucky	6	Forfeiture of usury with costs
Ohio	6	Contract void
Indiana	6	Two times usury, 10% legal
Illinois	6	Three times interest
Missouri	6	Forfeiture of interest
Michigan	7	Forefeit usury and one-fourth principal
Arkansas	6	Forfeit usury, 10% legal
Florida	8	Forfeit interest
Wisconsin	7	Three times usury, 12% legal
Iowa	7	Three times usury, 12% legal

Note: A percentage listed in penalty column denotes that if both parties agreed to the interest rate in writing it could be as high as the rate indicated.
Source: Hunt's Merchants' Magazine 4 (1841), p. 268

ship with an important credit source. No systematic investigations of antebellum court records have been made to see how often usury suits were filed, but John James's finding for the postbellum period probably held in the earlier era. "Although bank customers could file suits against banks violating the usury limit," wrote James, "few suits were actually filed probably because most customers [and their attorneys] were afraid of being black-listed by the banks and thus unable to borrow."[23]

Legal rates were probably ignored when economic conditions warranted higher rates. On 19 August 1851, the "Money Market" column in *Bicknell's Counterfeit Detector, Banknote Reporter, and General Prices Current* quoted the going rate on first class paper at 1 percent per month and noted that it was twice the legal rate. But Philadelphia banks, at least, could lend at these extraordinary rates without fear of violating usury limitations. While the city's banks could not make loans directly at these rates, a Pennsylvania court's decision specifically stated that banks could buy commercial paper in the secondary market at any rate. The court had ruled that "a fair *purchase* may be made of bond or note, even at twenty or thirty per cent. discount, without incurring the danger of usury."[24] Even if banks were constrained by usury laws in their direct dealings with customers, the banks could easily avoid the limitation by rationing regular clients and purchasing commercial paper on the street.

There were, as well, other legal methods of collecting interest in excess of rates allowed by usury laws. Banks often demanded that borrowers maintain compensating deposit balances. Stephen Girard, as noted in the preceding chapter, instructed his cashier to allocate loans in proportion to the borrowers' deposits. It was unlikely that Girard represented an exceptional case. Demanding depositors to maintain compensating balances, of course, reduced the effective loan size and raised the effective interest rate. Another common method of extracting interest in excess of lawful rates was to demand that borrowers keep the borrowed funds on deposit at the bank for a few days before withdrawing them. This practice effectively shortened the term of a loan and again raised the effective interest rate paid by the borrower.

The most often employed method of avoiding usury violations, perhaps, was charging (or overcharging) for so-called sight exchange. A common lending instrument was the bill of exchange

23. James, *Money and Capital Markets*, p. 82.
24. *An Abridgement of the Laws of Pennsylvania* (1811), quoted in Tooker, *Nathan Trotter*, pp. 177–8.

drawn on a distant city. To make the argument, concrete consider a bill of exchange drawn by a tobacco factor in Kentucky in favor of a Louisville merchant on the Philadelphia Bank, payable in sixty days at Philadelphia. As the Kentucky merchant was unlikely to be in Philadelphia in sixty days to collect the bill, he would rediscount the bill with one of Kentucky's banks. The discount charged by the Kentucky bank would include an amount above and beyond the opportunity cost of the money that reflected the cost of collection – the "sight" exchange. The going rate of exchange might range between one-quarter of one percent to as much as five percent and was widely reported in the financial press. With a sight exchange of 1.5 percent (a fairly typical exchange charge between Louisville and Philadelphia), the bank would accept a $100 note at $98.50 and then charge a discount reflecting the interest on a sixty-day loan.

The effective interest rate on bills of exchange can be broken down into its two component parts: the interest rate and the sight exchange, or the cost of bringing the money home after sixty days. It was through the use of sight exchange that usury laws could be rather easily circumvented.[25] If a borrower accused a bank of usury, the bank's best defense was that only the legal interest was charged and the excess represented the cost of repatriating the funds. When usury allegations did surface, they usually resulted from borrower complaints about excessive sight exchange charges. Sometimes, disgruntled borrowers claimed that banks had forced them to offer bills of exchange instead of locally payable promissory notes so that an explicit sight exchange charge could be added. A investigation by Massachusetts' legislature in 1840 uncovered the practice of charging sight exchange on Boston drafts and reported the rates of Boston exchange charged by Massachusetts country banks, which averaged about one-half of one percent.[26]

The results of a similar investigation by a Kentucky legislative committee concerned with abuses of the system also found its way into the legislative record. In questioning officers of the Northern Bank of Kentucky at Louisville, the committee asked if the bank had ever

25. Rockoff, "Origins of the Usury Provision."
26. Massachusetts General Court (1840).

forced a borrower to fraudulently disguise a promissory note as a bill of exchange so as to extract sight exchange. The bank's officers claimed they had not. But when asked: "Have not individuals applied for accommodations on notes, and been refused, where they received the same upon a bill of exchange," the bank's officers simply replied, "Yes in some cases, but not generally."[27] Yet, it appears that the legislature, having uncovered the practice, did nothing to stop it. Morton Horwitz's claim that "it was widely possible by the time of the Civil War to arrange usurious transactions in such a way as to entirely avoid running afoul of the usury laws," seems correct.[28] While this evidence does not rule out some effect from usury laws, it is unlikely that the laws proved truly effective in restraining bank behavior, and it is, therefore, doubtful that they explain much of the congruence in the regional interest rate series.

A second alternative explanation for the apparent equality of regional interest rates may be differences in bank cost functions. It may have been the case that actual lending rates differed significantly between regions, but banks in the South and West faced higher administrative or other costs so that net rates of return masked differences. In other words, it may have been that banks did not equalize loan interest rates; rather, they strove to equalize rates of return to equity. The essence of this potential objection is that shareholders and equity market conditions drove managerial behavior more so than borrowers and short-term capital market conditions.

The extant evidence is spotty, but what there is suggests that administrative costs did not vary significantly across regions. Table 4.6 shows that total bank expenses varied between about 1.5 and 2 percent of loans and discounts in the late 1820s. Costs declined in all regions through the 1830s and 1840s to about 0.75 to 1 percent. And by the late 1850s, they had risen to about 1 to 1.5 percent. The important point, however, is that they were nearly equal in such widely separated places as Boston, Charleston, and Louisville. While much more evidence needs to be uncovered before any definitive conclusions can be drawn, these spotty and largely impressionistic statistics suggest that the regional pattern of interest rates did not result from differential regional bank costs.

27. U.S. House, 25th Congress, 2d Session, *House Executive Document No. 79*, pp. 768–9.
28. Horwitz, *Transformation of American Law*, p. 244.

Table 4.6. Bank costs as a percent of outstanding loans, 1829-1859

	1829	1834	1839	1844	1849	1854	1859
Massachusetts Bank (Boston)	--	--	0.91	0.79	0.87	0.90	1.07
Bank of Charleston (South Carolina)	--	--	0.72	0.97[1]	0.79[2]	--	1.43[3]
Bank of State of S. C. (Charleston)	2.06	--	--	1.57	--	--	--
Bank of the Commonwealth (Kentucky)	1.08	--	--	--	--	--	--
Bank of Kentucky (Louisville)	1.46	1.13	--	--	1.33	--	--
Northern Bank of Kentucky (Louisville)	--	--	0.91[4]	--	0.79	--	--

Notes: [1] based on data from 1845; [2] from 1848; [3] from 1858; [4] from 1837
Sources: Gras, *Massachusetts First National*, pp. 627-31, 670-95; Bank of Charleston, *Proceedings*, 1839, 1844, 1858; U.S. House, 29th Congress, 2d Session, *Executive Document No. 120*; U.S. House, 31st Congress, 1st Session, *Executive Document No. 68*; South Carolina, *Compilation*, p. 484; Kentucky, *Senate Journal* (1828, 1837); Kentucky, *House Journal* (1828, 1833); Kentucky, *Legislative Documents* (1849)

ADDITIONAL EVIDENCE OF INTEGRATION: COMMERCIAL PAPER RATES

In addition to developing interest rate proxies from bank reports, it was also possible to develop several independent regional interest rate series from information printed in the antebellum financial press. Several newspapers appeared in American port cities in the 1780s and 1790s that provided detailed reports of prices of goods at auction as well as rates on sterling bills of exchange, shipping movements, and news from European markets. By the 1830s, several new financial papers appeared with significantly expanded coverage of market news and information. Although auction prices remained the principal concern and afforded the most space, publishers began to include such things as corporate stock prices, government bond prices, rates of foreign and domestic exchange, banknote discounts, and discount rates on commercial paper. Many newspapers aimed at general audiences also began to include "Money Market" columns that reported, albeit in less detail, the same information. The expansion of interregional trade in the 1820s and 1830s also created a demand for news from distant markets, and local papers supplied it. Merchants therefore had access to timely information on both local and distant markets, making it easier for them to coordinate their market activities.[29]

Using these sources it is possible to reconstruct a portrait of regional interest rates that complement the bank-rate series reported in Tables 4.2 and 4.3. The series of annual average discount rates on first-class commercial paper and bills of exchange for six cities are reported in Table 4.7.[30] The Boston rates are Bigelow's series of discount rates in Boston and New York and Joseph Martin's Boston rates, both reprinted in Macaulay.[31] Interest rates for New York and Philadelphia were drawn from weekly "Money Market" columns appearing in the *New York Tribune* between 1842 and 1859 and from *Bicknell's Counterfeit Detector, Banknote Reporter, and General Prices Current* published in Philadelphia between 1837 and 1857. Southern rates were found in the *New Orleans Price Current*, the New Orleans *Daily Picayune*, and the *Charleston Mercury*. Rates in the Cincinnati market were taken from Berry's study of western prices.[32]

Because local discount rates were not explicitly reported, interest rates for Charleston and New Orleans (between 1836 and 1854) were calculated from prices of inland bills of exchange. Bills were sold either "at sight" or "at time." Sight bills were payable upon presentation (with three days' grace being standard legal practice) at the collection office; time bills were payable after a specified period. The most common were 30 and 60 day bills, payable either 30 or 60 days after presentation (again with 3 days grace) to the drawee (the person on whom the bill was drawn). Holders of these bills rarely wished to wait 60 days for their funds, so banks and exchange brokers often purchased them at a discount that represented the costs of collection,

29. Pred, *Urban Growth*. This section is drawn largely from Bodenhorn, "Capital Mobility."
30. The monthly series underlying the annual rates reported in Table 4.7 can be found in Bodenhorn, "Capital Mobility," pp. 603–9.
31. Macaulay, *Movement of Interest Rates*.
32. Berry, *Western Prices before 1861*, p. 493.

Table 4.7. Average annual commercial paper rates, 1836-1859

Year	Boston	New York City	Phila- delphia	Charles- ton	New Orleans	Cincinnati
1836	20.30%	--	--	6.38%	11.00%	--
1837	14.39	--	12.94%	8.88	18.93	--
1838	8.54	--	--	18.57	15.40	--
1839	13.96	13.58%	13.69	13.40	17.18	--
1840	7.38	--	7.34	12.92	12.83	--
1841	6.88	7.16	9.52	11.63	9.10	--
1842	8.46	8.01	10.34	9.05	13.66	--
1843	4.17	3.24	4.59	7.36	8.10	--
1844	4.83	4.65	5.08	6.31	6.63	--
1845	5.95	5.87	7.01	5.63	6.30	--
1846	8.29	6.79	8.52	7.58	7.22	--
1847	11.50	7.15	8.38	6.24	10.97	--
1848	15.27	9.80	11.23	11.65	12.93	--
1849	10.18	6.42	8.05	7.83	7.76	--
1850	8.00	5.65	6.98	5.99	7.43	--
1851	10.07	7.00	9.17	5.50	8.94	--
1852	6.27	5.07	6.57	6.31	7.09	10.00%
1853	10.70	7.51	9.22	6.13	10.00	11.75
1854	10.96	9.39	12.99	9.69	11.91	11.90
1855	9.46	6.80	9.28	8.00	7.46	10.00
1856	8.71	7.59	9.35	7.81	6.01	9.64
1857	13.06	10.94	9.41	11.42	13.11	12.38
1858	4.84	4.52	--	10.04	7.47	8.88
1859	7.02	5.57	--	8.96	6.00	10.89

Note: Annual averages of monthly discount rates
Sources: Boston: Macaulay, *Movement of Interest Rates*, pp. A246-47; New York City: *New York Tribune*, various issues, 1839-1859; Philadelphia: *Bicknell's Counterfeit Detector*, various issues, 1837-1857; Charleston: *Charleston Mercury*, various issues, 1836-1859; New Orleans: *Daily Picayune*, various issues, 1840-1859 and *New Orleans Price Current*, various issues, 1836-1840; Cincinnati: Berry, *Western Prices*, p. 493

a small commission (usually 0.5 percent), and an implicit interest charge. If the interest charge on sight bills was essentially zero – that is, the discount represented only commission and collection charges – interest rates on 60-day bills can be calculated from the spread

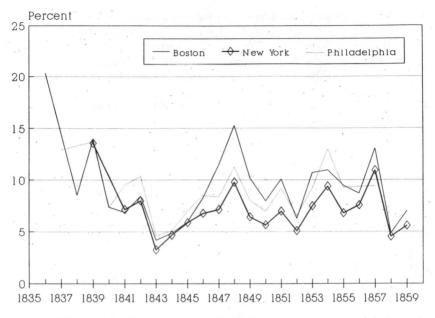

Figure 4.4. Average annual discount rates on commercial paper in northern cities, 1836–1859

between the long and short discount charges. This method was used to calculate rates in New Orleans and Charleston.[33]

Figures 4.4 and 4.5 plot annual averages of the monthly rates generated using the procedure outlined above. As the results of the previous section would lead us to believe, commercial paper rates in the Northeast and Middle Atlantic regions were nearly equal and moved in similar ways throughout the period. But, again, interest rates in the South and West are of particular interest because much previous research on postbellum capital markets has demonstrated that these regions failed to integrate into the national market until early in the

33. Schubert used this method to calculate short-term interest rates in eighteenth-century Britain. Interest charges implicit in a 60-day bill were calculated as:

interest rate = 6 * 100 * [(long rate − short rate)/ short rate]

   If, for example, 60-day bills were discounted at 3 percent and sight bills at 1 percent, the cost of obtaining $100 payable in New York in 60 days was $103; $100 at sight cost $101. The implicit interest charge on a 60-day bill was, then, 6*100*(2/101) or 11.88 percent. See Schubert, "Arbitrage in Foreign Exchange Markets," pp. 3–4 for a derivation and further justification for the use of this procedure.

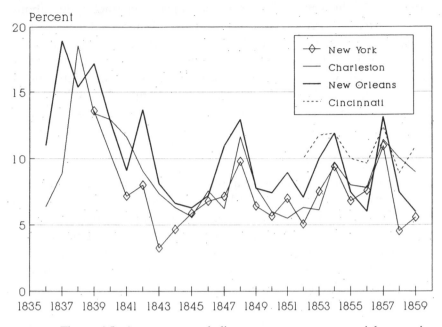

Figure 4.5. Average annual discount rates on commercial paper in southern and western cities, 1836–1859

twentieth century. These rates for the antebellum era reveal a pattern remarkably like that found for the post-Civil War period. During the decade between 1836 and 1845, short-term rates in southern cities exceeded those in northern cities by 2 to 3 percentage points. After 1845, however, rates in all six cities were similar and movements in northern rates were mimicked in southern and western markets. During several periods in the 1850s, in fact, southern interest rates on short-term financial instruments were marginally lower than those in Middle Atlantic port cities.

It does not appear that anything notable occurred in the 1840s to bring about an increased integration of regional capital markets. As the bank-derived interest rate proxies suggested, short-term capital markets had been pulled together by the early 1830s, if not earlier, but those early ties remained fragile. The disparity in rates between 1836 and 1845 resulted from the financial dislocations caused by failure of the Bank of the United States of Pennsylvania, the Bank of England's discount policies, and the resulting commercial depression of 1837 through 1843. During the depression, uncertainty about the security of borrowers and their collateral increased, and lenders became less willing to lend in markets where information arrived only after a lag. Markets were sundered and local interest rates followed similar but separate paths because they were then determined by local supplies of and demands for loanable funds. With the trough of the depression dated at 1843 by the National Bureau of Economic Research, reintegration by 1845 demonstrates the real strength of the ties binding these markets together and their ability to recover and reintegrate quickly following a large, long-lasting shock.[34]

During the panics of 1847–8 and 1857–8, regional markets did not disintegrate as they had in 1837. This may have resulted from improved bank coordination among southern branch banks. Charles Calomiris and Larry Schweikart found that the movement of funds both within and between regions slowed during the panic of 1857, but did not altogether cease as it had during the panics of 1837 and 1839.[35] In addition, the arrival of the telegraph improved communication, and bankers could have determined with greater confidence the creditworthiness of distant borrowers. It is equally plausible that the later panics were less severe, shorter-lived, and therefore less disruptive to capital flows.

Regardless of the exact cause, by the late 1840s short-term capital markets were bound together, sometimes to the chagrin of contemporary bankers and other capitalists. In September 1857, when interest rates in New York City rose to 24 percent and higher in the early stages of the panic, the New Orleans *Daily Picayune* reported that local bankers and brokers had "little concern for the goings-on on Wall Street." They believed that the panic was the result of "overtrading" by several New York banks and would remain localized. No one in New Orleans felt that a widespread panic loomed and the 10 percent discount rate on "prime, endorsed" commercial paper bore out that optimism. Less than four weeks later, however, the panic had spread and interest rates in New Orleans reached 24 to 36 percent. Given the pervasive uncertainty about the extent or expected length of the panic, the *Daily Picayune* reported few buyers of even the best bills, and banks had ceased discounting altogether. The mood among

---

34. See Abramovitz, "Long Swings," pp. 424–5 for the NBER's dating of nineteenth-century business cycles.
35. Calomiris and Schweikart, "Panic of 1857," pp. 824–32.

merchants, the paper reported, was an "overall feeling of depression."
Financial integration, it seemed, could be both a blessing and a curse.

A FURTHER TEST OF THE INTEGRATION
HYPOTHESIS

Though suggestive, equality or near equality of regional interest rates
is neither a necessary nor a sufficient condition for financial market
integration. Interest rates in two areas could have been equal and yet
those areas could have constituted distinct markets. Usury laws, risk
differentials, or mere coincidence may have underlain the apparent
integration of markets. More, formal tests, however, support the
impression that early American credit markets were, in fact,
integrated.

Stigler and Sherwin propose a test based on the correlation of
prices; the more correlated price, the more integrated were regional
markets.[36] Table 4.8 reports correlation coefficients for the monthly
commercial paper rates underlying Figure 4.4. Most of the correlation coefficients are significant at usual confidence levels and support
the impression that the United States, east of the Mississippi River
at least, was served by an integrated national network of short-term
capital markets.[37]

Yet some might still question the integration hypothesis. Although
markets that might generally be believed to have been integrated –
say Boston and New York – do, in fact, correlate quite highly, other
markets do not. The correlation coefficients between Boston and
Charleston and between Charleston and Cincinnati, for example, are
only one-fourth as great as the correlation between Boston and New
York City. These relatively low correlations of regional interest rates
between the South and the Northeast leave open the question of
whether a national credit market existed in the antebellum era.

Lance Davis argued that northeastern markets were integrated
early in the century because New York bankers and brokers regularly transferred funds to other cities when interest rates there were
greater than at home. This arbitrage, requiring the transfer of funds,

36. Stigler and Sherwin, "Extent of the Market."
37. I thank La Croix and Grandy, "Financial Integration," for pointing out an earlier error
    in interpreting these results.

Table 4.8. City pair correlations of commercial paper rates, 1835-1859

City pair	Correlation coefficient	N	City pair	Correlation coefficient	N
Boston-New York	0.87 (24.89)	201	New York-Cincinnati	0.72 (8.62)	71
Boston-Philadelphia	0.72 (15.21)	217	Philadelphia-Charleston	0.47 (7.90)	222
Boston-Charleston	0.21 (3.43)	257	Philadelphia-New Orleans	0.52 (8.91)	216
Boston-New Orleans	0.47 (8.30)	245	Philadelphia-Cincinnati	0.50 (4.04)	51
Boston-Cincinnati	0.69 (7.80)	69	Charleston-New Orleans	0.59 (11.46)	248
New York-Philadelphia	0.84 (20.89)	184	Charleston-Cincinnati	0.21 (1.74)	68
New York-Charleston	0.56 (9.65)	206	New Orleans-Cincinnati	0.72 (8.62)	71
New York-New Orleans	0.71 (14.54)	210			

Notes: t-statistics in parentheses; N = number of monthly observations
Sources: See Table 4.7 and Bodenhorn, "Capital Mobility," pp. 603-8

would only have occurred when regional interest differentials exceeded the costs of arbitrage. Arbitrage costs, therefore, created a range of interest rates in one market, within which it would be unprofitable to import funds. The low correlations uncovered above may reflect just that; that it was unprofitable to arbitrage on any existing differences. As such, interest rates could move independently, but within a narrow band defined by the costs of arbitrage. It was only when rates in one city exceeded, say, those in New York City by more than the costs of arbitrage that funds flowed between cities and brought divergent rates back into line. This example brings into sharp relief the fundamental difference between capital *mobility* and capital *movement*. Capital can be highly mobile and yet very little of it actually moves. But mobility depends, critically and ultimately, on the possibility that it can and will move when conditions (like pronounced and sustained interest differentials) warrant its movement.

Rates of domestic exchange defined the costs of interregional arbitrage, and Table 4.9 provides evidence that regional interest rate differentials were, in fact, limited by arbitrage costs. The table reports quinquennial average net rate of return differentials between New York City and several other regions. The upper figure in each cell represents the average differential between net rates of return in a particular city, state, or region; the lower figure represents exchange costs between New York and a particular region. To make the example concrete, consider the Philadelphia cell for 1840–4. The upper value implies that, during that quinquennium, rates in Philadelphia were lower than New York City rates by an average of 1.22 percentage points. It would have made little sense, however, for Philadelphians to arbitrage on this rate differential because the cost of moving funds (one way, moving funds there and back would effectively double the lower value) would have represented 2.37 percent of the total value of funds transferred. While the Philadelphian could earn an extra \$1.22 on \$100 remitted to and invested through a New York City correspondent, the cost of doing so was \$2.37. It made little sense, then, to arbitrage on the existing differential. Other cells in the table demonstrate that rate of return differentials between New York and other regions were generally confined to bounds defined by the costs of arbitrage.

The information displayed in Figure 4.6 provides an illustrative portrait of how arbitrage operated and kept geographically separated markets linked. The figure plots the difference between monthly commercial paper rates in Charleston, South Carolina and New York City between 1844 and 1859. Bold lines define the long-run average upper and lower "arbitrage points" between the two cities.[38] If rate differentials moved outside these points, it was profitable for banks and brokers to purchase exchange on the other city and request a correspondent to invest it at the higher rate. It is readily seen that rate differentials fluctuated randomly around zero, and only on rare

---

38. As Table 4.9 demonstrates, exchange costs or arbitrage points were relatively high during the financial depression of the late 1830s and early 1840s. By the mid-1840s, however, exchange costs stabilized and remained relatively constant throughout the remainder of the period. The use of the long-run average simplifies the diagram.

Table 4.9. Average quinquennial interest rate differentials and the costs of arbitrage, 1840-1859

	Region or City Rate - New York City Rate (Arbitrage Costs = Exchange and Commission Charges)			
	1840-44	1845-49	1850-54	1855-59
Boston	--	-0.08%	-0.02%	-0.08%
	--	(0.82)	(0.79)	(0.78)
Philadelphia	-1.22%	0.52	0.10	-1.11
	(2.37)	(0.73)	(0.79)	(0.89)
Virginia	-1.67	-1.29	-0.77	-0.25
	(3.57)	(1.88)	(1.84)	(2.20)
South Carolina	0.43	-0.06	1.46	0.21
	(2.09)	(1.63)	(1.62)	(2.04)
New Orleans	1.73	0.60	2.26	--
	(3.18)	(0.97)	(1.31)	--
Kentucky	-0.15	0.53	1.94	0.72
	(5.47)	(2.28)	(1.85)	(2.40)
Tennessee	0.89	-0.21	-0.52	0.64
	(8.13)	(2.91)	(3.06)	(2.68)
Old Northwest	0.12	1.85	1.25	--
	(5.74)	(2.38)	(2.05)	--

Notes: Arbitrage costs equal sum of average exchange charges and a 0.5 percent commission charge (assumed constant throughout the era). Virginia exchange rates are for Richmond; South Carolina rates are for Charleston; Kentucky rates are for Louisville; Tennessee rates are for Nashville; and Old Northwest rates are for Cincinnati.
Sources: Interest rate differentials calculated from Tables 4.2 and 4.3. Exchange charges are from *Commercial and Shipping List*, various issues, 1840-1859

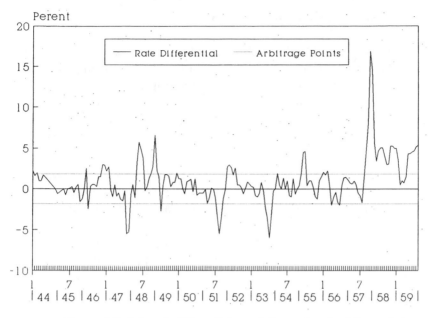

Figure 4.6. Interest differentials and the costs of arbitrage between New York City and Charleston, South Carolina, 1844–1859

occasions did rate differences move outside the arbitrage points. When they did, the divergence was short-lived. Not until the panic of 1857 did Charleston rates persistently exceed rates in the nation's financial center. But prior to that shock, rates in this southern city closely resembled rates in the Northeast.

This is how an efficient, integrated market should operate. The law of one price need not hold perfectly to be operative. Prices may occasionally diverge, but market forces should quickly and efficiently eliminate any significant departure from regional price equality. So long as antebellum short-term capital markets were functioning normally (non-panic periods), they eliminated substantial interest rate differentials. Being in constant communication with distant correspondents and tracking interest rate movements in other markets, antebellum bankers were ever vigilant and stood ready to profit on higher rates elsewhere. As a result, regional interest rates were brought into near equality by the late antebellum era and probably much earlier.

CONCLUDING REMARKS

The most important finding of this chapter is illustrated in Table 4.10, which reports differences in interest rates between each of four regions and New York City in the antebellum and postbellum eras. It is clear that three of the regions – New England, Middle Atlantic, and South Atlantic – were (using the usual definition of a small rate differential) integrated with New York City long before the outbreak of the Civil War. Interest differentials in 1835, 1845, and 1855 were similar to and in several cases smaller in absolute value, than those realized in 1875, 1885, and 1895. The South provides a particularly instructive case, given that most studies of postbellum capital markets have focused on its anomalous experience. But the South was not always an anomalous case. Interest differentials between that region and the Northeast were significantly lower before the war than after. If anything, rates there were marginally lower than in the Northeast. This provides particularly strong evidence that America's regional financial markets were linked very early. Most financial historians would probably agree that American short-term capital markets were effectively integrated by the turn of the century. Yet regional interest rate differentials were generally smaller before 1860 than after 1900. Moreover, the evidence uncovered here suggests that antebellum capital markets may well have been effectively integrated as early as 1820. Rates calculated (but not reported) as far back as 1815 demonstrate a similar equality. "Even at these early dates the simplest interpretation seems to be that the market was integrated."[39]

   The Old Northwest's experience, however, remains troublesome as rates there exceeded those in New York by as much as 295 basis points even as late as 1845. But evidence for this region is dominated by rates at the Bank of the State of Indiana, a bank that enjoyed a considerable amount of monopoly power until Indiana enacted free banking in 1852. Limited evidence from Ohio – a competitive, chartered banking state – show that rates there were more in line with those in the Northeast. Still, the conclusion that rates in this region exceeded those elsewhere cannot be easily dismissed. A "frontier" effect reflecting either higher risks or capital scarcity may

39. Bodenhorn and Rockoff, "Regional Interest Rates," p. 184.

Table 4.10. Interest rate differentials with New York City, selected years

Year	New England	Middle Atlantic	South Atlantic	Old Northwest
1835	-0.07	-0.16	-0.29	0.48
1845	-0.41	0.03	0.89	2.95
1855	-0.40	-0.20	-0.56	--
1875	1.59	1.14	1.33	1.99
1885	0.37	0.92	1.59	1.77
1895	0.57	1.23	1.09	0.79
1905	0.48	0.44	2.41	0.82

Note: Figures represent regional bank rate less New York City bank rate.
Sources: Tables 4.2 and 4.3; Davis, "Investment Market"

have been in effect. Only further research can shed light on these possibilities.

Finding early American capital markets integrated should come as no surprise to students of other early capital markets. A series of studies by Larry Neal demonstrated that stock markets in London and Amsterdam were integrated by the 1720s.[40] Only wars and severe financial shocks sundered these markets and, even then, they reintegrated quickly thereafter. The American Civil War may have been expected to have had a similar effect. Yet, American markets apparently failed to reintegrate quickly after the war. Historians have long believed that dislocations caused by the Civil War were responsible. The war destroyed or crippled most southern banks. The Civil War-era National Banking Acts thrust banks under a common regulatory

40. Neal, "Integration of International Capital Markets"; Neal, "Integration and Efficiency"; and Neal, *Rise of Financial Capitalism*.

umbrella and Reconstruction-era federal legislation forced this unnatural system to reintegrate under the strain of policies aimed at gradual specie resumption. As desirable as these policies may have been on other grounds, they surely failed to smooth the way to financial reintegration after the war.

All this leads to a final question: at what date did American capital markets integrate? While considerably more work is required to push interest rate measures further back in time, it may be reasonable to conjecture that American capital markets were always integrated. The notion of geographically distinct centers of savings and investment being gradually merged into a single entity is probably an inappropriate way to envision the process. Instead, it may be better to view the process as one in which the frontier pushed westward as capitalists chose to invest in new regions. This is not to imply that westerners sat awaiting the eastern capitalist to bring with him an appropriate financial structure and deliver unto them access to a national capital market. As noted at the outset, antebellum America is probably best thought of as a number of regional markets that were unified through a complex institutional structure (to be detailed in the next chapter). Pioneers certainly brought with them some ideas of an appropriate financial structure and then adapted it to their own purposes and preferences – Michigan's free banking being a notable example.[41] Once these institutions were in place, however, they were not immediately incorporated into the regional or national network. Acceptance into the institutional superstructure required information, the passing of tests and ultimately trust, all of which occurred in time. In the short-run, though, many western and southern financial institutions operated in a region – the frontier – beyond the pale for established eastern capitalists and the "frontier, to use Frank Knight's terminology, was the line that separated risk from uncertainty."[42] In time, the frontier moved on and institutions once beyond it were brought within it, and incorporated into the web of American finance.

41. Rockoff, "New Evidence on Free Banking."
42. Bodenhorn and Rockoff, "Regional Interest Rates," p. 187.

5 Banks, Brokers, and Capital Mobility

A man brings money to the bank to meet a payment which he desires to make a great distance, and the bank, having a connection with other banks, sends it to where it is wanted. As soon as bills of exchange are given upon a large scale, this remittance is a very pressing requirement.

Walter Bagehot (1906)

In addition to the profits which a bank derives from discounting paper . . . it also, occasionally, sells its own drafts on distant banks for a premium, – it having been previously arranged between them, that they would accept each other's drafts.

George Tucker (1839)

By 1810 American banks had become part and parcel of a banking system.

Fritz Redlich (1947)

The term *global village* is now commonly employed to describe what is widely seen as a new international economic reality. Implicit in this term is the notion that the world economy is growing increasingly integrated. Stock markets throughout the world rise and fall in unison. Domestic producers can view their home turf as neither their own nor sufficiently large to support their operations. Whether the economic world of the late-twentieth century has, in fact, undergone some remarkable transformation, or whether the change is simply one of perception is arguable. Certainly, western Europe's principal stock markets were integrated by the first quarter of the eighteenth century, as Larry Neal's work so clearly demonstrated.[1] Similarly,

1. Neal, *Rise of Financial Capitalism*, chapter 7.

165

Brinley Thomas's work showed that, while the world's labor markets may not have been truly integrated, trans-Atlantic migration ebbed and flowed with changing economic conditions on both sides of the ocean.[2] And large North American companies, such as Singer Sewing Machines and American Tobacco, while perhaps not representative of business generally, recognized the need for world-wide distribution of their products by the late nineteenth century.[3]

No term equivalent to *globalization* surfaced in the antebellum era to describe a similar economic transformation taking place within the United States. That the United States was growing increasingly economically unified seems indisputable. Interregional trade was growing at unprecedented rates. Between 1820 and 1840, the real value of goods received at New Orleans from the interior grew at an average annual rate of 7.05 percent.[4] Although part of that impressive growth was a result of starting from a small base, growth in the subsequent score of years still averaged 5.75 percent per annum in real terms. Between 1836 and 1860 the raw tonnage of goods transported from the West to New York over the Erie Canal increased at an annual average rate of 12.45 percent.[5] Table 5.1 demonstrates that New Orleans and the Erie Canal were not unrepresentative of general patterns. Between 1840 and 1860, the volume of trade moving from the Old Northwest to the Northeast increased at an average annual rate of 13.42 percent; from Northeast to Old Northwest at 11.19 percent. Growth in trade between other regions did not grow as quickly, but it still increased at a significant pace.

Simultaneous with an increasing volume of interregional trade, the United States was experiencing fundamental economic transformations as the share of agriculture in employment and value added was falling relative to manufacturing and commerce. Gross economic output, too, was accelerating at a modest pace. Clearly, events in the real sector of the economy were placing severe stresses on the financial sector. Regardless of whether one accepts the supply-leading or demand-following frameworks discussed in Chapter 1, banks and financial intermediaries mattered in that they either actively promoted economic change and development or they, at the

2. Thomas, *Migration and Economic Growth*.
3. Chandler, *Visible Hand*, chapters 7–11.
4. New Orleans trade data from North, *Economic Growth*, pp. 250–2; nominal figures deflated by "Farm Products" index reported in Warren and Pearson, *Prices*, table 3, pp. 25–6.
5. North, *Economic Growth*, pp. 250–1.

Table 5.1. Average annual rates of growth of interregional trade by region of origin and destination (in percent)

Origin	Destination		
	North	West	South
North	--	11.19	4.68
West	13.42	--	5.42
South	2.83	6.02	--

Note: Calculated from regional import/export data in current dollars
Source: Fishlow, "Antebellum Interregional Trade," p. 360

very least, needed to respond to the demands placed on them. Chapters 2 and 3 suggested that the financial sector promoted economic development in that it allocated short-term capital in response to changing sectoral demands in a reasonably efficient manner. Chapter 4 suggested that the self-same system brought about an efficient geographic allocation. This chapter outlines the organizational and institutional developments occurring in the first half of the nineteenth century that allowed for an appropriate financial response to changes in the real sector. The financial sector, as the previous chapter demonstrated, was integrated and interdependent by the 1850s and probably much earlier. This chapter, then, picks up where the last chapter left off in that it considers those institutions and organizations that promoted and realized that integration.[6]

6. The distinction between institutions and organizations may seem trivial to some, but within the so-called "new institutional economics" the distinction is of considerable importance. Douglass North defines institutions as the "humanly devised constraints that shape human interaction . . . [and] reduce uncertainty by providing structure to everyday life." North insists that *institutions* thus need to be differentiated from *organizations*, which are humanly devised groups (firms, labor unions, governments) that must play by the rules. North, *Institutions*, p. 3. Others, such as Mancur Olson, use the term *institutions*, but are referring to organizations in North's terminology. See, for example, Olson, *Logic of Collective Action*.

The chapter proceeds by first considering antebellum organizations believed to have influenced the geographic allocation of capital. It first considers the strategies pursued by Nicholas Biddle as head of the era's prominent financial institution – the Second Bank of the United States – in bringing about the integration of antebellum American financial markets. Evidence suggests that while the Bank was the dominant player in the nation's financial markets, its interregional activities were not indispensable to the integration of the country's regional markets.[7] That is, the Second Bank did not embark upon a series of original or innovative practices, though it may well have extended the use of some practices into regions in which they were previously unknown or unused. The chapter then turns to a consideration of the role of private bankers, brokerage houses and state-chartered commercial banks and the intricate web of correspondent relations developed by these organizations. Finally, we turn to a series of fundamental institutional changes effected by reinterpretations of commercial codes by state and, especially, the federal courts. Without the changes wrought by the courts, which were growing increasingly supportive of interregional trade by overturning laws inimical to it, antebellum financial markets probably would not have allocated capital as efficiently as they did.

THE SECOND BANK AND REGIONAL INTEGRATION

When Nicholas Biddle assumed the presidency of the Second Bank of the United States in 1823, he took command of an organization whose ability to control the monetary affairs of the country had been considerably diminished. Before Biddle took the helm, Langdon

---

7. The uppercase "Bank" is used when referring to the Second Bank of the United States. This saves space and should cause no confusion as other banks are referred to with the lowercase "bank." Similarly, the term "Second Bank" is used as a descriptive shorthand. Technically, the Bank's corporate name was "The President and Directors of the Bank of the United States." It was, however, the second such bank chartered by Congress; the first obtained a twenty-year charter in 1791. The First Bank's charter was not renewed and the Second Bank was granted a twenty-year charter in 1816. While contemporaries referred to both as the Bank of the United States, it has become common practice among historians to differentiate between them by the terms "First" and "Second." For the sake of simplicity and brevity, that usage is adopted here.

Cheves (pronounced "chivis") contracted the Bank's operations in order to retrench and correct mistakes made under the previous leadership that had nearly bankrupted the institution.[8] Though all the Bank's branches labored under Cheves' directives, it was the southern and western branches that were most affected. Cheves assigned each branch its own capital, and the branches were expected to operate in accordance with their capital allocation. That is, the Bank's branches were to issue notes and discount paper in amounts that their capital would sustain and hold reserves sufficient to meet redemptions of its own notes. Cheves had effectively taken a national organization and transformed it into a network of independent banks operating under the loose direction of the parent institution in Philadelphia.

When Nicholas Biddle took control, he planned to reverse Cheves' actions and establish the Second Bank's primacy in the nation's financial affairs. His primary goal was the establishment of a truly national currency. To that end he initiated policies designed to decrease the discounts on depreciated state bank notes and to facilitate exchange between regions. Having accumulated a large volume of state bank notes during Cheves' administration, the Bank reigned in the state banks by presenting their notes for redemption. As a consequence, the remaining circulation was made redeemable and banknote discounts were significantly reduced. Lowering the costs of – and thereby facilitating – interregional exchange was accomplished by using the Bank's branch network to extend and dominate the market in both the purchase and collection of inland bills of exchange. Biddle's Bank pursued the latter goal by first pegging interregional exchange rates and then making a market in domestic bills at those rates.[9]

Biddle preferred bills of exchange to locally payable promissory notes for a variety of reasons. One was that he envisioned a division of labor in the banking system. The Second Bank would, capturing the cost advantages of its branch network, specialize in bills of exchange and leave the discounting of promissory notes to the state

---

8. For a complete discussion of Cheves' actions and the problems he inherited from the previous administration see Womack, *An Analysis*, chapter 5; and Catterall, *Second Bank*, chapter 4. The story is too complex to do justice to it here, and it would take us far afield.

9. Catterall, *Second Bank*, p. 132.

banks.[10] And Biddle, ever desirous of placing his Bank in a favorable light, argued that the benefits of this division would be reaped by all. In a report to the Bank's stockholders in 1831, Biddle laid out a defense of his policy:

These operations too are fortunately of the highest benefit to the community; they give the most direct encouragement to industry, by facilitating the purchase and interchange of all its products, they bring the producers and consumers into more immediate contact by diminishing the obstacles which separate them, and they specially adapt the Bank to the wants and interests of each section of the Union, by making it alternatively a large purchaser among the sellers of bills, and a large seller among the purchasers.[11]

During a partisan congressional investigation of the Bank in 1832, Biddle again emphasized the domestic exchange operations of the Bank. They were, he argued, the Bank's most important financial operation, important not only to the Bank, but to the country as well. The majority report refused to accept that the Bank was of much value, but the drafters of the minority report underscored Biddle's contention. The Bank was, the minority wrote, "certainly an invaluable institution. It has not only annihilated time and space [by moving funds between regions], but it has done something more. It has produced such a state of exchanges, that it is much easier for a man in New York to pay a thousand dollars in St. Louis than to pay it in Wall Street."[12] Although perhaps overstated, the Second Bank *had* between 1823 and 1832 reduced some of the costs associated with domestic exchange. By 1832 rates on domestic exchange were generally at par between northeastern cities and between one and one and one-half percent between western and southern cities.

While Biddle emphasized the benefits accruing to the public from the Bank's exchange operations, engaging in and expanding the scope of the business allowed Biddle to extend the Bank's reach and increase its profits. Through its domestic exchange operations, the Bank reduced reserve pressures placed on eastern branches by western and southern offices. Notes issued by the western and southern branches gravitated toward eastern offices, which then became responsible for their redemption. Eastern branches, therefore, faced

10. Redlich, *Molding*, p. 126.
11. *Report of the Proceedings of the Triennial Meeting of the Stockholders of the Bank of the United States* (1831), pp. 13–14, quoted in Redlich, *Molding*, p. 129.
12. U.S. House, 22d Congress, 1st Session, *House Report No. 460*, p. 313.

discounting constraints because their reserves were effectively ear-marked for the redemption of western and southern note issues. Cheves had attempted to solve the problem by allocating each branch a specific capital and requiring that each operated within bounds appropriate to that capital. Cheves' method failed because it neither reduced the northeastern flow of notes nor transferred reserves to northeastern branches. Biddle quickly abandoned Cheves' ineffective solution and replaced it with extensive exchange operations.

It was a fact that branch issues gravitated to the north and east, but it was also true that much of the produce flowing out of the Mississippi River valley moved in the same direction and most southern and western bills and notes were drawn to facilitate this movement of goods. The Bank's difficulty lay in that under Cheves' direction, southern and western branches continued to discount promissory notes payable at their office rather than bills of exchange payable where the goods were destined. Upon taking control of the Bank, Biddle instructed branch cashiers to reduce the value of discounted notes and replace them with bills of exchange drawn on the East. When the bills matured, under this system, payment was made at an eastern office, which provided eastern branches with the necessary specie to redeem the branch drafts that found their way to eastern offices. Western branches thereby accommodated their clients without unduly checking the lending capabilities of eastern offices.[13] Not only did the Bank attempt to establish a division of labor within the banking system generally, it also divided the labor between its own offices. Southern and western branches were active purchasers of domestic bills; northern and eastern offices were active sellers.

As natural as was Biddle's interest in bills of exchange, it never-theless represented a revolutionary policy change at the Second Bank and may have prompted similar changes at some state-chartered

---

13. Biddle described the process in a more convoluted manner: "The course of western business is to send the produce to New Orleans, and to draw bills on the proceeds, which bills are purchased at the several branches, and remitted to the branch at New Orleans. When the notes issued by the several banks find their way in the course of trade to the Atlantic branches, the western branches pay the Atlantic branches by drafts on their funds accummulated at the branch at New Orleans, which there pay the Atlantic branches by bills growing out of the purchases made in New Orleans on account of the northern merchants or manufacturers, thus completing the circle."

   U.S. House, 22d Congress, 1st Session, *House Report No. 460*, p. 313. See also Womack, *An Analysis*, p. 368 for a description of Biddle's policy.

banks. When asked about the subject in 1818, the cashier of the Philadelphia office knew of only one other local bank that dealt in domestic exchange. And other evidence supports the claim that the Second Bank effectively pioneered the use of domestic exchange, especially between North and South. Prior to the mid-1820s and the ascension of Nicholas Biddle, the collection of inland bills of exchange was carried out through independent brokers, private bankers and, to a lesser extent, state banks. Although the bill market had, by 1820, extended itself into the western hinterlands, as references to "note-shavers" (a pejorative term for brokers) appeared in *Niles Register*, the markets remained relatively provincial.[14] An advertisement by the Boston brokerage firm of Gilbert & Dean, appearing in 1812 publicized that it would "collect bills for a reasonable compensation" at New York City, Philadelphia, and Baltimore, but its interior collections were limited to parts of Massachusetts, Rhode Island, and Connecticut.[15] Commercial columns appearing regularly in the *New York Price Current* between 1811 and 1817 similarly reported current rates of domestic exchange only on Boston, Philadelphia, and Baltimore.[16] This does not, of course, imply that interregional exchanges were unknown in the early antebellum era, but they must have been limited. If the volume or extent of these transactions had been substantial, buyers and sellers of exchange would have required information on prices and volumes, and contemporary newspapers probably would have supplied it.

So, too, prior to the Second Bank's entry into the market, the reasonableness of domestic exchange charges were often questioned by contemporaries, and claims of usury were common. *Niles Register* reported in 1818 "that in ordinary cases where the security is good, and the paper undoubted, they don't charge more than two per cent. per month." A discount rate of 24 percent per annum undoubtedly included both the interest and exchange charges, and it is likely that *Niles Register* reported exceptional or noteworthy rates rather than less spectacular, but typical, rates, which averaged around 7 percent interest and one to three percent exchange. But rates in excess of 20 percent also suggest that the market for domestic

14. See "The Farmer and the Broker," *Niles Register* (22 August 1818); "Brokers," *Niles Register* (8 May 1819); and "Shaving," *Niles Register* (9 October 1819).
15. *The Pilot* (Boston), 12 October 1812.
16. *New York Price Current*, various issues, 1811–1817.

Table 5.2. Rates of domestic exchange on drafts
sold in Boston, end of April, 1811-1815

	1811	1812	1813	1814	1815
New York					
30 days	0.5%	0.5%	0.5%	0.5%	5.0%
60 days	1.0	1.0	1.0	1.0	--
Philadelphia					
30 days	1.0	0.5	0.5	0.5	6.0
60 days	1.0	1.0	1.0	1.0	--
Baltimore					
30 days	0.5	0.5	0.5	0.5	--

Note: All values are percent discounts from face
value of bills of exchange.
Source: *Ming's New York Price Current*, various
issues, 1811-1815

exchange remained immature, speculative, and thin. Table 5.2 presents a series of domestic exchange discounts at Boston on three
other Atlantic port cities in April of each year from 1811 to 1815.
During periods of normal commercial and financial activity, domestic exchange charges were relatively modest, ranging from one-half
of one to one percent. With the financial panic of 1814, when
most banks outside Boston suspended specie payments, exchange
charges rocketed upward. The significant rise in exchange charges
during the suspension (lasting from 29 August 1814 through 20 February 1817 in Philadelphia) reflects the increased costs and risks associated with exchange operations. Because bills drawn on Philadelphia
were paid in local banknotes, exchange charges of 5 to 6 percent

accounted for the depreciation in the specie value of Philadelphia banknotes.[17]

As noted in the previous chapter, charges of usury were inevitable when exchange fees reached five or six percent on a 30- or 60-day bill of exchange. Critics were, as Nicholas Biddle explained, confusing "two things distinct in themselves, but necessarily blended in the same operation," the exchange charge and the discount rate.[18] Exchange was undoubtedly used (even abused) on occasion to extract higher than legal rates without running afoul of usury laws, but such occurrences were probably resorted to only when usury ceilings became binding. It was easier, and not uncommon, for banks and brokers to simply ignore the laws, which they regularly did, than force a customer to discount a bill of exchange instead of a locally-payable note. Moreover, banks got around usury laws by entering the rediscount market in which usury laws did not apply, buying bills and drafts at a significant discount that reflected higher real interest rates.

Under Biddle's leadership in the decade following 1823 the Second Bank emerged as the dominant player in the domestic exchange market. In 1820 the Bank purchased less than $6 million in domestic exchange. By 1833 it purchased nearly $70 million in exchange, more than twice the total value of trade passing through New Orleans from the Upper Mississippi and Ohio River valleys during that year.[19] Yet, historians may have overestimated the Second Bank's importance. Biddle, and the Bank's supporters, claimed that this volume of exchange dealings was made possible through the utilization of the Bank's extensive branch network. Financial historians, like Davis Dewey and Fritz Redlich, accepted Biddle's contention that his Bank captured scale economies other banks could not and that the Bank passed these cost savings along to its clients.[20] Evidence presented in Table 5.3 appears to support that conclusion. Rates of domestic exchange charged by the Second Bank's New York City office were consistently lower than rates charged by the city's banks and exchange brokers. While the New York office of the Second Bank

17. Because New York and Philadelphia banknotes had depreciated, relative to specie, by five percent in May 1815 and Baltimore banknotes by 14 percent, the exchange charges see reasonable, if not too low to be profitable. U.S. Comptroller of the Currency, *Annual Report* (1876), p. LXXXIX.
18. U.S. House, 22d Congress, 1st Session, *House Report No. 460*, p. 47.
19. North, *Economic Growth*, p. 250.
20. Dewey, *State Banking*, p. 167; Redlich, *Molding*, p. 133; Smith, *Economic Aspects*, p. 4.

Table 5.3. Rates of exchange on selected cities in New York City charged by New York City branch of the Second Bank of the United States and by state banks and brokers in New York in 1830 (percent discount)

	Second Bank New York	State Banks and Brokers
Boston	par	0.25
Philadelphia	par	0.25
Baltimore	par	0.50
Richmond	par	1.00
Fayetteville, NC	par	2.00
Charleston	0.25	1.50
Savannah	0.75	1.50
Mobile	1.50	--
New Orleans	1.00	1.00
Nashville	0.75	--
Louisville	0.50	--
Cincinnati	1.00	--

Note: All values are percent discount from face value of bill of exchange. Par implies that no discount was charged. *Sources*: U.S. House, 22d Congress, 1st Session, *House Executive Document No. 147,* p. 60; U.S. Comptroller of the Currency, *Annual Report* (1876), p. LXXXVII

purchased exchange on Atlantic coast cities at par, banks and exchange brokers discounted such bills at rates varying between 0.25 and 1.50 percent. Biddle, in fact, explained that most of the animosity toward his Bank originated among those whom the Bank had driven out of business by its low rates.

Although the Second Bank's posted and pegged exchange rates

were par on eastern cities and about 1 to 2 percent in the South and West, the Bank's profits from exchange dealings (exclusive of interest charges) between 1830 and 1834 averaged 2.2 percent.[21] Biddle's Bank probably disguised its higher than posted exchange discounts with its commission charges. Commission fees on bill collections among exchange brokers in the post-Second Bank era were a nearly uniform 0.5 percent.[22] Given the spread between the Second Bank's posted exchange rates and its actual returns, its commissions must have exceeded 1 percent, effectively raising the costs of transferring funds between regions. This raises serious questions about Biddle's self-portrayal as a benevolent monopolist.

Financial historians, however, have largely accepted Biddle's self-portrayal as an innovative entrepreneur who recognized and exploited a profitable opportunity that state banks had long ignored. Bray Hammond, for example, argued that the Second Bank adopted in its domestic exchange operations a method well established in foreign trade and that only after observing the Second Bank's success did state banks follow.[23] In his history of the Philadelphia Bank, Nicholas Wainwright claimed that "in 1836, it [the Philadelphia Bank] entered a new field, one hitherto monopolized by the Bank of the United States – the purchase of domestic exchange."[24] It may, in fact, have been that several banks entered the industry only after the Second Bank had shown them the way, but it was unlikely that the Bank was indispensable to the process. As previously noted, brokerage houses though small had arisen early in the century and, as Peter Temin argued, "if the Second Bank had not existed, other means would have been found to transfer credit from one place to another."[25] Even Redlich, who himself represented the Second Bank as a necessary precondition for the expansion of interregional exchange operations, reported that by 1800 "inter-bank deposits and incipient correspondent relations" between state banks were developing to facilitate interregional transactions. And most bankers recognized the overarching importance of nurturing and furthering these ties.[26]

---

21. Calculated from information reported in Catterall, *Second Bank*, pp. 504–5.
22. *New Orleans Price Current*, various issues, 1840–1842; and *Commercial and Shipping List* (New York), 3 January 1852.
23. Hammond, *Banks and Politics*, p. 700.
24. Wainwright, *History of the Philadelphia National*, p. 72.
25. Temin, *Jacksonian Economy*, p. 39.
26. Redlich, *Molding*, p. 16.

The real driving force, perhaps, behind the Second Bank's increased interest in domestic exchange was an unprecedented increase in the number and types of financial instruments. Prior to 1820 the volume of interregional trade was small, relative to mid-century at least, and gave rise to limited amounts of domestic exchange. Transportation improvements, like steamboats, canals and, later, the railroads, which facilitated interregional trade and prompted a westward shift in the locus of foodstuff production, may have had a far greater influence on the utilization of domestic bills than the Second Bank's policies. By the early 1830s, during the very height of the Second Bank's dominance, the market for domestic exchange had grown so competitive that many banks were forced to abandon their long-standing practice of discounting notes and bills one or two days per week. Exchange rates fluctuated daily and businessmen were no longer willing to wait several days to learn if their bill would be discounted and what the exchange rate might be.

While Biddle's Bank may have dominated the domestic exchange market, it was never a pure monopolist. An intricate network of state banks and exchange brokers entered the market nearly concurrently with the Second Bank. The Bank apparently extended and dominated the market in domestic exchange, but it was not indispensable to the process. Instead, the rising volume of domestic exchange operations were likely the result of an increased supply of domestic bills as the flow of southern and western produce expanded after 1820. The Second Bank's role in fostering exchange markets and integrating both the financial and real sectors of the economy were not trivial – financing $70 million in produce shipments in 1833 was hardly trivial – but its influence should not be exaggerated and the activities of other important players ignored.

PRIVATE BANKERS AND EXCHANGE BROKERS: PREDECESSORS OF THE COMMERCIAL PAPER HOUSE

Lance Davis based his explanation of postbellum interest rate convergence on the extension of the commercial paper market into relatively remote (financially speaking) western and southern regions and the increased capital mobility brought about by the commercial paper house.[27] But these specialized intermediaries did not suddenly arise in the 1880s. Their roots can be traced directly to antebellum America's earliest exchange brokers. Unlike postbellum era commercial paper houses that purchased paper outright and then marketed it in secondary markets, antebellum exchange brokers were exactly that – brokers. They did not buy commercial paper outright from their customers. Rather, brokers accepted notes and bills on consignment and forwarded the proceeds to the maker of a bill when a buyer was found.[28] Outright purchases of commercial paper by bill brokers was apparently not a common practice until initiated by Henry Clews in the late 1850s.[29]

There is substantial evidence, however, that note brokerage arose early in the nineteenth century. The business grew gradually from the turn of the century until the Second Bank's entry in the 1820s.[30] Although some historians, like Redlich and Hammond, claimed that the Second Bank's actions preempted the existing business and stymied the further development of a private, competitive market, Albert Greef argued that the Second Bank's actions actually encouraged entry and promoted growth in note brokerage.[31] By making a market in bills of exchange, particularly those originating in the South and West and drawn on the East, the Second Bank supported the operations of private brokers and state banks in the exchange market. With the Second Bank standing ready to buy good bills, its actions increased the liquidity of good bills, making them more attractive investments. In addition, the Second Bank's extended branch network facilitated and simplified the collection of bills on distant cities.

Whether the Second Bank promoted or stymied the development of private brokerage is open to debate and deserves further research. It is clear, however, that the Bank's closure in 1836 left a yawning void in the business of collecting exchange. After the Second Bank's demise, brokers entered the market with seeming abandon. In 1836 and 1837 at least fourteen newly established brokerage houses adver-

---

27. Davis, "Investment Market," p. 372.
28. Myers, *New York Money Market*, pp. 55–7.
29. Greef, *Commercial Paper House*, p. 31.
30. Klein, "*Development of* Mercantile Instruments," p. 531.
31. Greef, *Commercial Paper House*, p. 31.

tised their services in a single Philadelphia newspaper.[32] If the contention that the Second Bank displaced and drove from the business most of the exchange brokers operating in 1823 is correct (which seems unlikely), then the post-Bank growth in the market was nothing short of phenomenal. In 1842 a New York City directory listed seventy-six exchange offices, almost all of which were located in lower Manhattan around Wall Street.[33] In New Orleans there were at least thirty exchange offices.[34] Even more remarkable was the spread of brokerage outside the country's urban, commercial centers. Newspaper advertisements from such geographically dispersed places as Pittsburgh, Cincinnati, Nashville and Natchez appeared regularly, publicizing the activities and rates charged by local brokers.[35] By 1859 the market found its way into remote towns like Camden, Arkansas which supported McCallum & Graham's brokerage house.[36]

Because the business of bill brokers was accepting commercial paper on consignment, offering it around to potential buyers, and collecting bills forwarded from correspondents in other cities, the explosion in the number of brokers in the post-Second Bank era is not particularly surprising. The business required a minimal initial capital investment since a typical broker purchased very little paper outright. Paper was accepted from commission merchants, wholesale grocers, manufacturers and others and then peddled around to potential buyers. A study of the rediscount market would be fascinating in its own right as buyers formed as varied a group as could be found anywhere. The largest buyers in New York, for example, were out-of-town banks and capitalists with money to lend at short term. The private banking house of Thomas Branch & Company of Petersburg, Virginia, as previously noted, rediscounted notes with three chartered banks, two savings banks and a handful of private capitalists. South-

---

32. *Bicknell's Counterfeit Detector*, various issues, 1836–1837. While it is not entirely clear that all were newly established brokerage houses, no mention of them was found in earlier city directories nor were newspaper advertisements found in earlier issues of this or other newspapers. It seems likely, therefore, that these were new entrants to the business.
33. *Longworth's American Almanac* (1842).
34. *New Orleans Annual* (1842).
35. Broker advertisements can be found in any contemporary commercial newspaper. The ones referred to above appeared in *Daily Picayune* (New Orleans), *Bicknell's* (Philadelphia), and *Journal of Commerce* (New York).
36. Advertisement by McCallum & Graham, *Daily Picayune*, 19 April 1859.

ern cotton and tobacco factors were also large buyers and sellers depending on the season. In the autumn they sold bills drawn on produce shipments.[37] In the spring and summer they purchased bills to keep surplus funds invested during the slow seasons. Most commercial paper was short-term so the funds would be realized and available before the next season's crop shipments again monopolized the factors' funds.

The Second Bank's success in its domestic exchange operations is largely attributed to its branch and agency network and this route to success was not lost on bill brokers and private bankers. Brokers were quick to form correspondent relationships with brokers in other cities so as to facilitate the collection of exchange. The Natchez brokerage of J. P. Waddell, for example, advertised that it maintained correspondent relationships with brokers in Boston, New York, and New Orleans. The St. Louis broker L. A. Benoist listed correspondents in Philadelphia, New York, and Cincinnati; and G. A. Cooke, a Pittsburgh broker, maintained correspondents in Philadelphia, New York, and Baltimore.[38]

Private bankers developed and nurtured more-advanced correspondent relationships than the exchange brokers. S. & M. Allen, for example, originally built their business on the sale of lottery tickets for such varied projects as Harvard College and the Washington Monument, but the Allen's business quickly grew into a full-fledged private bank that "dealt in bank notes from all parts of the country, promissory notes, [and] 'Eastern and Southern bills.'"[39] These sorts of transactions required connections in distant places. S. & M. Allen developed these connections by organizing branch partnerships throughout the country. By 1828 there were partnership or agency offices in Portland (Maine), Providence, Boston, Albany, Pittsburgh, Philadelphia, Baltimore, Washington, D.C., Richmond, Fayetteville (North Carolina), Savannah, Mobile, and New Orleans.

The history of E. W. Clark & Company of Philadelphia followed a similar path. By the early 1840s the Clark house was one of the most renowned names in the domestic exchange market and became one of the nation's largest dealers. In 1839 Clark's firm was brokering

37. Greef, *Commercial Paper House*, pp. 26–35.
38. Correspondent relations taken from business advertisements appearing in *Bicknell's*, various issues, 1836–1837.
39. Larson, *Jay Cooke*, p. 27.

about $1 million in domestic exchange and making a "clear profit of $40,000 or $50,000 a year," in doing so.[40] By the mid-1840s, its business had grown so much that the firm opened partnerships in the principal regional commercial and financial centers such as St. Louis, New Orleans, New York, and Boston, as well as such seemingly out-of-the way places as Springfield, Illinois and Burlington, Iowa.[41]

Although better known for its foreign exchange operations, the merchant banking house of Alexander Brown & Sons of Baltimore was also a major player in the market for domestic bills of exchange, and to expedite its bill operations it opened branch offices or agencies in Philadelphia, New York, New Orleans, and most of the country's other principal ports. When sufficient foreign exchange could not be had to keep the firm's funds employed, the Browns typically turned to short-term domestic exchange.[42] By the 1850s the Brown's domestic bill business ebbed and flowed with seasonal trade patterns. Between May and November, the Brown's northern branches sold foreign exchange to importers and invested the cash in short-term commercial paper. But as the cotton crop began moving to market in the late autumn, the firm liquidated its commercial paper holdings and placed the funds at the disposal of its southern agencies.[43]

Not to be outdone by its cross-town rival, the private banking house of J.I. Cohen, Jr. & Brothers of Baltimore had branches and agencies scattered throughout the eastern United States as the following reproduced advertisement demonstrates.[44]

J. I. Cohen, Jr. & Brothers, having offices in New York, Philadelphia, Baltimore, Richmond, Norfolk and Charleston, and agencies throughout the Eastern and Western States, are enabled to collect drafts &c. on the most favorable terms on the following places –

Portland	Gettysburg	Winchester
Boston	Carlisle	Norfolk
Providence	Harrisburg	Petersburg
Hartford	Lancaster	Newburn

40. Ibid., pp. 41–2.
41. Ibid., pp. 54–5.
42. Perkins, *Financing Anglo-American Trade*, p. 32.
43. Ibid., pp. 108–9, 147.
44. *Philadelphia Price Current*, 28 June 1828.

New Haven	Baltimore	Wilmington
New York	Washington	Fayetteville
Albany	Georgetown	Raleigh
Cincinnati	Alexandria	Charleston
Pittsburgh	Richmond	Savannah
Chambersburg	Lynchburg	Augusta

And Bank bills of the above places and most others of the country, taken at most moderate rates of discount.

J. I. Cohen, Jr. & Brothers
35 South Third Street

Private bankers and brokers were, in addition to bill brokerage, involved in several businesses. Accepting deposits, discounting and buying bills of exchange and promissory notes, and brokering state banknotes were probably the most common, especially among those bankers located in more remote locations. Those located in larger cities also dealt in corporate securities and government debt. Because they were precluded from issuing banknotes, they were forced to finance these activities with private capital or by cultivating a deposit business. J. I. Cohen & Brothers did both. The private bank's Philadelphia agency advertised in April 1839 that it would pay 5 percent interest on ninety-day deposits, 4 percent on thirty-day deposits, and 3 percent on demand deposits if at least $500 was deposited.[45]

Except for a few prominent, probably unrepresentative, cases like those described above, private banking represents one of the great voids in our understanding of antebellum American financial markets. It is known, however, that the industry was important, if not large. In 1853 the *Bankers' Magazine* identified 460 private banks operating from Battle Creek, Michigan to Zanesville, Ohio. Cincinnati alone supported 23; New Orleans, 16; St. Louis, 15.[46] By 1860, the *Merchant's and Banker's Register* listed 920 private banks scattered across the country.[47] Richard Sylla, however, argued that these sources seriously understate the true size of the industry.[48] He estimated, by combining separate sources, that there were about 1,260 private banks in 1860 operating on a total capital of $38.6 million and

45. *Bicknell's*, 2 April 1839.
46. *Bankers' Magazine* 4 (July 1854), pp. 19–23.
47. *Merchant's and Banker's Register for 1860*, pp. 28–41.
48. Sylla, *American Capital Market*, pp. 264–5; Sylla, "Forgotten Men of Money," p. 185.

holding $102.7 million in deposits. Private banks then accounted for nearly one-third of all banks and one-fourth of all capital invested in banking. Certainly, the industry warrants increased attention for, as Jay Cooke pointed out, the 1840s and 1850s were "a grand time for brokerage and private banking."[49]

By Sylla's estimate, the average private banker had invested about $30,500 in the business and held about $81,300 in deposits. While histories of such private banking houses as those of Stephen Girard, E. & W. Clark, and Alexander Brown are interesting and informative, clearly they are not representative of antebellum private banking generally.[50] Most loaned small sums to small traders and, while familiar to local merchants, farmers and manufacturers, they were not commonplace names in New York and London financial circles. Most private bankers loaned and labored in relative obscurity and have passed so into history. That something is known about a half dozen or so exceptional bankers underscores the depth of our ignorance, not our understanding.

While the private banking house of Branch & Sons of Petersburg, Virginia may not be representative of the industry either, its records provide insights into the business of one private banker whose scale and scope was probably more representative of the industry than the houses of Girard or Cooke or Brown.[51] Like many antebellum private bankers, Thomas Branch began as an auctioneer and commission merchant, but as his fortune increased he turned to money lending as an outlet for his surplus capital. On 1 January 1846, Branch & Sons held deposits for 167 clients amounting to about $31,600 and had allowed another 55 clients to overdraw their accounts by $16,800. By this measure, then, Branch & Sons was about half the size of Sylla's estimated average bank.

More to the point, however, Branch & Sons played an important role in importing capital into antebellum Virginia. Table 5.4 shows that in 1848/49, Branch & Sons discounted nearly $74,000 in bills of exchange drawn on correspondents in distant cities, nearly half of which was used to finance the shipment of tobacco and grains to Liv-

49. Jay Cooke, *Memoirs*, quoted in Tooker, *Nathan Trotter*, p. 191.
50. For some representative studies of unrepresentative private bankers, see Adams, *Finance and Enterprise*; Larson, *Jay Cooke*; Tooker, *Nathan Trotter*; and Perkins, *Financing Anglo-American Trade*.
51. This section draws heavily on Bodenhorn, "Private Banking in Antebellum Virginia."

Table 5.4. Drafts on correspondents at the banking house
of Branch & Sons of Petersburg, Virginia

Location of correspondent	Amounts drawn	
	1848/49	1859/60
Boston	$ 0	$18,607
Providence	0	128,194
Other New England	0	11,799
New York City	5,684	217,243
Philadelphia	2,831	84,594
Wilmington, Del.	9,900	90,888
Baltimore	4,590	17,233
Other Mid-Atlantic	0	0
Richmond	3,667	196,422
Lynchburg, Va.	702	80,505
Other South Atlantic	0	26,315
Liverpool	35,363	0
Totals	$73,480	$879,416

Sources: VHS, Branch & Company Records, *Letterbook,
1846-1849; Draft Book, 1859-1862*

erpool. By 1859–60, the firm drew for more than $879,000 and the
locus of Branch's business had changed. He was no longer drawing
bills and hence importing capital from England. Most of the firm's
drafts were drawn on New England and Middle Atlantic cities, with
New York City and Providence being the most prominent correspondent cities. It is also noteworthy that Branch was also drawing

on clients within the South as well. More than $195,000 had been drawn on Richmond; more than $105,000 on other southern cities. Sylla's contention then that private banking was an integral, if often overlooked, component of early American banking appears to be correct. While largely overlooked, these bankers played an important role "in the exchange business on which private bankers often specialized."[52]

Clearly not all private bankers and exchange brokers were as largely involved in the exchange market as Branch & Sons (if Branch & Sons were "average," the total volume of domestic exchange purchased by 1,263 private banks would have been $1.1 *billion* in 1859–60), but their ability to provide local residents with accommodation through bills of exchange was undoubtedly an important factor in the process of financial integration. Correspondent relationships between private bankers and brokers were probably not as effective as the geographically diversified twentieth century commercial paper house in mobilizing funds and arbitraging on regional interest rate differentials, but these relationships allowed for and facilitated capital movements between regions. Country bankers and brokers could loan against balances held by city correspondents; and if these city correspondents allowed country brokers overdraft privileges, rural brokers could increase their discounting operations when conditions warranted by discounting bills payable at the office of their eastern correspondent. These debts were then extinguished when the produce collateralizing the bill was sold and the bill redeemed. These relationships undoubtedly played a significant role in the integration of antebellum financial markets and promoted the equalization of regional interest rates.

COMMERCIAL BANKS AND COMMERCIAL PAPER

State-chartered banks, as well as private bankers and exchange brokers, actively participated in the domestic exchange market. Banks faced two outlets for their loanable funds. Promissory notes and bills of exchange were handed over their counters for discount,

---

52. A more detailed study of Branch's operations can be found in Bodenhorn, "Private Banking." Quote from Sylla, "Forgotten Men of Money," p. 180.

but if these offerings proved insufficient to fully employ their funds they could purchase commercial paper in the open market. As the century wore on, the extent of their commercial paper operations expanded.

In the early nineteenth century, most banks viewed themselves as local, or at most regional, enterprises. The by-laws of the Philadelphia Bank adopted in 1812, for example, stated that "To entitle a note or bill to be discounted at this Bank, the maker or acceptor thereof, must usually reside in the city of Philadelphia."[53] It was a rule of Stephen Girard's, too, that his private bank in Philadelphia would only discount the notes of Philadelphia businessmen, and only those who maintained accounts with his bank.[54] Country banks, however, could rarely adopt such rigid policies. The economic environment was such that produce tended to move toward the coast and, if rural banks were to finance that trade, they were forced to discount bills payable in coast cities. Soon after opening for business, the president of the Westmoreland Bank of Pennsylvania (located in western Pennsylvania, south of Pittsburgh) made an arrangement with a Philadelphia bank to honor drafts drawn upon it by the Westmoreland Bank with the latter paying an exchange charge of one-half of one percent on all such drafts.[55] By the 1840s, the market had evolved and rural banks no longer simply drew on city correspondents. They moved into city markets and bought and sold on their own account. When, in 1844, the Bank of Delaware County found itself accumulating surplus funds, the board directed the bank's president to purchase up to $20,000 of paper with good collateral from Philadelphia firms.[56]

In the 1830s, the market witnessed a dramatic transformation evinced by the Bank of Delaware County's actions. Country banks purchased paper in the open market from bills brokers and city banks, too, purchased such paper as well as rediscounting acceptable paper offered by country banks. In 1836, the Mount Vernon Bank of Foster and the Smithfield Limerock Bank of Smithfield, both in Rhode Island, were reproached for loaning a large portion of their funds in Providence. It was believed by many that these actions proved a great "injustice to the respective towns in which they were

53. Wainwright, *History of the Philadelphia National*, p. 19.
54. Adams, *Finance and Enterprise*.
55. Holdsworth, *Financing an Empire*, p. 297.
56. Ibid., p. 362.

situated."[57] Despite criticism for these activities, the extent of the behavior continued to increase. By the 1840s, Massachusetts' bank commissioners complained bitterly about the practice of many of that state's banks investing in commercial paper originating in New York and peddled by Boston's State Street brokers. The commissioners believed that any paper "travelled for" was a poor credit risk.[58] Moreover, several Massachusetts' banks, in the absence of branches, employed agents who travelled the country discounting good notes. Believing these to be de facto branches, the bank commissioners condemned them as antithetical to both law and morality:

Banking institutions have a locality to which their operations are designed to be confined. It is a perversion of such design if the officers are sent into the money market in other places in pursuit of paper which, under the form of exchange, will give a higher rate of interest than it would be prudent for them to exact of the business community in their own neighborhood; it is an interference with the rights and interests of other banks, and the practice is frequently attended with loss on account of the true character of the paper. The increased facility of communication have a tendency to concentrate business in the metropolis. Managers of banks in the country, established for local convenience, should be at all times aware that to discount paper, receive checks, and exchange their bills through an agency in the city is an infringement upon the foregoing statute.[59]

Despite the commissioners' warnings about the illegality of these practices, they expanded during the decade. The commissioners' 1859 report also included several strictures against the increased tendency of country banks to purchase commercial paper in Boston.[60]

Developments in Connecticut proceeded along the same lines. In 1837 the Exchange Bank of Hartford, for example, purchased $45,000 in commercial paper from New York brokers.[61] The Phoenix Bank of Hartford, on the other hand, went farther south for business. The effects of the panic of 1837 on the prospects of Alabama and Louisiana bankers so troubled the Phoenix's directors that they sent two of their own on a tour of the region to investigate. The bank's net losses from accommodations in the South ultimately amounted to $15,520.[62] Other of the state's banks extended their reach westward. Connecticut's bank commissioners were critical of several

57. Stokes, *Chartered Banking*, p. 40.
58. Miller, *Banking Theories*, pp. 181–2.
59. Massachusetts Bank Commissioners (1852), quoted in Dewey, *State Banking*, pp. 141–2.
60. Massachusetts Bank Commissioners (1859), quoted in Citizen, *Village Bank*, pp. 16–17.
61. Greef, *Commercial Paper House*, pp. 16–17.
62. Burpee, *First Century of the Phoenix National Bank*, p. 54.

banks for making loans and buying exchange in the West, particularly that of Ohio canal and railroad companies. Some Connecticut banks eventually wrote off bad loans made to these enterprises, but the state's bank commissioners were far less critical of the practice, generally, than were Massachusetts' commissioners.[63] So long as the banks purchased double-name paper issued by reputable borrowers and then only after local credit demands had been satisfied, Connecticut's commissioners had few problems with the practice. Most importantly, however, was that the banks' westward movement of available capital integrated markets and, as William Hasse noted, "states like Ohio grew because Connecticut people and Connecticut banks helped financially."[64]

While New England's country banks were stretching out regionally, the region's city banks were taking on a more national character. In June 1836, the Suffolk Bank met southern drafts totaling $140,000, though it remains unclear if this was a regular activity or a typical amount.[65] Until about 1850, for example, the usually conservative Massachusetts Bank remained almost exclusively engaged in local discounting.[66] Financial innovation is nothing new, however, as in 1856 the Mechanics Bank of Philadelphia's discount committee reported that it "felt a mortification that our merchants generally are obliged to resort to New York . . . for the purchase of Foreign . . . [and] Domestic bills" and recommended "that both these lines of legitimate and profitable business be more steadily and extensively pursued than heretofore."[67] The Mechanics Bank followed that advice as did the conservative Massachusetts Bank. By 1857, nearly one-third of the Massachusetts Bank's loans were extended on paper originating outside the city of Boston, principally New York and Philadelphia.

Other Boston banks, however, had adapted to these changes earlier and, by the mid-1850s, were already extensively engaged in the commercial paper and exchange markets. They regularly dealt with banks and brokers from such far-away places as Baltimore, Charleston, Mobile, New Orleans, Cincinnati, and St. Louis.[68] In 1855, for

---

63. Miller, *Banking Theories*, p. 182.
64. Hasse, *History of Money and Banking in Connecticut*, p. 38.
65. Whitney, *Suffolk Bank*, p. 26.
66. Spencer, *First Bank of Boston*, p. 17.
67. Quoted in Holdsworth, *Financing an Empire*, p. 207.
68. Gras, *Massachusetts First National*, p. 126.

example, the State Bank of Boston received $28,000 in exchange income. The Shawmut in excess of $8,500; the New England about $7,500; and the Massachusetts $4,300. Assuming an average exchange charge of 1.5 percent, the State Bank then bought about $1.8 million in southern exchange in 1855; the four banks combined about $3.2 million. Obviously those banks willing to expand their southern exchange business found it to be quite profitable. Moreover, the pursuit of those profits promoted, as Adam Smith's invisible hand simile would lead us to expect, the larger social good. The pursuit of profit helped integrate the several regional financial markets.

As involved as were northeastern urban banks in interregional short-term capital transfers, it was rural western banks that most utilized the exchange and commercial paper markets to take on a more national aspect. In addition to the previously noted activities of several Pennsylvania country banks, a Pittsburgh bank in November 1843 shipped $166,300 in specie by steamboat to New Orleans for deposit in the Bank of Louisiana to be used for the purchase of bills of exchange on New York and Philadelphia the following winter. Apparently, these transactions proved profitable as the following autumn similar specie shipments of gold totalling $118,000 were sent to New Orleans in care of exchange brokers there for the purchase of similar bills.[69]

Southern banks, too, made constant and profitable use of exchange and commercial paper markets. In December 1845 the Northern Bank of Kentucky reported purchasing $115,894 in bills of exchange in the Cincinnati market, most of which were payable in New Orleans, New York and Louisville.[70] It is not clear from whom the exchange was purchased, but it was probably obtained through a broker or agent in Cincinnati.

The extent to which Kentucky's banks availed themselves of the brokers' services and the importance of these operations were summarized by Virgil McKnight, president of the Bank of Kentucky, in response to an interrogatory from a legislative committee.

Some checks [bills of exchange] have been sold in New York and Philadelphia on New Orleans at a discount, and premiums paid in New Orleans for checks. . . . The object of buying and selling exchange, is to facilitate the trade and commerce of the country, and the providing an available fund to redeem our circu-

69. Holdsworth, *Financing an Empire*, pp. 281–2.
70. Kentucky, *Legislative Documents* (1845), p. 710.

lation. . . . The checks bought by the Bank and Branches payable within and without the State, we estimate as nearly equal to one half the amount of Bills of Exchange purchased by the Bank and Branches, and we estimate the Exchange branch of business to be more profitable to the Bank, if prudently conducted, than an equal amount employed in the discount of notes, and to be essential to a bank of circulation.[71]

The purchase of bills other than those offered directly over the bank's counter, then, accounted for about one-half of the bank's purchases of exchange. If that proportion remained relatively stable, it implies that the bank purchased about $1.5 million worth of commercial paper in the open market in 1836 and about $2 million in 1841. By the mid-1850s, the bank regularly held in excess of $4 million in exchange at year end, implying that the bank may have discounted as much as $12 million in exchange during any given year.[72] Other banks in the Old Southwest and Old Northwest were similarly engaged. In 1836 the Planters Bank of Tennessee sold about $1.7 million in eastern exchange.[73] The Shawneetown branch of the Bank of Illinois likewise reported that it had made extensive purchases of bills of exchange most of which were payable in New Orleans "at short dates, and will be collected without renewal or delay."[74]

Evidence from Virginia also suggests that state-chartered banks actively participated in a well-functioning secondary market for negotiable instruments. The Farmers Bank of Virginia, being one of the state's largest banks, was a major buyer and seller of commercial paper. In the fourth quarter of 1843, it bought or sold $326,800 in domestic bills; paying premiums of $2,908 for its purchases and receiving $2,461 in income through its sales. The bank's operations in exchange markets during the fourth quarters of 1844 and 1845 amounted to nearly $247,700 and $248,100. Similarly, the Bank of Virginia in January 1840 reported that its exchange dealings for the previous year (1839 being a panic year so that its purchases probably declined relative to preceding years) exceeded $4.4 million, and discounts and premiums received from these transactions amounted to $75,300 implying that exchange and commission (typically 0.5 percent) charges averaged about 1.7 percent.[75]

71. Kentucky, *Legislative Documents* (1842), p. 380.
72. U.S. House, 25th Congress, 2d Session, *Executive Document No. 79*, p. 758.
73. Ibid., p. 709.
74. Ibid., p. 780.
75. Virginia, *House Documents* (1840–1845).

Exchange dealings were confined to neither the largest banks nor those in large commercial centers. Reports from the Northwestern Bank of Virginia, based in Wheeling (now West Virginia), show that it too had rather extensive dealings in exchange. Between 1840 and 1845 the bank's average semi-annual (six months ending 1 January) profits arising from exchange operations averaged slightly less than $3,500.[76] This value implies, on average and assuming an average 1.5 exchange discount, that the Northwestern Bank purchased about $233,000 in exchange during the second half of the year. Neither the bank's profits nor its exchange dealings are as impressive as those done by the Bank of Virginia, but they were proportionate given its smaller size.[77]

By the 1850s exchange and commercial paper dealings had even invaded the smaller towns of Virginia's interior. The Monticello Bank of Charlottesville in 1853 bought $103,755 in domestic exchange; it sold $99,910, probably to other banks and brokers and local merchants who needed exchange to pay debts to northern and eastern suppliers. The Merchants Bank of Lynchburg, too, in 1854 purchased $130,712 in exchange at discounts ranging from three-quarters of one to one and one-quarter percent. And these exchange operations represent a significant proportion of the bank's business as it held only $372,483 in bills and notes as of January 1855.[78]

Certainly, many more instances could be compiled to yield a more vivid portrait of the range of exchange and commercial paper activities engaged in by antebellum state-chartered banks, but this brief glimpse into their activities demonstrates that exchange dealings constituted a significant share of their business. The antebellum commercial paper market consisted of a complex network of state-chartered banks, exchange brokers, private bankers and speculators. Although the antebellum market was not as sophisticated as the commercial paper market that developed after the Civil War, with its broad-based commercial paper house, antebellum institutions performed the critical function of linking geographically dispersed markets into a unified whole.

76. Ibid.,
77. The Northwestern Bank had only 14 percent of the Bank of Virginia's assets and earned 11 percent as much in exchange operations.
78. Virginia, *House Documents* (1854–1855).

STATE BANKS, CORRESPONDENT RELATIONS, AND CAPITAL FLOWS

Denied the ability to branch across state lines, state-chartered banks were forced to develop ties with banks in other states and cities before they could participate in large-scale domestic exchange and commercial paper operations. Very often, the development of these ties represented one of the first actions undertaken by a new bank. Redlich found that as early as the 1790s, country banks kept deposits with Boston banks which, in turn, maintained deposits with banks in Philadelphia and New York. Sufficient data have survived, wrote Redlich, "to prove that inter-bank deposits and incipient correspondent relations existed . . . as early as the 1800's."[79] As the century wore on banks expanded these ties beyond their immediate region. No longer satisfied to limit their dealings to a compact geographic circle, banks reached out across vast spaces to profit from discounting bills generated in the lucrative southern cotton and tobacco and western grain trades. The simplest way to do this was to contract with a correspondent to assist them. The result of expanding this network was that banks "simplified the process of making payments over long distances" and "increased the interdependence of the banking system."[80]

One of the earliest acts of the Philadelphia Bank after opening in 1804 was to enter into correspondent relationships with the Merchants Bank and the Manhattan Company, both of New York.[81] The Merchants Bank, in turn, came to agreements with the New York State Bank of Albany in 1803 and the Newark Banking and Insurance Company of New Jersey in 1805.[82] Early on, these relationships were designed to facilitate note exchange and redemption agreements, which explains their provincialism as banknotes probably did not stray too far from home. Within a short time, however, banks recognized that these relationships could be exploited in exchange operations. Once they came to this realization, bankers' correspondent agreements provided for the collection of bills of exchange payable in the other bank's city, for the purchase and sale of foreign and

79. Redlich, *Molding*, p. 16.
80. Adams, *Finance and Enterprise*, p. 80.
81. Holdsworth, *Financing an Empire*, p. 161.
82. Hubert, *Merchants National Bank*, pp. 77, 81.

domestic exchange in the other bank's city, and for interest to be paid on surplus balances held with a correspondent.

Possibly following the lead of Stephen Girard's bank that had within a few months of opening in 1812 come to correspondent agreements with banks in New York, Boston, Baltimore, and Charleston, the Philadelphia Bank during the 1820s developed relations with banks in the South and West.[83] It extended large credits to banks in Georgia, Alabama, New Orleans and Cincinnati. The Philadelphia Bank's agreement with the Carrollton Bank of New Orleans may have been typical. In return for the Carrollton acting as the Philadelphia Bank's collection and purchasing agent in New Orleans, the Philadelphia Bank agreed to collect without charge the Carrollton's drafts on New York, Philadelphia, and Baltimore; to receive installments on the Carrollton's stock; to open books for the transfer of the Carrollton's stock in Philadelphia; to redeem the Carrollton's notes; and to open a credit line of $100,000 to be used for the purchase and collection of commercial bills.

When, by the 1830s, northeastern banks had developed an extensive intra-regional complex of correspondent agreements, their attention turned westward and southward, particularly toward New Orleans through which an ever increasing amount of Mississippi and Ohio River valley produce was flowing. When the Carrollton Bank fell into bankruptcy during the financial panic of 1837 and sharply curtailed both its local and distant operations, the Philadelphia Bank scrambled to develop relations with a sound correspondent. Within a few months, the Philadelphia Bank reached an agreement with the Citizens Bank of New Orleans that included the following provisions:[84]

1. The dealings of both Institutions with the city where the other is located shall be strictly confined to operations on joint account.
2. The operations of the Philad[a] Bank shall be limited to the purchase of Bills on & notes of the State of Louisiana and such other of the neighboring states as may [be] hereafter determined; and of the Citizens' Bank shall embrace Foreign as well as domestic Exchange upon places where the Citizens' Bank has

---

83. Adams, *Finance and Enterprise*, pp. 2, 71–3; Wainwright, *History of the Philadelphia National*, pp. 61–2.
84. Tulane University, *Citizens Bank of Louisiana Minute Book*, 2 April 1838 and 4 June 1838.

no similar arrangements – Each Bank guaranteeing to the other its purchases.

3. As it is not probable the purchases in Philad[a] of Exchange on the South can keep pace with purchases in N. Orleans of Foreign & domestic Exchange the Citizens' Bank will by means of checks on Philad[a] keep a proper equilibrium in the advances of the other Bank.

6. The Bank collecting the others [sic] remittances on any other point than the place where it is located shall make no other charges to the joint account than the actual cost of transferring the funds to the point where said Bank is located.

7. The accounts shall be settled twice a year. Vis, on the 1st Jan & 1st July and the profits shall be divided equally.

In June 1838, the Citizens Bank entered into a similar agreement with the Bank of Charleston. It was the Commercial Bank of New Orleans, however, that was probably the southern bank most actively engaged in exchange-based correspondent relationships. The Commercial maintained accounts with seventy-one banks and had an "active correspondence" with forty of those.[85] Though generally viewed favorably as a source of profits, some commentators considered these relationships inherently dangerous. It was believed that New Orleans banks, holding large amounts of domestic exchange remitted by and deposits maintained by distant correspondents, were ever subject to the control of out-of-state banks that may have, at any time, withdrawn their funds.[86] This presented a particular danger during a panic. But when such situations arose, New Orleans banks protected themselves just as banks in other regions did; they simply suspended specie payments until the panic subsided.[87]

While New Orleans established itself as the prominent southwestern banking center in the 1830s, New York emerged as the preeminent northeastern center. Challenging New Orleans' Commercial Bank's extensive network was the Mechanics Bank of New York, which maintained correspondent relationships with fifty-four banks in seventeen states in 1833. The Union Bank, too, had sixteen correspondents in eight states; the Manhattan Company, twenty-six corre-

85. Green, *Finance and Economic Development*, p. 73.
86. Redlich, *Molding*, p. 52.
87. Tulane University, *Citizens Bank of Louisiana Minute Book*, 2 April 1838, 4 June 1838; Green, *Finance and Economic Development*, p. 73; Redlich, *Molding*, p. 52.

spondents in ten states.[88] By 1850, New York had, in fact, become the financial center of the country. Margaret Myers claimed that of the approximately 700 banks operating in the United States nearly 600 had a New York City correspondent.[89]

New York's dominance is unquestioned and is most readily seen in the volume of bankers' balances held there by country correspondents. Table 5.5 presents the dollar value of net bankers' balances held in five Atlantic commercial centers. By 1835 New York City had already demonstrated its comparative advantage in attracting such deposits. In that year, New York City banks held in excess of $4.4 million. Philadelphia banks held about $2.4 million; Boston banks, about $1.0 million; Baltimore and Providence, less than $1.0 million. The real and significant growth in bankers' balances occurred in the 1850s. By 1858, New York City banks held more than $19.2 million; Philadelphia about $2.5 million; Boston, $3.7; while Baltimore and Providence continued to attract less than $1.0 million.

This relatively rapid growth in the volume of bankers' balances held in New York City were not evenly or proportionately distributed between the city's banks as there were nine banks that held disproportionately large amounts of these balances.[90] This disparity probably resulted from the payment of interest on such balances by those nine banks. It is well known that New York bank presidents regularly met to discuss the payment of interest on bankers' balances and that the majority of the banks disapproved of the practice. Many simply refused to pay interest. Adopting a no-interest policy probably limited these banks' ability to attract country bank deposits and develop a network of foreign correspondents, but it is impossible to verify that assumption. But, as Margaret Myers noted, it was the consolidation of interbank deposits within the city rather than its distribution among the city's banks that represented a significant financial development. Interest payments may have determined which banks gathered the largest share of these deposits. "The actual flow of funds to the city was brought about by much more fundamental causes related to the trade of the country."[91]

Natural trade patterns inevitably brought banknotes from all over

88. Redlich, *Molding*, p. 52.
89. Myers, *New York Money Market*, p. 115.
90. Ibid., p. 117.
91. Ibid., p. 120.

Table 5.5. Net bankers' balances held in selected eastern cities, 1835-1859 (in $ millions)

	New York	Philadelphia	Boston	Baltimore	Charleston
1835	$4.40	$2.93	$1.03	$0.33	$0.08
1836	3.55	2.71	0.96	0.51	-0.14
1837	-1.26	0.11	1.83	0.09	0.28
1838	3.55	1.60	--	--	0.22
1839	0.94	0.15	-0.13	0.44	0.19
1840	1.92	3.51	1.55	-0.15	-0.15
1841	1.65	-1.54	--	-0.23	0.05
1842	6.02	0.83	--	-0.06	-0.11
1843	7.51	0.97	--	-0.15	-0.15
1844	6.77	1.32	--	0.62	0.07
1845	4.81	1.91	2.26	--	0.20
1846	4.65	1.98	1.97	0.55	0.29
1847	8.30	2.70	4.81	1.16	0.49
1848	2.80	1.62	--	--	-0.26
1849	9.50	2.14	2.39	1.09	0.34
1850	12.51	2.45	4.17	1.14	0.41
1851	8.99	1.31	--	--	0.34
1852	16.75	3.00	5.53	0.45	0.38
1853	10.17	1.62	4.26	1.31	0.27
1854	20.74	1.42	2.20	0.02	0.20
1855	9.29	1.55	1.95	0.28	0.29
1856	9.30	1.66	1.23	0.00	0.66
1857	8.74	2.95	0.85	1.42	0.52
1858	19.26	2.54	3.37	0.89	0.10
1859	12.29	1.70	3.69	0.00	--

Sources: See Table 4.2.

the country into Atlantic port cities and interbank deposits provided for the redemption of wandering banknotes. As early as 1831, New York's bank commissioners noted this phenomenon. "The city of New-York," they wrote, "being the great exchange for the monitary [sic] as well as mercantile operations of the country, both of which invariably flow in the same channel, it is there that the reservoir is kept upon which most of the banks draw for the redemption of their notes as the exigencies of business require."[92] As notes travelled away from their issuing bank, their value in exchange decreased proportionately with distance (or costs of returning them to their home range) and the increased risk of accepting them, which was also related to distance from their home market as information about banks became scarcer the further away it was. Additionally, counterfeiters tended to counterfeit notes of distant banks as fewer people would be familiar with more-distant notes.

To maintain their notes' integrity and exchange value, country banks entered into redemption agreements with city banks. In return for maintaining a redemption balance with a city correspondent, the city correspondent agreed to redeem the country bank's notes at or close to par. Redemption agreements benefitted all involved parties. City banks benefitted because they could invest some fraction of these balances at short-term and profit from the investment. Country banks benefitted "because it [gave] their notes a more extended circulation; and by the bill holder . . . because it save[d] him the expense of transportation."[93]

Another reason for a country bank holding interbank deposits in an Atlantic commercial center was to profitably employ excess funds. Funds that could not be loaned at a reasonable compensation or at acceptable risk in a home market could be transferred to an urban correspondent to be invested in high-grade commercial paper or in the emerging call-loan market. Bagehot, indeed, found this to be the case in England in the late nineteenth century. He argued that "[f]or the most part, agricultural counties do not employ as much money as they save; manufacturing counties, on the other hand, can employ much more than they save; and therefore the money of Norfolk or Somersetshire is deposited with the London bill-brokers, who use it to discount bills of Lancashire and Yorkshire."[94]

The same thing was happening in the antebellum United States. To employ but one instructive example, the Merchants and Mechanics Bank of Wheeling, Virginia reported holding $214,300 in eastern bankers' balances in 1841. In 1846, it held $227,400; in 1847, $114,100; in 1848, $118,000.[95] The 1841 figure represented more than 15 percent

---

92. New York, *Assembly Document No. 69* (1831), p. 4.
93. Ibid.
94. Bagehot, *Lombard Street*, p. 287.
95. Virginia, *House Documents* (1842, 1847–1849).

of the bank's total assets and it seems unlikely that a bank would have tied up such a large proportion of its funds in an unremunerative or unduly risky employment. Moreover, maintaining a correspondence with urban, particularly New York City, banks opened up otherwise unobtainable investment opportunities. Commercial paper or bills of exchange bearing prominent New York names were more desirable than those bearing names of small local merchants because the former were considered less risky and more marketable. Should a country bank unexpectedly need funds, New York bills were readily salable; bills on a Wheeling house were not. By trading in paper issued by prominent urban merchants, country banks effectively diversified their portfolios.

Richard Sylla argued that a positive aspect of the Civil War-era National Banking Acts was the development of the reserve pyramid.[96] Pyramiding legitimized the holding of city deposits by country banks, facilitated the transfer of funds from rural, agricultural regions to urban, manufacturing centers, and promoted economic growth by directing funds to high-growth industries. It is evident that the concentration of interbank deposits in a few banks in New York City was not an outgrowth of the National Banking Acts.[97] It represented the culmination of a process that had begun long before. "Truly modern bankers' balances," noted Fritz Redlich, "came into existence in the networks of correspondents which some New York banks built up in the second half of the 1820's and in the first half of the 1830's."[98] Additionally, New York's emergence as the locus of correspondent relationships should not blind us to the development and exploitation of these relations elsewhere in the country. Certainly, most country banks maintained relations with New York or New Orleans or both, but country banks also tapped into regional financial centers by fostering relationships with bankers in Pittsburgh, Cincinnati, Louisville, Richmond, St. Louis, Savannah, and other, lesser, commercial cities. The development of financial ties and, hence, financial integration was a sweeping, pervasive process involving the majority of the country's banks.

96. Sylla, *American Capital Market*, p. 209.
97. Myers, *New York Money Market*, p. 118.
98. Redlich, *Molding*, p. 51.

INTEGRATION AND THE LAW: LEGAL
DEVELOPMENTS IN THE ANTEBELLUM ERA

The nearly concurrent development between the mid-1820s and early-1830s of extended networks and markets in commercial paper and bills of exchange, of interbank balances and broad-based private banking still requires explanation. As noted above, financial historians have attributed this confluence to Nicholas Biddle's entrepreneurial spirit and his effective use of the Second Bank's national branch network in pursuing his design. A close study of the record, however, fails to provide clear and persuasive evidence of that interpretation; nearly coincident timing of two events does not, of course, imply causation. In fact, banks and brokers had constructed correspondent networks and engaged in limited exchange and commercial paper transactions before Biddle's full-scale entry into the market. True, the market expanded and matured during and after the Second Bank's tenure, but legal developments beyond the Second Bank's control were central to many of these developments.

Histories of early American commercial law emphasized its unsettled nature and state-to-state variations; variations that certainly limited the volume of interstate trade. Lawrence Friedman, for example, argued that any study of the relationship between the law and the economy of the early antebellum era required "close study of local law."[99] Such wide state-to-state variations were particularly detrimental to the sale, purchase and collection of bills of exchange. "Rivalry among state legislatures and the unsettled conditions of local law," wrote Tony Freyer, "contributed to uncertainty in the commercial law of the states, which generated challenges to the transferability of negotiable instruments around the country."[100]

Uncertainties surrounding the legal standing of creditors created disincentives to invest in bills of exchange payable in distant regions. Furthermore, in many states local justices chosen by popular election tended to favor residents when hearing cases pitting resident debtors against nonresident creditors.[101] But the Constitution and the Judi-

---

99. Friedman, *History of American Law*, p. 157.
100. Freyer, "Negotiable Instruments," p. 436.
101. Ibid., pp. 446, 448.

ciary Act of 1789 had created an institution – the federal judiciary – capable of knitting together these local courts and generating a consistent body of commercial law. Being relatively independent of local influences, federal courts were able to aid interstate trade through the development of a commercial law more concerned with its ramifications for economic efficiency than with protecting the interests of local residents.[102] A series of decisions issued by the United States Supreme Court between the 1820s and 1840s, in fact, laid the basis for more-integrated financial markets by more clearly delimiting the rights and obligations of creditors and debtors engaged in interstate trade.

The first issue requiring resolution was that of the negotiability of financial instruments, especially promissory notes and bills of exchange. By the outbreak of the American Revolution each colony had developed its own version of English common law. Some colonies had incorporated elements of the English "merchant courts" into the rubric of their common law, others had not. Neither independence nor adoption of the Constitution brought order out of this chaos. Through "reception" statutes the newly independent states recognized various parts of English common law as the basis of local jurisprudence. Few of these laws were dutifully copied and implemented. Most were subject to local customs and idiosyncracies and a multitude of alterations were included to meet the demands of state legislatures. The effect of this diversity in the law of commercial transactions was a great deal of uncertainty among holders of promissory notes and bills of exchange about their exact legal standing.[103]

Establishing a consistent rule of negotiability, a necessary prerequisite to the development of extensive interstate markets in bills and notes, required that courts resolve the issue of "privity" in the exchange of financial instruments as the "common law requirement of privity presented an insurmountable conceptual barrier to negotiability."[104] In other words, how could Adams, who had given a promissory note to Belcher, be sued by Connors, to whom Belcher had transferred the note, when no consideration or explicit agree-

---

102. The so-called "Law and Economics School" has developed a large literature contending that the evolution of common law results from concerns with economic efficiency as much as from legal equity. See, for example, Posner, *Economic Analysis of Law*; and Cooter and Ulen, *Law and Economics*.
103. Freyer, "Negotiable Instruments," p. 444.
104. Horwitz, *Transformation*, p. 213.

ment had passed between Adams and Connors. Because no consideration had passed between them and no agreement reached, reasoned some lawyers, no contract existed between the two parties. At common law, therefore, Connors had no legal recourse to Adams. In other cases, the reasoning became even more convoluted. If Connors, for example, had subsequently endorsed the note over to Duncan, could Duncan sue Belcher as a prior endorser if Adams defaulted?

Even before this fundamental question could be definitively answered, a subsidiary question needed resolution. Could Duncan, a subsequent endorsee, hold a better title than Belcher? If Belcher sued after Adams had defaulted on a promissory note, Adams could offer various defenses to excuse himself of the obligation to pay. Adams could, for example, have argued that there had been a lack of consideration on Belcher's part, or fraud, or usury, or any of a host of other valid defenses. But subsequent endorsees, such as Connors or Duncan, would necessarily be ignorant of any mistakes or frauds involved in the original contract and unable to offer a defense. If promissory notes were to circulate freely, innocent subsequent endorsees needed assurance that the obligation would be met regardless of any defects in the original bargain between Adams and Belcher. Questions of privity such as these could be and were, in some instances, overcome by statutory law allowing for assignment. Absent statutory enactments, consistent judicial rulings were considerably less certain.

Of course, in cases involving bills of exchange most of these questions had been resolved in British law by the eighteenth century, if not earlier. In the United States, however, the law was not nearly as settled on this point, especially for promissory notes. After independence, banks arose ready to extend credit on negotiable financial instruments, but the lack of legal standing, particularly for promissory notes, limited the ability of banks to transfer or assign these notes so that a secondary market in promissory notes never developed. Eventually, courts in every state were forced to come to grips with the issue as banking and trade expanded. By 1800 only five states recognized a full negotiability standard, but three important commercial states – Massachusetts, Pennsylvania, and Virginia – refused to adopt this standard.[105]

---

105. Ibid., pp. 214–15.

In this instance, the federal courts were of little help in unifying differing state doctrines. The first important case addressing the rights of remote endorsees came before the United States Supreme Court in 1803.[106] Two later endorsees, having failed to get satisfaction from the notes' maker, sued a prior endorser. Because Virginia law did not recognize a full negotiability doctrine, they lost. Unsatisfied with the decision of the state court, the endorsees sued in a federal court in the District of Columbia. This court, in a divided decision, held that if a maker of a note failed to pay, endorsees could recover from prior endorsers, a result contrary to both existing Virginia statute and common law precedent. This case quickly found its way to the United States Supreme Court, which overturned the lower court's decision. Chief Justice Marshall, a principal actor in the establishment of Virginia's anti-negotiability common law doctrine, argued that, without an express Virginia statute recognizing negotiability, subsequent endorsees had no claim against prior endorsers. More importantly, however, Marshall laid out a rule that federal courts should apply the specific law of the state.[107] It was not within the purview of the Court, in Marshall's philosophy, to establish a general, nationally uniform commercial law. States' rights were primary and were not to be trod on for the sake of economic interests.

Marshall's states' rights philosophy undoubtedly influenced his decision. Its ramifications, however, extended beyond states' rights as it limited opportunities available to those interested in engaging in interstate transactions as differential treatment often placed nonresident creditors at a decided disadvantage when a note went into default. In 1810, one contemporary legal analyst commented on the lack of a consistent, interstate negotiability doctrine, an inconsistency that remained for decades.[108] Even as late as 1845, United States Supreme Court Justice Story wrote in his *Commentaries on the Law of Promissory Notes* that the question of the negotiability of promissory notes remained "clogged with positive restrictions, or practical difficulties, which greatly impede[d] their use and value, and circulation."[109]

---

106. For details of the case, see *Riddle v. Mandeville* 1 Cranch 95 (1802); and *Mandeville v. Riddle* 3 Cranch 290 (1803).
107. Horwitz, *Transformation*, pp. 220–1.
108. Ibid., p. 215.
109. Quoted in ibid, p. 225.

While the law of promissory notes remained inconsistent across states, the law of bills of exchange, following the British tradition, was somewhat more settled. In the discussion of usury laws and their evasion in Chapter 4, it was argued that banks preferred to discount bills of exchange to promissory notes because the former allowed for exchange charges above and beyond usury limits. While the possibility of earning usurious rates was undoubtedly one source of the banks' preference, the unsettled question of the negotiability of promissory notes was another. With no consistent law of negotiability and, consequently no significant secondary market in promissory notes, banks may have preferred bills because of their better legal standing when assigning them. Should a bank face liquidity problems, its possibilities were limited if it held a portfolio consisting primarily of promissory notes. With an adequate supply of good bills of exchange, on the other hand, liquidity could be restored quickly and easily by rediscounting them with another bank or selling them in the secondary market. Not only did charter restrictions, general banking laws, and other statutes press upon the lending opportunities and portfolio choices of antebellum banks, the generally unsettled state of the common law of commercial instruments did as well.

Even in the law of bills of exchange, it was not until the 1820s and 1830s that federal courts developed a particularly rigorous and consistent body of legal decisions laying out the rights and obligations of makers, acceptors and endorsers. During the 1820s, expansion in the volume of interregional trade, noted at the beginning of this chapter, brought ever more cases before the federal judiciary as United States Supreme Court decisions in 1816 and 1821 had made it easier for litigants to move cases from state to federal courts.[110] Moreover, in a series of cases decided in the mid- and late 1820s, the high court established more-uniform principles concerning the law of bills of exchange so that by 1833, Justice Story wrote that the import of the Supreme Court had been to "increase confidence . . . between the commercial and agricultural states."[111]

110. See *Martin v Hunter's Lessee* 1 Wheaton 304 (1816); and *Cohens v. Virginia* 6 Wheaton 264 (1821) for cases allowing for easier removal to federal courts.
111. Among the more important cases involving bills of exchange and interstate collection are *Coolidge v. Payson* 2 Wheaton 75 (1817); *Wayman v. Southard* 10 Wheaton 46 (1825); *United States Bank v. Smith* 11 Wheaton 547 (1826); *Townsley v. Sumrall* 2 Peters 68 (1829); and *Bank of the United States v. Weisiger* 2 Peters 129 (1829). Justice Story quoted in Freyer, "Negotiable Instruments," p. 436.

Two of the most important cases involving the rights of nonresident creditors on bills of exchange were handed down in 1839 and 1842. *Bank of Augusta v. Earle*, decided in 1839, established an important precedent concerning bills of exchange that affected not only banks, but corporations throughout the United States.[112] Joseph Earle, a Mobile, Alabama businessman, whose business was apparently suffering from the ravages of the panic of 1837 fixed upon an ingenious "solution to his cash flow problems."[113] Owing on two bills of exchange drawn on Mobile, one of which had been purchased by an agent for the Bank of Augusta (Georgia), the other by a banking subsidiary of the New Orleans and Carrollton Railroad Company (the Carrollton Bank), Earle refused to pay at maturity. His defense was that neither bank had been chartered under Alabama law and was therefore operating illegally when their agents purchased bills payable in Mobile. Alabama's Supreme Court found for Earle, as did the federal Circuit Court in Alabama. Both courts found that the foreign banks had violated Alabama's constitutional prohibition of any bank operating within the state except those specifically chartered by Alabama's legislature.

As the financial panic deepened, other creditors, emboldened by the courts' decisions in the Earle case, began testing the waters. One was William Primrose who owed on a bill due at the Mobile branch of the Bank of the United States. Primrose refused to meet it on grounds that the Bank of the United States had also violated Alabama's constitutional prohibition. Attorneys for the Bank of the United States sued and the case reached the Supreme Court along with appeals from both the Bank of Augusta and the New Orleans and Carrollton Railroad.

The Court considered all three cases together and the case attracted some of the country's most renowned and talented lawyers. D. B. Ogden represented the Bank of Augusta and the New Orleans and Carrollton Railroad; Daniel Webster, the Bank of the United States; Charles Jared Ingersoll represented Earle; and a Mr. Crawford filed a brief on behalf of Primrose.[114] Arguing for the state banks,

---

112. *Bank of Augusta v. Earle* 13 Peters 522–3.
113. Schweikart, *Banking*, p. 145.
114. David Bayard Ogden was a noted attorney who argued several cases before the U.S. Supreme Court. The Mr. Crawford listed in the brief is not further identified, but it may have been George Walker Crawford (1798–1872), who was governor of Georgia (1843–1847), Attorney General of Georgia (1827–1831) and U.S. Congressman (1843). See Johnson, *Dictionary of American Biography*, III, pp. 520–3; XIII, pp. 638–9.

Ogden asserted that, if the lower court's decision was allowed to stand, a deep wound would be "inflicted on the commercial business of the United States" for the Circuit Court's decision would "prevail to the full extent of inhibiting the same purchases in other States, and thus exclude the principal operations of commerce between the States of the Union."[115]

While laying out the case in terms of its implications for interstate trade, Ogden's legal argument surrounded the doctrine of "comity" – one sovereignty recognizing another's laws.[116] The Circuit Court had held that comity did not apply to corporations and that they were restricted to operating within the jurisdiction that had chartered them. But Ogden argued that Alabama's constitutional prohibition had not explicitly denied comity and, since comity was assumed unless specifically denied, the Circuit Court's decision had been faulty. Alabama, as well as most other states, had recognized comity with foreign governments and should it not, therefore, be reasonable that they should do the same with the governments of adjoining states. Webster, too, presented the comity argument and then expanded upon it.[117] Representing the Bank of the United States, Webster asked for a liberal interpretation of corporations – that being composed of citizens, they retained all the rights and responsibilities of citizens. It was not illegal under Alabama's constitution, argued Webster, for foreign citizens to purchase bills of exchange drawn on Alabama so it should not be illegal for a group of individuals, under corporate auspices, to do likewise. Ingersoll represented Earle and supported a restrictive interpretation of corporate powers.[118] Being constructions of local legislatures, he argued, corporations carried no contractual powers outside the jurisdiction of their creators.

Chief Justice Roger B. Taney delivered the Court's opinion and skillfully sidestepped the liberal versus restrictive theory of corporations. To Taney the case turned upon Ogden's comity argument. "The intimate union of these States," wrote Taney, "as members of the same great political family; the deep and vital interests which bind them so closely together, should lead us, in the absence of proof to the contrary, to presume a greater degree of comity, and friendship, and kindness towards one another, than we should be authorized to presume

115. *Bank of Augusta v. Earle* 13 Peters 523.
116. Ibid., 590–1.
117. Ibid., 549–67.
118. Ibid., 568–84.

between foreign nations."[119] But Taney was unwilling to put forward a completely "liberal" view of corporations. It was only because Alabama had not explicitly denied comity that the Court overturned the prior decision. States could, if they chose to do so, positively deny it. Taney noted, for example, that New York and Pennsylvania had enacted specific statutes prohibiting out-of-state corporations from contracting for fire insurance within their states. The Court would accept these sorts of specific limitations. Because Alabama had enacted no such law concerning the discounting of bills of exchange, the Court could only assume that Alabama implicitly recognized the right of foreigners, whether individuals or corporations, to purchase or collect bills of exchange within its boundaries.

Without referring specifically to *Earle*, Bray Hammond argued that Taney's judicial record demonstrated his willingness to give state-chartered corporations freer reign than they had formerly enjoyed. In rejecting a completely "liberal" interpretation of corporate powers – he left open the door to explicitly deny comity – Taney had made his decision "compatible with agrarian doctrine [but] its real affinity was with laisser-faire."[120] It was a monument to Taney's success in walking this line, wrote Larry Schweikart, that he satisfied both sides with a pseudo-liberal interpretation that resulted in the "absence of any significant southern protest" over the decision.[121] Taney's decision should have "rattled the rafters" in Alabama, yet it was accepted rather calmly. But Alabama's rather complacent acceptance of the decision should not have been particularly surprising. Even the most rabid states' righters surely recognized the importance of a well-functioning, interstate market for bills of exchange. Without such a market supporting the state's principal industry, king cotton would have been reduced to viscount status as foreign credit was indispensable in bringing the crop to market.

Where the *Earle* decision guaranteed as expansive an exchange market as contemporary institutions would allow, the Court's 1842 decision in *Swift v. Tyson* ensured consistent and predictable interstate practice.[122] For the market in exchange to operate efficiently it

119. Ibid., 590–1.
120. Hammond, *Banks and Politics*, p. 337. Hammond preferred to illustrate Taney's pro-corporate attitude through Taney's opinion delivered in *Charles River Bridge v. Warren Bridge* 11 Peters 419.
121. Schweikart, *Banking*, p. 147.
122. *Swift v. Tyson* 16 Peters 1.

was not enough that banks and brokers everywhere could purchase exchange anywhere and be assured of payment. It required as well a set of consistent, or at least predictable, rules of collection. *Swift* finally and definitively guaranteed the rights of later endorsees as promissory notes and bills of exchange repeatedly changed hands.

On its face *Swift v. Tyson* appeared to be a typical, rather innocuous commercial dispute. Tyson, a New York City merchant, had accepted a bill of exchange made by Keith and Norton of Maine based upon the sale of several parcels of land, which Keith and Norton claimed to be in their possession. In fact, Keith and Norton did not have title to the land, so they had neither the right to sell it nor the right to use it as collateral for a bill of exchange. Tyson subsequently endorsed the bill and handed it to Swift in exchange for a preexisting debt. Keith and Norton failed to meet the bill at maturity and Swift sued Tyson for payment.

Tyson's defense was twofold. On one hand, argued Tyson's attorney, the bill had been originally based upon a fraudulent transaction. Since New York law did not consider an agreement based upon a fraud at its inception a valid contract, the bill was void and Swift had no recourse to Tyson. It was Swift's responsibility to know the origin of the transaction. On the other hand, the bill had been endorsed and handed over to meet a preexisting debt – Swift had returned a protested bill on Tyson in return for the bill made by Keith and Norton. New York's common law precedents were equivocal on this point. The state's Court of Errors, then New York's highest court, had handed down some decisions stating that such an agreement lacked consideration, making the contract void. In other cases, the Court of Errors had held that a pre-existing debt did, in fact, represent consideration because an existing debt represented a legitimate claim on resources and hence made it a valuable consideration.[123]

Swift's attorney countered Tyson's defense on two points. He argued that Swift did not know of the fraudulent basis of the bills, nor could he have or should he have been expected to have known. It was a long-standing tradition in the laws of bills of exchange, dating back to England's merchant courts, that subsequent endorsees who accepted a bill in good faith were protected from previous frauds or mistakes and thus had recourse to prior endorsers when a maker

123. Ibid., 9–14.

failed to meet the obligation. Secondly, argued Swift's attorney, it was imperative for commercial stability that the ambiguities in New York's case law be cleared up. Even more important to future commercial stability was a United States Supreme Court decision applicable to all cases in all states. Swift's attorney put the argument most forcefully when he argued that:

> Congress, and Congress alone, has the power to regulate commerce between the States. But it will be impossible for Congress to regulate commerce between the States, if it be left to State courts to declare authoritatively in the absence of any statute upon the point, the force, and meaning of, and the rights of parties under that most important instrument of such commerce – the bill of exchange, when drawn and held in and by a citizen of one State, and accepted and payable in and by a citizen of another State.[124]

To Justice Story, who rendered the Court's decision, the facts were simple and the law straight-forward. Agreeing with Swift's attorney, Story wrote:

> There is no doubt that a bona fide holder of a negotiable instrument for which a valuable consideration, without any notice of the facts, which impeach its validity . . . holds the title unaffected by these facts, and may recover thereon. . . . This is a doctrine so long and so well established, and so essential to the security of negotiable paper, that it is laid up among the fundamentals of the law.[125]

On this matter, the Court had held definitively before and Story simply followed precedents already laid down.[126]

But Justice Story refused to stop there. He wished to establish the federal judiciary as the final arbiter of commercial law and used this case to establish its primacy. In that sense, the Court's *Swift* decision represented a watershed in the role of the federal judiciary in commercial matters. The 34th Section of the Judiciary Act of 1789 required the Supreme Court to recognize and follow local *law* when considering cases dealing with local issues. For decades prior to *Swift*, the Court had interpreted this clause to mean both statutory enactments and common law decisions. Justice Story, however, rejected this construction of the 1789 Judiciary Act. He explicitly rejected the notion that the decisions of local courts constituted law. "They are,"

---

124. Ibid., 9.
125. Ibid., 15.
126. See *Coolidge v. Payson* 2 Wheaton 75 (1817); and *Townsley v. Sumrall* 2 Peters 68 (1829) for the relevant precedents.

he wrote, "at most, only evidence of what laws are, and are not of themselves laws. They are often re-examined, reversed, and qualified by the courts themselves, whenever they are found to be either defective, or ill-founded, or otherwise incorrect."[127] As such the Court was not bound by the holdings of "local tribunals." The Court was only compelled by the 1789 Act to follow the dictates of local legislatures. Since New York's legislature had nothing to say on the issue at hand, the Court was free to follow its own judgement. Given a lack of explicit statutory law, the Court generally, and Story in particular, was bound to follow the general principles and doctrines of commercial law. The law of bills of exchange and promissory notes, believed Story, was simply too important for the national welfare to be left in the hands of local courts. "The law respecting negotiable instruments," he said, "may be truly declared . . . to be in a great measure not the law of a single country only, but of the commercial world."[128]

Legal scholars, such as Freyer and Horwitz, have argued that the *Swift* rule represented the culmination of efforts by the federal judiciary to establish a uniform and consistent body of law governing the negotiability of financial instruments in particular, and to assert its primacy in commercial law in general.[129] The *Swift* decision was the first case in which the Supreme Court "clearly and bluntly" asserted its power in deciding which sets of laws would govern interstate transactions – and its decision was that the Court would follow the traditions of general commercial practice rather than the idiosyncracies of local law. In establishing this policy, the Court made it clear that the federal judiciary was charged with the responsibility of protecting the rights of nonresident creditors and debtors from the prejudices of local courts. Some forty years in the making – taking Marshall's 1803 decision in *Mandeville v. Riddle* as the starting point – Story's 1842 decision in *Swift* finally "provided businessmen with predictability and uniformity in cases involving the interests of nonresidents."[130] As such, it certainly improved the functioning of the antebellum exchange market and further promoted an integrated, national market for short-term capital.

127. *Swift v. Tyson* 16 Peters 18.
128. Ibid., 19.
129. Horwitz, *Transformation*, p. 245; Freyer, "Negotiable Instruments."
130. Freyer, "Negotiable Instruments," p. 245.

CONCLUDING REMARKS

Ultimately it would be difficult, if not impossible, to completely unravel the web of events and institutional changes occurring in the first half of the nineteenth century which brought about the integration of short-term American capital markets. This chapter, however, has laid out a plausible chain of events. With the development of new transportation technologies like the canal, the steamboat and the railroad, trade, especially interregional trade, expanded rapidly in the period after 1820. Southern planters produced and shipped increasing volumes of cotton to northern and European ports. Western farmers, too, produced and shipped ever larger volumes of grains, pork and other primary products to distant cities via the Mississippi River and the Erie Canal. Consequent upon the growing volume of interregional trade came a need for methods of financing it. Though in the midst of a so-called transportation revolution, shipment and storage remained a relatively expensive proposition. The bill of exchange, actually dating far back into antiquity, quickly presented itself as a viable method of financing produce shipments. Drawn to finance the shipment of goods, bills of exchange used the commodity itself as collateral. In this way, the farmer, factor or broker was not forced to provide the up-front costs. By tendering a bill, the shipper financed the movement of goods with few out-of-pocket expenses, receiving instead the proceeds net of shipping costs at the time of sale.

As important as the widespread adoption of the inland or domestic bill of exchange was for producers, it was at least equally important for financial intermediaries. Bills of exchange, guaranteed as they were by an attached bill of lading, reduced the risks of lending as they offered an attractive alternative to promissory notes guaranteed by collateral (like land, structures or produce) with only provincial appeal and a necessarily limited market. Before the bill of exchange could be a widely used financial instrument, it was necessary that methods of repatriating funds be developed. Bills were drawn and payable in distant locations – wherever the produce was destined. Having funds in New Orleans or New York meant little to a Tennessee cotton planter or an Ohio wheat farmer or their factors if those funds could not be realized at home. The institutional or organizational response was the development of a complex network of state banks, private banks, exchange brokers, produce factors – even the preeminent Second Bank of the United States – and others who developed correspondent relationships allowing for the reasonably efficient movement of funds. In a complex structure even Adam Smith would have admired, all this private self-interest resulted in a clear social benefit, which was, of course, that short-term capital was mobilized and allocated to those regions of the country where they were most in demand.

Explanations of the post-Civil War convergence of regional interest rates have been as varied as the number of scholars investigating the issue, but organizational change and legal developments have taken center stage. This chapter offered an explanation of pre-Civil War integration based on similar factors. Organizational developments included a progression from state banks and specialized exchange brokers operating within limited orbits which were overshadowed, if not supplanted, in the mid-1820s by the entry of the Second Bank into the domestic exchange market. While the Second Bank's operations were certainly coincident with a sweeping extension the market, it remains unclear whether the Bank's activities expanded the market or whether Biddle and his Bank profitably exploited a fundamental shift in the technology of regional trade. With the demise of the Second Bank in 1836, state banks, private banks and exchange brokers entered on a large scale and served those sectors previously reliant upon the Second Bank for their far-flung financial transactions. The continued ability of the markets to maintain a near equality of regional interest rates in the post-Second Bank era suggests that these organizations provided the necessary financial services. By developing intricate networks of correspondents, banks and their agencies and branches efficiently mobilized and transferred short-term capital throughout the country or, at least, that part of the country east of the Mississippi River.

Before banks and brokers could exploit these developments, however, they required a consistent and predictable institutional complex. Legal developments in the score of years between 1820 and 1840 provided it. During that period, federal courts provided an impetus to interregional trade and financial operations by reversing some early federal decisions and in preempting local courts and by clearly establishing the rights and obligations of creditors and debtors connected only indirectly through their purchase and sale of various financial instruments. This is not to argue that without a federal judiciary, that was growing increasingly pro-business, that the web of banks and brokers would not have developed nor the markets integrated. But it is unlikely that these events would have occurred as readily as they did in the absence of a set of uniform and predictable rules.

6   Conclusion: How Banks Mattered

In 1857 Amasa Walker published his history of a fictional New England bank in which he satirized the then conventional wisdom concerning banks. Depicting the small-town American as an individual unschooled in the complexities of financial markets and too ready to accept the fantastic, Walker wrote that he was "told what a fine thing it [would] be to have a bank in the town; how it [would] furnish capital for the merchants, manufacturers and farmers; how it [would] 'build up the village,' make real estate advance in value, and add to the importance and respectability of the place; besides which he [would] get *eight per cent.* dividends."[1] And credulous as he was, he believed it. To Walker, however, the fallacy of the argument was apparent and the gullibility of the public beyond belief. Establishing a bank could not, in and of itself, bring prosperity to the countryside. The reality would never approach the promise.

The central conclusion of this monograph is that the very premise Walker ridiculed was largely correct. Banks and other financial intermediaries could and did matter in the process of economic growth and development. Intermediaries formed an important link because they expanded the borrowers' financial capacity. By overcoming impediments to the flow of funds between savers and investors, intermediaries made it possible for borrowers to obtain more credit and on better terms than they could have had they been forced to negotiate with ultimate savers. In this regard, financial intermediaries

---

1. Walker, *History of the Wickaboag Bank*, p. 54.

213

provided a "vital service" to the economy and allowed it to expand at a pace unattainable in their absence.[2]

The ways in which financial intermediaries pushed the economy toward a realization of its potential were varied. Most important perhaps was their influence on the nature of capital. In many developing economies (nineteenth-century America included), wealth was commonly held in the form of inventories of foodstuffs and other primary products, livestock, and land or land improvements. The share of producer durables was relatively low, while that of consumer durables remained high. Reasons for this were varied but they may have included a societal value that equated prestige with land holdings or it may have been indicative of risk avoidance as large proportions of the populace were unfamiliar with alternative, notably financial, assets. More important, perhaps, was that in financially underdeveloped countries inventories of foodstuffs and livestock represented the only assets which were reasonably liquid and divisible and offered some protection against the vagaries of price and output fluctuations. But this response to risk was costly to both the individual and society as storage and spoilage costs were high and hoarding inhibited resources from moving to more productive employments.

The important element in the early evolution of financial markets, then, was not that they encouraged households and other economic units to exchange one type of financial instrument for another. Rather, their importance lay in that they encouraged households to exchange real productive assets that others could employ more efficiently for financial assets representing claims to those assets. In the earliest phases of development such changes in the composition of wealth were critical. With an increasing share of household wealth taking the form of financial instruments, investors and entrepreneurs could hold more, and more-productive combinations of, real assets.

In the earliest phases of American development this change was wrought by the simplest of financial instruments – the banknote. The appearance of the banknote on (even within) the frontier allowed households to hold money instead of perishable but productive assets. Monetization of an economy coaxed productive resources from hoards, facilitated trade, and hastened development. In modern times and developed nations, a monetized economy is taken as a

2. Gertler, "Financial Structure," p. 564.

datum. It was not always so, and the fundamental changes wrought by the introduction of bank-supplied currencies are belittled only at great risk to our understanding of the sweeping changes that took place in the earliest stages of development. The fundamental change wrought by monetization was clearly indicated by the reaction of Kentuckians upon the receipt of their first banknotes. When banknotes were obtained:

> They were handled with care and admired for the fine pictures upon them. If an old farmer got hold of one of them he showed it to his wife and children and enjoyed their wonder and admiration. It was laid away between the leaves of the family Bible, and kept smooth and nice until a pressure, not to be borne, extorted it for debt, or it went for something that had to be bought.[3]

Banknotes, therefore, performed their role as both a medium of exchange and a store of wealth. And the use of the banknote in both roles represented a development critical to economic change. In the absence of banknotes, currency on the American frontier (sometimes even well within it) consisted of a rag-tag mixture of foreign and domestic coins, land warrants, tobacco warehouse receipts, even animal pelts, which increased the costs of transacting over what they were with the use of banknotes. Secondly, accepting a banknote and slipping it between the pages of the family Bible implied the potential that resources were being moved to more-productive uses.

Money in the form of the banknote was far from neutral in a developing economy. Its introduction and use represented a fundamental institutional change and reinforced an emerging commercial ethos. Banknotes inculcated a habit and a willingness to exchange paper claims for real assets. While many have argued that savers in the nineteenth century gradually, sometimes grudgingly, became ever more willing to accept scraps of paper in exchange for real assets, the focus has been on equities, bonds, commercial paper and other, relatively sophisticated scraps of paper. Richard Sylla and his colleagues claimed that the period 1790 to 1815 represented a financial watershed because eastern investors rapidly increased their equity holdings.[4] This certainly represented an elemental shift, but it should not be forgotten that the same period was one of the most fecund periods in the growth of banking institutions, which occurred only because

---

3. Duke, *History of the Bank of Kentucky*, p. 9.
4. Sylla, Wilson and Jones, "U.S. Financial Markets"; Sylla, Wilson, and Wright, "America's First Securities Markets."

Americans were becoming increasingly willing to accept and hold banknotes instead of inventories of productive assets.

This is not to say that financial development alone was the wellspring of economic development. Development was too complex a process, one too easily derailed by any number of factors, to have been driven by a single sector. Nevertheless, neglecting the essential role of financial intermediaries may represent a greater error of omission than exaggerating their importance represents one of commission. The financial sector, as Edward Shaw noted, was "unique in the degree to which its markets, prices, institutions, and policies impinge[d] upon all others."[5] Money was the only good that regularly traded against all others. And interest rates were the relative prices that had the most pervasive relevance to all intertemporal economic decisions; and ultimately, all economic decisions are intertemporal.

Despite much bitter controversy among contemporaries about the appropriate scale and scope of the banking system, forces supporting the continued development of the sector generally carried the day. And the American financial sector grew increasingly complex and interconnected in the antebellum era. In Chapter 2 we saw why contemporary supporters of banking fought so diligently for its establishment and expansion and then encouraged its activities by granting banks favors (like corporate status) often unavailable to other types of enterprises. While the evidence about the concurrent growth of the financial and real sector remains ambiguous, the evidence clearly supports the contention that the presence of banks was a critical precondition for subsequent economic growth. Over the long run, a one percent increase in the initial value of loans per dollar of state-level gross domestic product increased the subsequent rate of growth by about one percent. In the short run, the influence of banks was even greater. But statistical relationships, as instructive and informative as they can be, often obscure as much as they illuminate. Although the process of growth and development across time and place has many common characteristics, they are not, as Simon Kuznets wrote, so invariant as to amount to nothing "more than a mere statistical generalization or mechanical coincidence."[6]

It is the underlying explanation that matters as it ultimately shapes

---

5. Shaw, *Financial Deepening*, p. 3.
6. Kuznets, *Six Lectures*, pp. 109–10.

our perceptions and focuses our thinking. The explanation offered here was that banks and other financial intermediaries represented a necessary precondition for economic growth. For early America, I offered a modification of the so-called "supply-leading" hypothesis. Under this view, banks designed to meet the needs of a traditional merchant class were established and initially catered almost exclusively to the mercantile sector. But as the economy matured and artisanal shops gradually transformed themselves into proto-industrial enterprises, banks designed to meet the needs of other groups similarly transformed themselves to meet the needs of incipient manufacturers. Despite the provocative nature of the hypotheses offered by Joseph Schumpeter and Alexander Gerschenkron, support for the supply-leading hypothesis has been lacking, largely because most growth theorists and other economists tend to accept the opposite view – that economic growth pulls financial institutional along on its coattails.

Kuznets, to note but one prominent example, accepted the so-called "demand-following" view. The rise in the shares of financial intermediaries during development resulted, Kuznets wrote, from "far-reaching changes in the pattern of economic and social life," changes to which the financial sector passively responded.[7] In another place, Kuznets went so far as to calculate the elasticity of financial sector output to GDP growth.[8] While he found finance to be relatively responsive (elasticities of 1.10 to 1.68, or about the same as manufacturing), the answer to whether finance is "supply-leading" or "demand-following" remains complex and clouded.

Evidence presented herein supports the former, but the latter was probably operative as well. Nor need the two views necessarily be mutually exclusive. It was likely that prior to the onset of modern development an economy must have been monetized to some extent and some, however limited, credit channels must have been in place. There had to have been, as Schumpeter argued, some organization(s) willing to interrupt the equilibrium circular flow and divert resources into innovative, if untested, enterprises. It was, perhaps, in the earliest stages of development that this function was most critical. Once the process was set in motion, however, other organizations appeared

---

7. Kuznets, *Capital in the American Economy*, p. 422.
8. Kuznets, *Economic Growth of Nations*, pp. 110–12.

which took advantage of the opportunities afforded by the actions of a few innovative, risk-taking bankers and other intermediaries. There may, in fact, have been an effective division of labor between the two, not unlike the division between venture capitalists and commercial banks (among a host of others) today.

While the formal model and statistical techniques employed in Chapter 2 suggest a causal link between financial development and subsequent economic growth, evidence presented in Chapter 3 investigated the operation of that link. Growth, and development in particular, is typically associated with growth in the manufacturing and service sectors relative to agricultural and primary product sectors. The historiography of Anglo-American banking is that the industry's support of manufacturing was limited. Committed to short-term commercial lending, banks financed an insignificant fraction of fixed-capital investment in manufacturing. Recent research into the mechanics of the First Industrial Revolution, however, suggests that most early manufacturers were not squeezed by shortages of long-term capital as long-term capital represented a small fraction of most manufacturers' total investment. Far more important was the financing of inventories and work-in-progress, both of which required access to sources of short-term or working capital.

Micro-level evidence collected from a handful of banks, while limited, lends support to the modified supply-leading hypothesis. A well-established stylized fact of American banking history is that the earliest banks were founded by and for the benefit of merchants. Merchants received the lion's share of the banks' credit, but then merchants dominated the commercial landscape in 1790 and for several decades thereafter. By mid-century, however, incipient manufacturing – sometimes labeled proto-industrialization – was making itself felt in many places and beginning to overshadow mercantile activities in some.

Several questions remain: How did the banks respond to this change? Did they promote it by lending to new enterprises, or did they remain servants to the past? Certainly some, sometimes prominent, banks responded slowly to wider economic change; others adapted quickly, still others were in the vanguard. In his history of the Bank of North America (America's first), Lawrence Lewis, asserted the 1830s were a time when business "was very active, a thousand new industries were developing themselves in all parts of the country, and the need of banking capital [credit] was pressing in the extreme."[9] Yet the venerable old bank clung to antiquated methods and found itself unable to compete successfully with younger banks that were exploiting, perhaps even uncovering, new opportunities. Lewis believed it fortuitous (for the bank, at least) that several of the bank's aged directors either resigned or died with their places taken by younger men more acquainted with the changing needs of business.

By mid-century, bank lending had changed. Nowhere was that more evident than in the changing names of banks. The historical progression of bank names, in and of themselves, would make an intriguing sociological study. The earliest banks, for example, commonly adopted names like the Massachusetts Bank or the Bank of Virginia, reflecting their close connection with and underlying support from the state itself. But the earliest banks were quickly dominated by an established mercantile elite who typically ignored the demands of business arrivistes, which resulted in public outcry for banks more responsive to the needs of small traders, artisans and farmers. The result was a wave of banks that adopted names like the *People's Bank* or the *Citizens Bank* or the *Freemans Bank*, names meant to reflect their wide accessibility and names that reflected the democratic, egalitarian mood in Jacksonian America. So, too, many newly established banks adopted names which signified the occupational group or groups to which they catered. In the 1820s, innumerable banks adopted names like the *Commercial & Farmers Bank* or the *Merchants and Planters Bank* or the *Traders Bank*. Beginning in the 1830s, and continuing through the 1850s, ever more newly established banks adopted names like the *Mechanics Bank* or the *Manufacturers & Mechanics Bank*, reflecting a shift in both sectoral shares and lending patterns. Other bank names reflected an increasing division of labor, if you will, with such names as the *Leather Manufacturers Bank*, the *Butchers & Drovers Bank*, or the *Grocers & Producers Bank*.

No longer closely tied to the mercantile community, banks became increasingly specialized and offered credit to organizations in proportion to their representation within the local business community. Merchants no longer received the bulk of the banks' funds, nor did

9. Lewis, *History of the Bank of North America*, p. 93.

they receive credit on more favorable terms than others. Manufacturers, in fact, while receiving loans in slightly smaller amounts than
merchants, typically obtained them at lower rates and somewhat
longer terms.

Contrary to the historiography of early American banking, manufacturers did not labor under shortages of short-term capital because
banks preferred mercantile and agricultural lending. Agriculture,
while it remained the dominant American industry, if anything,
received far less bank credit than is commonly presumed. Of course,
the evidence was drawn from a sample of city banks and rural banks
surely focused on agricultural lending. Though spare, the evidence
indicates that "in this game an ounce of data is better than a pound
of econometric technique."[10] Clearly more research is required
before firm conclusions can be drawn, but evidence presented here
suggests an interpretation of Anglo-American banking contrary to its
long-held characterization, namely that it did much to assist industrialization in the earliest stages of development.

Yet another stylized fact of early American banking is that financial
organizations, principally banks, failed to promote or bring about an
efficient geographic allocation of capital. Again the results reported
here contradict that view. The degree of financial integration can be
measured in any number of ways, but the simplest measure is the
extent to which rates in the hinterlands tended toward rates in the
commercial and financial centers. Statistics constructed from contemporary bank reports suggest that bank loan rates throughout the
eastern half of the country were usually within one to two percentage points of rates in New York City and Philadelphia (the nation's
financial centers), and they demonstrated largely synchronous
movements.

Regional commercial paper rates, too, demonstrated near equality
and similar time-series properties, rising and falling in unison after
1840. That the nation was becoming increasingly integrated financially can be seen in the pattern of regional interest rate movements
in three panic periods. In the panic of 1837, interest rates in the
nation's principal commercial cities diverged and followed notably
different paths until about 1840 or 1841. The panic of 1848, on the
other hand, pushed rates everywhere higher, but more so in some

10. Mokyr, "Are We Living," p. 39.

cities than others. Similarly, the panic of 1857 pushed rates higher, but they increased by about the same amount in all six cities. By 1850, if not several decades before, America's financial markets were effectively integrated.

Although this result may be startling to those familiar with the literature on postbellum financial markets, it should come as no surprise to those familiar with antebellum financial institutions and organizations. The Second Bank of the United States has often been credited with attempts to unify the nation's currency and financial markets, and while its efforts were important, they were not critical to the development of an integrated financial community. Prior to the Second Bank's entry, exchange brokers, private bankers, even commercial banks, promoted integration by fostering correspondent relationships with bankers in distant cities. Initially, these relationships were often formed to allow for interbank settlements and regional clearing of banknotes. As interregional trade increased, the economy grew more integrated, and the Second Bank passed from the scene, the scope of these ties expanded and their nature and function changed. While correspondents still served as efficient mechanisms for the clearing of banknotes, they were also used to collect bills of exchange and to exploit regional arbitrage opportunities. As such, these correspondent networks in the antebellum era represented the embryonic stages of the geographically diversified commercial paper house of the late nineteenth and early twentieth centuries that Lance Davis credited with bringing about regional interest rate convergence in the late postbellum era.[11] Southern and western banks and brokers exploited these correspondent relations and drew on their eastern correspondents to arbitrage on interest rate differentials when local rates exceeded those in eastern markets or to transfer funds to city correspondents when the reverse was true.

It is important to note that events outside the financial sector were occurring simultaneously with the development of correspondent relations and the integration of financial markets, and may well have encouraged the development and exploitation of these ties. Legal developments between the 1820s and 1840s clarified the rights and obligations of those employing financial instruments in interstate trade. Greater certainty about one's legal standing, particularly the

11. Davis, "Investment Market," pp. 372–3.

leveling of the playing field for nonresident creditors, promoted the use of financial instruments and allowed for more impersonal trade. Both effectively widened the market, not only for goods, but for financial instruments as well.

A study of the institutional environment in which antebellum banks operated is critical to our understanding of the era's financial markets. And the evidence presented here suggests that the era's institutional complex was reasonably efficient. Douglass North argued that the "level of interest rates in capital markets is perhaps the most evident quantitative dimension of the efficiency of the institutional framework," because interest rates reflect how well institutions promote exchange and intertemporal allocation.[12] An equally important gauge of institutional efficiency is the sectoral and geographic dispersion of interest rates because it is possible to envision a situation in which interest rates were low while capital, because of institutional rigidities, remained immobile.

Advances in transportation and communications technologies, as well as institutional influences, were critical components in making capital mobile. Canals and steamboats hastened the movement of men and goods and quickened the flow of information. A cursory glimpse at contemporary newspapers makes evident larger changes underlying increased interregional trade. In 1800 newspapers generally reported events and prices in local or at most regional markets. A New York paper, for example, might report selected auction prices in New York and note a few prices in Philadelphia or Boston. By 1860, whole pages were given over to prices in New York and one or more columns were dedicated to information in such distant markets as New Orleans, Cincinnati, and St. Louis. The expansion of interregional trade in the 1820s and 1830s created a demand for news from distant markets and local papers supplied it. Merchants and manufacturers therefore had access to timely information on both local and distant markets, making it easier for them to coordinate their market activities. Long-distance trade was risky and the better and more timely the information the lower (or, at least, the more calculable) those risks.

Besides improvements in water transport, several other changes outside the financial sector impinged on financial transactions. Rail-

12. North, *Institutions*, p. 69.

roads moved information faster than canal boats. The telegraph, moving information at the speed of electricity, represented the first technology that allowed information to travel faster than man or animal. But the development and the installation of the telegraph was probably secondary, in the antebellum era, to the "penny post" initiated in the 1840s. Though business correspondence was probably price inelastic, lower postage costs increased the flow of information. Lower postage costs and more-regular service induced bankers to greater communication and bankers wrote volumes of letters to distant correspondents inquiring into the credit worthiness of prospective borrowers, asking of local market conditions, and searching out profitable opportunities.

The development of credit reporting agencies, too, lowered information costs as it reduced duplication of monitoring and standardized reporting. A recent issue of the *Economist*, in fact, noted that railroads, steamships and the telegraph were far more revolutionary in their day, compared to previously existing technologies, than satellite communications and the Internet are today.[13] All these changes, revolutionary or not, affected financial markets. Financial transactions, more so than most, depended on information. And the better and more timely that information, the larger the volume of financial transactions, assuming as most modern studies do that the supply of finance is information-intensive, hence, highly information-elastic.

Earlier, I suggested that integration can be defined and measured in any number of ways, the most common being the tendency toward interest rate equality, but however defined or measured, economic integration implies factor mobility. Although every attempt was made to deal with those factors likely to influence the mobility of capital in the antebellum United States, even the briefest reflection on the meaning of factor mobility forces us to realize that many of the theoretically relevant variables militate against econometric technique or even casual empirical observation, not the least of which is the absence of information on interregional flows of capital.[14] Capital mobility or immobility may result from either institutional or psychological factors. Institutional influences include government controls (like usury laws), the competitive condition of the financial

---

13. *Economist*, 28 September 1996.
14. Machlup, "Introduction," p. 2.

industry, and technological factors such as communications and information technologies. Psychological influences include the nature of expectations concerning profitability, risks and uncertainty, and tastes or preferences toward, say, risk and uncertainty. And it must be remembered that different individuals will respond to the same stimuli, say an x percentage point interest differential, in different ways. A capitalist in Boston or Louisville, for example, may have responded to a given interest differential more quickly and more completely than a capitalist in New Bedford or Bowling Green under one set of circumstances, but less quickly and less completely under another. Absent information on actual flows, we are reduced to outlining those forces likely to have influenced the mobility of capital and analyzing how a rational maximizing actor would typically respond. The conclusion to be drawn from this study is that the institutional complex which developed and evolved throughout the antebellum era, though not consciously designed to do so, made capital mobile.

Integration of America's regional financial markets, then, may be taken to mean that local borrowers and lenders had meaningful alternatives for sources and uses of funds in other localities.[15] Integration, defined as such, gave rise to at least two identifiable efficiencies. The first, perhaps best defined as *technical efficiency*, was that integration and capital mobility increased the effective size of the market and may have led to operational economies of scale. That is, the resources required to transform a given volume of savings into investment was reduced. This may have been accomplished by exploiting scale economies in attracting savings or allocating funds (large branch banks in the South and West), narrower specialization (commercial banks, private banks, exchange brokers, and so forth), lower costs per unit of information (the telegraph or expanded financial reporting in the press), or simply greater competition between financial intermediaries in markets previously insulated from outside competition.

The second set of benefits realized through integration may be labeled *allocational efficiencies*. With integration and capital mobility, borrowers in one locality had access to a broader spectrum of sources of funds and could tailor loan contracts to more closely meet their preferred repayment conditions. In addition, the risk-return

---

15. Hawkins, "Intra-EEC Capital Movements," pp. 54–5.

characteristics of various financial instruments may have been transformed by a widening and deepening of financial markets. Increased secondary market (i.e., commercial paper) activities by agents of distant banks, for example, may have reduced seasonal or cyclical movements in interest rates and thereby reduced risks and raised returns.[16] Secondly, increased integration and secondary market activity reduced liquidity risks and may have made both investment and saving more attractive.

In addition, by equalizing interest rates throughout the country, integrated markets permitted the optimum geographic location of industry. The movement of capital, as Raymond Mikesell noted, provided "a vehicle for distributing technical progress and productivity growth more evenly throughout" the United States.[17] An example noted previously was that Connecticut bankers loaned substantial sums to canal companies and merchants in Ohio. The movement of capital, in relative surplus in the East, westward allowed for the adoption of a new transportation technology which fostered the growth and development of commercial agriculture in the West. The locus of food production, resulting from lower transportation costs, shifted from marginal eastern lands to infra-marginal western lands. The effect of these capital transfers was to raise productivity in both regions.

The introduction of financial intermediaries and the evolution of financial markets during the antebellum era were, as Raymond Goldsmith noted, "so closely intertwined with the growth of the American economy; with its territorial expansion; with price and interest-level movements of long duration; with modifications of the structure of the economy, such as the declining share of agriculture and the hand trades; [and] with changes in the organization of business" that their influence can be ignored only at great risk to our understanding of the process of economic development. Banks monetized the economy, developed credit channels which fostered investment in new regions and new industries, and helped integrate a number of distinct regional markets into a unified whole. It may have been the latter that represented their real and lasting contribution to

16. To use a statistical analogy, integration may have reduced the time-series variance of interest rates and lowered the mean. The result, from the borrower's point of view, was greater certainty about the costs and risks of borrowing at varying maturities.
17. Mikesell, "Comment," p. 84.

the American economy – the reduction in the great dispersion of rates of return on various financial assets. To some writers, in fact, such reductions represent the sine qua non of economic development. An effective and efficient capital market's role in the economy is to monitor the efficiency with which the existing capital stock was employed by pushing returns on assets across both sectoral and geographic divisions toward equality. Ronald McKinnon went so far as to define economic development "as the reduction of the great dispersion in social rates of return to existing and new investments under domestic entrepreneurial control."[18] Evidence from the short-term capital market makes it clear that modern economic development was well underway in antebellum America and banks were a critical component in the process.

18. McKinnon, *Money and Capital*, p. 9.

Epilogue:
A Postbellum Reprise

Lance Davis's findings that short-term interest rates in postbellum America varied across regions by as much as 4 or 5 percentage points challenged the conventional wisdom that capital markets quickly and efficiently dissipate price differentials on credit instruments with similar risk characteristics.[1] Subsequent research has offered several hypotheses to explain this anomaly: legal restrictions on banks, differential risk, information and transportation costs, and the probability of bank failure.[2] Furthermore, though most researchers believe interest rates converged by World War I, they do not agree on what brought convergence about.[3] In any case, the theme running throughout the literature is that post-Civil War America did not benefit from an integrated capital market until the late nineteenth to early twentieth century.

Although a large (and still growing) literature demonstrates the persistence of interest rate differentials in the postbellum era, the evidence presented earlier suggests that antebellum markets distributed short-term capital to where it was demanded. Is it reasonable, therefore, to conclude that antebellum America was served by a single, nationwide capital market? Probably not. Short-term interest rates

1. Davis, "Investment Market."
2. Sylla, "Federal Policy"; James, "Banking Market Structure;" Stigler, *Organization of Industry*, p. 116; Keehn, "Federal Bank Policy;" Rockoff, "Regional Interest Rates; and Bodenhorn, "More Perfect Union."
3. In addition to studies listed in notes 1 and 2 see James, "Development of a National Money Market"; and Sushka and Barrett, "Banking Structure." Gene Smiley ("Interest Rate Movements") has even questioned whether rates converged by 1914.

227

on or beyond the frontier were considerably higher than those within it. In August 1850, when interest rates in the East averaged about 6 percent, short-term interest rates in St. Louis were reportedly as high as 24 to 30 percent; in San Francisco they were 72 to 96 percent.[4] In 1850 the Mississippi River probably formed the boundary between frontier and settlement, but newspaper columns noted the initial stirrings of a market in St. Louis for bills of exchange drawn on New York and other eastern cities.[5] San Francisco, however, lay far beyond the frontier and it would be several years before new communication and transportation technologies linked Pacific Coast markets to the East. But as Hugh Rockoff and I have noted elsewhere, it is probably erroneous to view the financial development of the United States as a process by which new technologies gradually knit isolated regional markets into a unified whole.[6] It may be more appropriate to think of American capital markets as always having been integrated; as settlement radiated outward, so, too, did the capital market.

The pronounced divergence in regional interest rates during the postbellum era then become even more vexing, particularly the South's different standing in the two eras. Southern interest rates before the Civil War were, within narrow bounds, equal to northern rates and capital flowed freely between the two regions. After the war, southern rates generally exceeded northern rates and at times were twice as high as rates in New York City. Capital flowed into the South after the war, but apparently not in sufficient quantities to eliminate short-term interest differentials. The Civil War, then, marks a sharp discontinuity in the history of American credit markets.

Three fundamental changes occurred during and after the Civil War, any one of which would have disrupted North-South capital flows. Operating in combination, they slowed the reintegration of the South into a national market to the pace of medieval siege. The most notable change was the large-scale failure of southern intermediaries.

---

4. *Missouri Republican*, 12 August 1850; *Commercial and Shipping List*, 27 July 1850.
5. *Missouri Republican*, various issues, 1850.
6. Bodenhorn and Rockoff, "Regional Interest Rates," p. 187. Odell, "Integration of Regional," and personal correspondence accept the gradual knitting together view when considering the Pacific Coast financial markets. Odell's interpretation for the Pacific Coast may be correct given its separation from eastern markets. Still, it may have been that the far western frontier pushed slowly eastward as San Francisco capitalists and those in other cities chose to invest in recently settled regions.

Compounding the effects of the disappearance of the region's commercial bank was the gradual displacement of the region's cotton and tobacco factors and the private banking industry they supported. The advance of the railroad and the changeover from plantation agriculture to tenant farming also fundamentally altered the financial landscape.

During the decade of the 1860s, as a result of the Civil War and Reconstruction-era legislation, the elaborate edifice of state-sponsored, state-chartered financial intermediaries that had required more than seventy years to construct was effectively destroyed by the federal government. With the closing of the Second Bank of the United States in 1836, the federal government had relinquished its control over the country's banking sector. The National Bank Act, passed in 1863, had roots dating back as least that far. Critics of state banking called for fundamental reform at every turn, citing the dizzying array of state banknotes – some 600 banks, each issuing several different denominations – and the high rate of bank mortality. While free banking had satisfied laissez faire proponents, critics viewed it as nothing short of monetary chaos. It was not until midway through the war, however, that Republicans who favored federal centralization were able to push through a meaningful reform bill. Secretary of the Treasury Salmon Chase was its foremost champion, recommending federal regulation on the grounds that it would create a uniform national currency, would assist the war effort by providing a market for government bonds, and would eradicate wide swings in the money supply. Still, a year elapsed between when Chase made his call for reform and when Congress enacted it. And it is highly unlikely that "the bill would have passed had the South, with its easy-money, antifederal outlook, still been represented in Congress."[7]

The 1863 act, as subsequently amended, created a national free banking system based on the model developed by New York's 1838 free banking law. Nationally chartered banks, under the supervision of the newly created Office of the Comptroller of the Currency, faced relatively high minimum capital requirements and were required to invest in U.S. government debt to secure their circulation, and the 10 percent tax placed on state banknote issues in 1865 virtually guaranteed that all banks would have to accede to these requirements.

7. Krooss and Blyn, *History of Financial Intermediaries*, p. 96.

Further, the act mandated a maximum aggregate banknote issue of $300 million with one-half that amount to be distributed proportionate to population, the other half in proportion to existing banking facilities.[8] It was unclear, however, that the aggregate circulation provision would be modified to take into account the banking needs of those states then in revolt should they be reintegrated into the national polity.

If reintegration of the Confederacy into the national polity was realized by the end of Reconstruction, its reintegration into the national economy was far in the future. In 1840, per capita income in the South Atlantic region stood at 70 percent of the national average.[9] But if slaves were treated as capital goods rather than consuming units, per capita incomes in the South Atlantic region were 96 percent of the national average.[10] By 1880, however, the South had fallen far behind the remainder of the country with per capita incomes as low as 45 percent of the national average. It was not until 1950, or nearly ninety years after the outbreak of the war, that South Atlantic incomes would attain the relative level achieved in 1840.

Perhaps no sector of the southern economy suffered as much as the financial sector. Although southern financial intermediaries were fully integrated into a national short-term capital market in the antebellum era, a large body of evidence demonstrates that three decades after the war the South still constituted a distinct, *dis-integrated* capital market. The most likely explanation of the South's inability to reintegrate into the nation's financial markets lies in the fact that the sundered financial links between the South and the remainder of the country "had to be completely replaced."[11]

Southern banks and the interregional and international connections they had so diligently developed and nurtured throughout the antebellum era failed to survive the war. Almost all southern banks invested heavily in Confederate and state securities which became virtually worthless even before the Appomattox armistice. By October 1865, for example, 41 percent of the Bank of the State of South Carolina's assets were tied up in Confederate securities.[12] Only

8. Ibid., pp. 96–7.
9. Easterlin, "Interregional Differences," p. 137.
10. Engerman, "Reconsideration," pp. 354–6; and Fogel, *Without Consent or Contract*, p. 85.
11. Davis, "Investment Market," p. 392.
12. South Carolina, *Reports and Resolutions* (1865).

12 percent of its assets were invested in private notes and bills, most of the remainder was in South Carolina securities. As the value of these government securities decreased, the bank's holdings of private securities was insufficient to support its liabilities, and the bank was forced to liquidate. William Royall cites the same cause for the failure of Virginia's banks.[13]

The pressures under which Tennessee's banks operated during the Civil War were probably representative of those faced by banks in other Confederate states. In January 1861, Tennessee's legislature authorized the sale of $5 million in state bonds to equip a provisional military force.[14] Encountering difficulty in placing the bonds in the hands of private investors, the state's three, broad-branched banks were approached and asked to buy the unsold, and apparently unsalable, securities. The partially state-owned Bank of Tennessee took up a considerable amount of the securities, but the two privately owned banks – the Union Bank and the Planters Bank – balked. The legislature and the governor equated their hesitation with treason. Any institution unwilling to demonstrate its unconditional support for the cause must have been opposed to it.

In testimony given during the bank's postwar bankruptcy hearings, Tennessee's ex-governor recalled personally calling upon the directors of the two recalcitrant banks:

> To make them clearly understand that the Union and Planters' Banks would not be permitted to pursue the policy which in previous interviews had suggested, but they would be compelled to cooperate with the Bank of Tennessee in meeting the financial necessities of the State.
>
> And while I do not now remember the language employed, I was satisfied then as I am now that I made those gentlemen understand that if they did not cooperate with the Bank of Tennessee in meeting these financial necessities, that I would compel them to do so, or take the assets of the Banks out of their hands and place them in the hands of a receiver who was friendly to the Confederate cause.[15]

Fearing that these banks, with strong ties to northern capitalists, would carry their funds out of Confederate reach where they may, ultimately, have been employed against the cause, Governor Harris felt he had no alternative but to demand their cooperation. No evidence was ever presented, of course, that either bank planned to

13. Royall, *History of Virginia Banks*, p. 39.
14. Campbell, *Development of Banking in Tennessee*, pp. 157–8.
15. Quoted in ibid, pp. 158–9.

support the Union instead of the Confederacy, but both banks were adamantly opposed to investing in Confederate securities. Governor Harris later claimed that "if no argument more potent than persuasion had been used that neither . . . bank would have invested a dollar in the War Bonds of Tennessee."[16] And his suspicion was well founded as Francis Fogg, director of the Planters Bank, testified before the bankruptcy court that:

I [knew] we [had] no money to loan and if we had, we ought not to loan it; but with a loaded pistol at my head, I say *aye* for the purpose of preserving if possible some of the assets of the Bank for the stockholders, as I [knew] they [would] all be destroyed in the hands of a receiver or of military authorities.[17]

Both the Union and the Planters Banks were quickly compromised. Though financially sound in 1860, neither recovered after they were forced to buy into this and subsequent Confederate loans. Both banks attempted to initiate liquidation proceedings during the war in order to salvage some part of the shareholders' investments, but the state wouldn't allow it. Forced to continue in a crippled condition throughout the war, both initiated liquidations as soon after the war as possible. By July 1865 their assets were in the hands of receivers. The partially state-owned Bank of Tennessee, which held nearly $8 million in worthless Confederate securities at war's end, quickly followed suit.[18]

Postwar failure rates were high in other states as well and the slow postwar reestablishment of banking in the South slowed the speed at which the region was pulled back into the national economy and diminished the effectiveness of its institutions as intermediaries and engines of growth. Virginia, with 65 banks and branches in 1860 with an aggregate capital in cxccss of $16 million, had but 19 banks with a combined capital of $2.5 million in 1867.[19] Kentucky's experience paralleled Virginia's. On the eve of the Civil War, Kentucky had one of the most stable, most respected state-sponsored systems in the Union, with 45 banks and branches and nearly $13 million in capital. In 1867 the state had 15 banks with less than $3 million in capital. But no two states were more completely stripped of their financial

16. Ibid., p. 160.
17. Ibid.
18. Ibid., p. 167.
19. U.S. Comptroller of the Currency, *Annual Report* (1876); Ransom and Sutch, *One Kind of Freedom*, table 6.4, p. 114.

intermediaries than the Carolinas. North Carolina with 50 branches and South Carolina with 20 in 1860 had combined, in 1867, only 7 banks with about $1 million capital. All told, by 1870 twelve southern states were served by only 69 national banks, compared to 1,545 banks serving the remainder of the country. Davis argued that, in the postbellum era, "the South almost certainly had the poorest banking facilities."[20] But the South's postbellum experience was without precedent, as the antebellum South's large, broad-based branch networks were admired by contemporary observers and subsequent generations of historians alike for their stability, soundness and, as we have seen, their ability to intermediate effectively and draw capital into a region chronically short of indigenously generated capital to be used in developing the region's resources and in support of its entrepreneurs.

The postwar rise in tenant farming and developments in transportation and communications also sundered another important link between southern credit markets and the outside world. In the antebellum era, cotton factors provided a host of marketing and credit services to planters.[21] Antebellum banks typically eschewed loans to planters because planters generally asked for long-term mortgage credit with property, slaves, or even the next season's cotton crop offered as collateral. Loans such as these presented a clear violation of the real-bills doctrine as they locked up loanable funds for long periods and had imperfect, at best, secondary markets. Moreover, offering credit to planters would have forced banks to gather a great deal of information on the credit worthiness of a large number of potential borrowers. Instead, banks preferred to deal with a small number of cotton factors who borrowed short on real bills drawn against cotton consignments and for whom credit information was more easily gathered. Factors then passed credit along to planters who required funds between the planting and harvesting seasons. As Woodman noted, bills drawn by some well-known factors were readily discounted throughout the country, and it was through the factor that "the world's money markets, like the world's commodity markets, became available to the cotton planter."[22]

20. Davis, "Investment Market," p. 389.
21. Woodman, *King Cotton*.
22. Ibid., p. 41.

Soon after the war the expansion of the railroad radically altered the cotton marketing system. Growers no longer had to ship their crop to factors in coastal cities to have it graded, classed, weighed, compressed, and shipped on consignment. By the 1870s northern buyers traveled throughout the southern hinterlands and purchased and shipped cotton very nearly from its point of origin to its northern destination.[23] And northern buyers avoided the need for credit by paying cash.[24] Tenant farmers still required credit between planting and harvest, but the few remaining factors were unwilling to grant it because growers rarely used their services in marketing the crop. Instead, furnishing merchants became the principal suppliers of rural credit and they, in turn, received most of their credit not from local banks but from northern manufacturers.[25] The cotton factors' marketing services became superfluous after the war and they gradually disappeared. With them went an important link in the antebellum chain of credit.

It was the achingly slow reestablishment of banking in the South combined with fundamental changes in the distribution of the region's principal crop that slowed the speed at which the South was reintegrated into the national economy. But it was the destruction of the region's antebellum banks and the laggard establishment of new ones that probably proved decisive, and the latter resulted from the federal government's wartime intervention in the financial sector. Minimum capital requirements for national banks were prohibitively high and the note issue limits negated the prospective banker's profit incentive.[26] Furthermore, the tax imposed on state bank notes made state banks equally unprofitable. The reestablishment of banking on a large scale in the South awaited the spread of deposit banking, the enactment of general banking laws in many states, and the lowering of capital requirements for national banks contained in the Gold Standard Act of 1900.[27] Until then, the few existing southern intermediaries could exploit their local monopoly, and monopoly power accounts for a significant fraction of postbellum interest rate differ-

23. Ibid., p. 272; and Ransom and Sutch, *One Kind of Freedom*, pp. 116–17.
24. Woodman, *King Cotton*, p. 275.
25. Ransom and Sutch, *One Kind of Freedom*, pp. 120–3.
26. Sylla, "Federal Policy," pp. 662–3.
27. James, "Development of a National Money Market," pp. 896–7.

entials.[28] In fact, the gradual reintegration of regional capital markets after passage of the Gold Standard Act and the revival of free banking in many states may have been little more than a return to the status quo ante bellum.

28. James, "Banking Market Structure," p. 459.

Appendix
Calculating State-Level Real Income

It should be stressed from the outset that the growth rates derived here are not detailed direct estimates of real per capita output in each state. Instead the estimates are derived by drawing together fragments of evidence produced by economic historians over the past several decades. Paul David, who generated the first set of "controlled conjectures" of the rate of growth of the U.S. economy in the antebellum period argued that the "instability of the rate of per capita real output growth during the antebellum era, like the swings in the U.S. growth rates found in subsequent periods, makes it a treacherous business to infer secular trends from observations drawn at arbitrary census-year intervals."[1] Keeping these pitfalls in mind, the following are designed to be suggestive rather than definitive estimates and their use in the econometric analysis in Chapter 2 is similarly suggestive.

Census-year estimates of real per capita gross domestic product and the subsequent growth rates are arrived at through the use of a simple identity. Using this identity, an index of per capita output can be derived from the product of two other indexes: one describing the sectoral composition of labor inputs; the second, the relative levels of labor productivity in each sector. That is, the first is the sector-specific labor participation rate, the second is the average sectoral output per worker. Estimating the relative levels of per capita product in any

1. David, "Growth in Real Product," pp. 156–7.

Table A1. State-level gdp estimates for 1830

| | Hundreds | | | Constant $1840 | | |
	Population	Labor force	Farm labor force	Farm output/ worker	Non-Farm output/ worker	Per capita output
Maine	3,995	1,080	799	153	357	55.7
New Hampshire	2,693	817	93	153	357	101.3
Vermont	2,807	780	662	153	357	51.1
Massachusetts	6,104	2,037	785	153	357	92.9
Rhode Island	972	335	140	153	357	93.7
Connecticut	2,977	940	559	153	357	74.4
New York	19,186	5,604	3,563	153	357	66.4
New Jersey	3,208	943	525	153	357	71.6
Pennsylvania	13,482	3,806	1,952	153	357	71.2
Delaware	767	225	173	153	357	58.7
Maryland	4,470	1,627	937	153	357	87.2
Dist. Columbia	398	105	9	153	357	89.6
Virginia	12,114	4,802	3,748	153	357	78.4
North Carolina	7,380	2,842	2,249	153	357	75.3
South Carolina	5,812	2,761	2,082	153	357	96.5
Georgia	5,168	2,169	1,687	153	357	83.2
Florida	347	155	128	153	357	84.2
Ohio	9,379	2,386	1,823	153	357	51.2
Indiana	3,430	803	725	153	357	40.5
Illinois	1,574	389	331	153	357	45.3
Wisconsin	--	--	--	153	357	--
Michigan	316	106	83	153	357	66.2
Kentucky	6,879	2,348	1,849	153	357	67.0
Tennessee	6,819	2,147	1,772	153	357	59.4
Mississippi	1,366	620	492	153	357	88.6
Alabama	3,095	1,261	996	153	357	79.8
Louisiana	2,157	1,093	729	153	357	112.0
Missouri	1,405	435	343	153	357	60.7

Note: For method of calculation see text.
Sources: U.S. Census Office, Ninth Census (1870), *Compendium*; Weiss, "U.S. Labor Force Estimates;" Weiss, "Economic Growth before 1860"

year can be decomposed into arriving at consistent measures of the two underlying magnitudes.[2]

David greatly simplified the analysis by dividing the economy into two sectors: agriculture and everything else. Generating estimates of per capita real output then involves estimating labor force participation rates in agriculture and everything else as well as estimates of output per worker in the two sectors. In his pioneering effort, David employed labor force estimates derived by Stanley Lebergott and

2. Ibid., pp. 158–60.

Robert Gallman's estimates of sectoral output per worker going back to 1840. In generating estimates for the period before 1840, David assumed that the growth in labor productivity in both sectors was equal to growth in labor productivity in the dominant activity – agriculture. Once these relatively small data demands are met, it is relatively easy to generate David's conjectural estimates of per capita output using the estimating equation:

$$O/P = (LF/P)[S_a(O/LF)_a + S_n(O/LF_n)] \tag{A.1}$$

Where O/P is output per capita; LF/P is the overall labor participation rate; $(O/LF)_a$ is output per worker in agriculture; $(O/LF)_n$ is output per worker in non-agricultural employment; S_a is the share of the labor force involved in agriculture; and S_n is the share of labor in non-agricultural activities.[3]

Since David developed his estimates a wealth of new information has come forth concerning labor productivity growth in the antebellum economy. Thomas Weiss, in a series of studies generated new estimates of the labor force and the participation rate at the state level. Fortunately, Weiss has reported his results in detail so it is a relatively straight-forward procedure to generate state-level estimates from the information he pulled together. Table A.1 reports a representative estimation of state-level estimates of output per capita using the information collected, corrected and reported by Weiss.[4]

These state-level estimates of real per capita output were then used to generate estimates of decadal growth rates used in the econometric analysis of Chapter 2.

3. Lebergott, "Labor Force and Employment"; Gallman, "Gross National Product"; David, "Growth in Real Output," p. 160; Weiss, "Economic Growth before 1860," p. 14.
4. Weiss, "Revised Estimates"; Weiss, "U.S. Labor Force Estimates"; and Weiss, "Economic Growth before 1860."

Bibliography

ARCHIVAL SOURCES

Charleston Library Society (Charleston, South Carolina). *Planters and Mechanics Letterbook, 1839–1847.* (microfiche)

Chester County Historical Society (Chester, Pennsylvania). *Records of the Bank of Chester County*, 1815–1818.

Robert Scott Small Library, Division of Archives and Special Collections, College of Charleston. *Records of the Bank of Charleston.*

Jefferson County Historical Society (Watertown, New York). *Records of the Black River Bank.*

Southern Historical Collection of the Manuscripts Department, University of North Carolina, Chapel Hill. *Bank of Cape Fear. Hillsborough Branch. Records, 1815–1846.*

Tennessee State Library and Archives (Nashville, Tennessee). Archives Division. *Bank of Tennessee, 1838–1865.* Record Group Number 47.

Tulane University. Records of Ante-Bellum Southern Plantations from the Revolution through the Civil War. Series H. Selections from the Howard Tilton Memorial Library, Tulane University and the Louisiana State Museum Archives. *Citizens Bank of Louisiana Minute Books and Records, 1833–1868.* Microfilm reels 13–17.

Virginia Historical Society (Richmond, Virginia). *Branch & Company, Richmond, Va. Records, 1837–1976.*

ARTICLES AND BOOKS

Abramovitz, Moses. "Long Swings in American Economic Growth." In *New Views on American Economic Development*, pp. 377–427. Edited by Ralph Andreano. Cambridge: Schenkman Publishing Company, 1965.

239

Adams, Donald R., Jr. "Portfolio Management and Profitability in Early-Nineteenth-Century Banking," *Business History Review* 52 (Spring 1978), pp. 61–79.

Finance and Enterprise in Early America: A Study of Stephen Girard's Bank, 1812–1831. Philadelphia: University of Pennsylvania Press, 1978.

Akerlof, George. "The Market for Lemons: Quality Uncertainty and the Market Mechanism," *Quarterly Journal of Economics* 84 (August 1970), pp. 488–500.

Anonymous (Nathan Appleton?). *A Defence of Country Banks; Being a Reply to a Pamphlet Entitled 'An Examination of the Banking System of Massachusetts, in Reference to the Renewal of the Bank Charters'*. Boston: Stimpson and Clapp, 1831.

Anonymous. "Banks of Massachusetts," *Hunt's Merchants' Magazine* 2 (February 1840), pp. 134–53.

Appleton, Nathan. *An Examination of the Banking System of Massachusetts in Reference to the Renewal of the Bank Charters*. Boston: Stimpson and Clapp, 1831.

Ashton, T. S. *The Industrial Revolution, 1760–1830*. Oxford: Oxford University Press, 1969.

Atack, Jeremy. "The Agricultural Ladder Revisited: A New Look at an Old Question with Some Data from 1860," *Agricultural History* 65 (Winter 1989), pp. 1–25.

and Peter Passell. *A New Economic View of American History*. New York: W. W. Norton & Company, 1994.

Atherton, Lewis E. "The Problem of Credit Rating in the Ante-Bellum South," *Journal of Southern History* 12 (November 1946), pp. 534–56.

Bagehot, Walter. *Lombard Street: A Description of the Money Market*. New York: Charles Scribner's Sons, 1906.

Bank of Charleston. *Proceeedings of the Stockholders of the Bank of Charleston, South Carolina, Held at Their Banking House*. Broadsides. 1837, 1839, 1840, 1841, 1844, 1845, 1858.

Barro, Robert J. "Economic Growth in a Cross Section of Countries," *Quarterly Journal of Economics* 106 (May 1991), pp. 407–43.

and Xavier Sala-i-Martin. "Convergence Across States and Regions," *Brookings Papers on Economic Activity* (1991), pp. 107–58.

"Convergence," *Journal of Political Economy* 100 (April 1992), pp. 223–51.

Bateman, Fred, James Foust, and Thomas Weiss. "The Participation of Planters in Manufacturing in the Antebellum South," *Agricultural History* 48 (October 1974), pp. 277–97.

and Thomas Weiss. "Manufacturing in the Antebellum South," *Research in Economic History* 1 (1976), pp. 1–44.

A Deplorable Scarcity: The Failure of Industrialization in the Slave Economy. Chapel Hill: University of North Carolina Press, 1981.

Bencivenga, Valerie and Bruce D. Smith. "Financial Intermediation and Endogenous Growth," *Review of Economic Studies* 58 (April 1991), pp. 195–209.

Bernanke, Ben S. and Mark Gertler. "Agency Costs, Net Worth, and Business Fluctuations," *American Economic Review* 79 (March 1989), pp. 14–31.

Berry, Thomas Sr. *Western Prices Before 1861: A Study of the Cincinnati Market.* Cambridge: Harvard University Press, 1943.

Bodenhorn, Howard. "Capital Mobility and Financial Integration in Antebellum America," *Journal of Economic History* 52 (September 1992), pp. 585–610.

"A More Perfect Union: Regional Interest Rates in the United States, 1880–1960." In *Anglo-American Financial Systems: Institutions and Markets in the Twentieth Century*, pp. 415–53. Edited by Michael D. Bordo and Richard Sylla. Burr Ridge: Irwin, 1996.

"Zombie Banks and the Demise of New York's Safety Fund System," *Eastern Economic Journal* 22 (Winter 1996), pp. 21–33.

"Private Banking in Antebellum Virginia: Thomas Branch & Sons of Petersburg" *Business History Review* 71 (Winter 1997), pp. 513–42.

and Hugh Rockoff. "Regional Interest Rates in Antebellum America." In *Strategic Factors in Nineteenth Century American Economic History: A Volume to Honor Robert W. Fogel*, pp. 159–87. Edited by Claudia Golding and Hugh Rockoff. Chicago: University of Chicago Press, 1992.

Bruchey, Stuart. *Enterprise: The Dynamic Economy of a Free People.* Cambridge, Mass.: Harvard University Press, 1990.

Bryan, Alfred C. *A History of State Banking in Maryland.* Johns Hopkins University Studies in Historical and Political Science, Series 17. Baltimore: Johns Hopkins University Press, 1899.

Burpee, Charles W. *First Century of the Phoenix National Bank of Hartford.* Hartford: privately printed, 1914.

Cable, John Ray. *The Bank of the State of Missouri.* Studies in History, Economics and Public Law, Volume 52, No. 2. New York: Columbia University Press, 1923.

Caldwell, Stephen A. *A Banking History of Louisiana.* Baton Rouge: Louisiana State University Press, 1935 (reprint New York: Arno Press, 1980).

Callender, G. S. "The Early Transportation and Banking Enterprises of the States in Relation to the Growth of Corporations," *Quarterly Journal of Economics* 27 (1903), pp. 111–62.

Calomiris, Charles W. "Deposit Insurance: Lessons from the Record," Federal Reserve Bank of Chicago *Economic Perspectives* 13 (May/June 1989), pp. 10–30.

and Larry Schweikart. "The Panic of 1857: Origins, Transmission, and Containment," *Journal of Economic History* 51 (December 1991), pp. 807–34.

Cameron, Rondo. With the collaboration of Olga Crisp, Hugh T. Patrick and Richard Tilly. *Banking in the Early Stages of Industrialization: A Study in Comparative Economic History.* New York: Oxford University Press, 1967.

(editor). *Banking and Economic Development: Some Lessons of History.* New York: Oxford University Press, 1972.

"Theoretical Bases of a Comparative Study of the Role of Financial Institutions in the Early Stages of Industrialization." In *Financing Industrialization*, vol. I, pp. 1–20. Edited by Rondo Cameron. Brookfield: Edwin Elgar, 1992.

Campbell, Claude A. *The Development of Banking in Tennessee*. Nashville: privately printed, 1932.

Catterall, Ralph C. H. *The Second Bank of the United States*. Chicago: University of Chicago Press, 1903.

Chaddock, Robert E. *The Safety Fund Banking System in New York, 1829–1866*. Washington, D.C.: Government Printing Office, 1910.

Chandler, Alfred. *The Visible Hand: The Managerial Revolution in American Business*. Cambridge: Belknap Press of Harvard University Press, 1977.

Citizen. *The Village Bank at Danvers. A Glance at its History with Other Relevant Matter, for the Consideration of the Stockholders and the Community Interested*. Boston: McIntire & Moulton, 1862.

Clark, W. A. *The History of Banking Institutions Organized in South Carolina Prior to 1860*. Columbia: The Historical Commission of South Carolina, 1922.

Conant, Charles A. *Wall Street and the Country: A Study of Recent Financial Tendencies*. New York: G. P. Putnam's Sons, 1904.

Cooter, Robert and Thomas Ulen. *Law and Economics*. 2d edition. Reading, Mass.: Addison-Wesley, 1997.

Court, William H. B. *A Concise Economic History of Britain from 1750 to Recent Times*. Cambridge: Cambridge University Press, 1962.

Daniels, Belden L. *Pennsylvania: Birthplace of Banking in America*. Harrisburg: Pennsylvania Bankers Association, 1976.

David, Paul A. "The Growth of Real Product in the United States Before 1840: New Evidence, Controlled Conjectures," *Journal of Economic History* 27 (June 1967), pp. 151–97.

Davis, Lance E. "The New England Textile Mills and the Capital Markets: A Study of Industrial Borrowing 1840–1860," *Journal of Economic History* 20 (March 1960), pp. 1–30.

"Capital Immobilities and Finance Capitalism: A Study of Economic Evolution in the United States, 1820–1920," *Explorations in Entrepreneurial History* Second Series 1 (Fall 1963), pp. 88–105. Reprinted in *Purdue Faculty Papers in Economic History 1956–1966*, pp. 581–95. Homewood, IL: Richard D. Irwin, Inc., 1967.

"The Investment Market, 1870–1914: Evolution of a National Market," *Journal of Economic History* 25 (September 1965), pp. 355–99.

and Robert E. Gallman. "Capital Formation in the United States during the Nineteenth Century." In *The Cambridge Economic History of Europe*, vol. 7, part 2, pp. 1–69. Edited by Peter Mathias and M. M. Postan. Cambridge: Cambridge University Press, 1978.

Deane, Phyllis. "The Role of Capital in the Industrial Revolution," *Explorations in Economic History* 10 (Summer 1973), pp. 349–64.

De Gregario, Jose amd Pablo E. Guidotti. "Financial Development and Economic Growth," *World Development* 23 (March 1995), pp. 433–48.

Dewey, Davis R. *State Banking Before the Civil War*. Washington, D.C.: Government Printing Office, 1910.

Diamond, Douglas W. "Financial Intermediation and Delegated Monitoring," *Review of Economic Studies* 51 (July 1984), pp. 393–414.

Dickens, Charles. *American Notes*. Glouchester, MA: Peter Smith, 1968.

Duke, Basil W. *History of the Bank of Kentucky, 1792–1895*. Louisville: J. P. Morton, 1895 (reprint New York: Arno Press, 1980).

Dunbar, Charles F. *The Theory and History of Banking*. New York: G. P. Putnam's Sons, 1929.

Easterlin, Richard A. "Interregional Differences in Per Capita Income, Population, and Total Income, 1840–1950." In *Trends in the American Economy in the Nineteenth Century*, pp. 73–140. Studies in Income and Wealth, Vol. 24. Princeton: Princeton University Press, 1960.

Engerman, Stanley L. "A Reconsideration of Southern Economic Growth, 1770–1860," *Agricultural History* 44 (April 1975), pp. 343–61.

  and Robert Gallman. "U.S. Economic Growth, 1783–1860," *Research in Economic History* 8 (1983), pp. 1–46.

Fama, Eugene F. "Banking in the Theory of Finance," *Journal of Monetary Economics* 6 (January 1980), pp. 39–57.

  "What's Different About Banks?," *Journal of Monetary Economics* 15 (January 1985), pp. 29–39.

  "Contract Costs and Financing Decisions," *Journal of Business* 63 (January 1990, Part 2), pp. S71–S91.

Fenstermaker, J. Van. *The Development of American Commercial Banking: 1782–1837*. Kent: Kent State University Bureau of Economic and Business Research, 1965.

  and John E. Filer. "Impact of the First and Second Banks of the United States and the Suffolk System on New England Bank Money, 1791–1837," *Journal of Money, Credit, and Banking* 18 (February 1986), pp. 28–40.

Fishlow, Albert. "Antebellum Interregional Trade Reconsidered," *American Economic Review Papers and Proceedings* 54 (May 1964), pp. 352–64.

Fogel, Robert W. *Without Consent or Contract: The Rise and Fall of American Slavery*. New York: W. W. Norton & Company, 1989.

Foner, Eric and John A. Garraty (editors). *The Reader's Companion to American History*. Boston: Houghton Mifflin Company, 1991.

Freyer, Tony A. "Negotiable Instruments and the Federal Courts in Antebellum American Business," *Business History Review* 50 (Winter 1976), pp. 435–55.

Friedman, Lawrence M. *A History of American Law*. New York: Simon & Schuster, 1985.

  Crime and Punishment in American History. New York: Basic Books, 1993.

Friedman, Milton and Anna J. Schwartz. *A Monetary History of the United States, 1867–1960*. Princeton: Princeton University Press, 1963.

  "Has the Government Any Role in Money?" *Journal of Monetary Economics* 17 (1986), pp. 37–62.

Fry, Maxwell J. *Money, Interest, and Banking in Economic Development*. Baltimore: Johns Hopkins University Press, 1988.

Gallatin, Albert. *The Writings of Albert Gallatin*. Edited by Henry Adams. 3 Vols. New York: Antiquarian Press Ltd., 1960.

Gallman, Robert E. "Gross National Product in the United States, 1834–1909." In *Output, Employment, and Productivity in the United States after 1800*, pp. 3–76. Edited by Dorothy S. Brady. New York: Columbia University Press, 1966.

"American Economic Growth before the Civil War: The Testimony of the Capital Stock Estimates." In *American Economic Growth and Standards of Living before the Civil War*, pp. 79–115. Edited by Robert E. Gallman and John Joseph Wallis. Chicago: University of Chicago Press, 1992.

Gerschenkron, Alexander. *Economic Backwardness in Historical Perspective*. Cambridge: Harvard University Press, 1962.

Gertler, Mark. "Financial Structure and Aggregate Economic Activity: An Overview," *Journal of Money, Credit, and Banking* 20 (August 1988, Part 2), pp. 559–588.

Gibbons, J. S. *The Banks of New York, Their Dealers, the Clearing House, and the Panic of 1857*. New York: D. Appleton & Company, 1859.

Goldsmith, Raymond W. *Financial Intermediaries in the American Economy since 1900*. Princeton: Princeton University Press, 1958.

Financial Institutions. New York: Random House, 1968.

Financial Structure and Development. New Haven: Yale University Press, 1969.

Golembe, Carter H. *State Banks and the Economic Development of the West, 1830–44*. New York: Arno Press, 1978.

Gras, N. S. B. *The Massachusetts First National Bank of Boston, 1784–1934*. Cambridge: Harvard University Press, 1937.

Greef, Albert. *The Commercial Paper House in the United States*. Cambridge: Harvard University Press, 1938.

Green, George D. *Finance and Economic Development in the Old South: Louisiana Banking, 1804–1861*. Stanford: Stanford University Press, 1972.

"Louisiana, 1804–1861." In *Banking and Economic Development: Some Lessons from History*, pp. 199–231. Edited by Rondo Cameron. New York: Oxford University Press, 1972.

Greenwood, Jeremy and Boyan Jovanovic. "Financial Development, Growth, and the Distribution of Income," *Journal of Political Economy* 98 (October 1990), pp. 1076–1108.

Gurley, John G. and Edward S. Shaw. "Financial Aspects of Economic Development," *American Economic Review* 45 (September 1955), pp. 515–38.

"Financial Intermediaries and the Saving-Investment Process," *Journal of Finance* 2 (May 1956), pp. 257–76.

Money in a Theory of Finance. Washington, D.C.: Brookings Institution, 1960.

Habakkuk, H. J. *American and British Technology in the Nineteenth Century*. Cambridge: Cambridge University Press, 1962.

Hammond, Bray. *Banks and Politics in America from the Revolution to the Civil War*. Princeton: Princeton University Press, 1957.

Harding, William F. "The State Bank of Indiana," *Journal of Political Economy* 4 (December 1895), pp. 1–36, 109–38.

Hasse, William F., Jr. *A History of Money and Banking in Connecticut*. New Haven: privately printed, 1957.

Hawkins, Robert G. "Intra-EEC Capital Movements and Domestic Financial Markets." In *International Mobility and Movement of Capital*, pp. 51–78. Edited by Fritz Machlup, Walter S. Salant and Lorie Tarshis. New York: Columbia University Press for National Bureau of Economic Research, 1972.

Helderman, Leonard C. *National and State Banks: A Study of Their Origins*. Boston: Houghton Mifflin Company, 1931.

Holdsworth, John Thom. *Financing and Empire: History of Banking in Pennsylvania*. Chicago: S. J. Clarke Publishing Company, 1928.

Homer, Sidney. *A History of Interest Rates*. New Brunswick: Rutgers University Press, 1963.

Horwitz, Morton J. *The Transformation of American Law*. Cambridge: Harvard University Press, 1977.

Hubert, Philip G. Jr. *The Merchants' National Bank of the City of New York: A History of its First Century Compiled from Official Records at the Request of the Directors*. New York: printed for the bank, 1903.

Huntington, Charles Clifford. *A History of Banking and Currency in Ohio Before the Civil War*. Ohio Archaeological and Historical Publications. Columbus: F. J. Heer Printing Company, 1915.

Jaffee, Dwight and Joseph Stiglitz. "Credit Rationing." In *Handbook of Monetary Economics* Volume II. Edited by Benjamin M. Friedman and Frank H. Hahn. Elsevier Science Publishers, 1990.

James, John. "Banking Market Structure, Risk, and the Pattern of Local Interest Rates in the United States, 1893–1911," *Review of Economics and Statistics* 58 (November 1976), pp. 453–62.

"The Development of the National Money Market," *Journal of Economic History* 36 (December 1976), pp. 878–97.

Money and Capital Markets in Postbellum America. Princeton: Princeton University Press, 1978.

Johnson, Allen (editor). *Dictionary of American Biography* 20 vols. New York: Charles Scribner's Sons, 1946.

Keehn, Richard. "Market Power and Bank Lending: Some Evidence from Wisconsin, 1870–1900," *Journal of Economic History* 35 (September 1975), pp. 591–620.

King, Robert G. and Ross Levine. "Finance and Growth: Schumpeter Might Be Right," *Quarterly Journal of Economics* 108 (August 1993), pp. 717–37.

"Finance, Entrepreneurship, and Growth: Theory and Evidence," *Journal of Monetary Economics* 32 (December 1993), pp. 513–42.

Klebaner, Benjamin J. *American Commercial Banking: A History*. Boston: Twayne Publishers, 1990.

Klein, Joseph J. "The Development of Mercantile Instruments of Credit in the United States," *Journal of Accountancy* 12 (September 1911), pp. 321–607.

Krooss, Herman E. "Financial Institutions." In *The Growth of American Seaport*

Cities, 1790–1825, pp. 104–38. Edited by David T. Gilchrist. Charlottesville: University Press of Virginia, 1967.

and Martin R. Blyn. *A History of Financial Intermediaries*. New York: Random House, 1971.

Kuznets, Simon. *Six Lectures on Economic Growth*. Glencoe, Illinois: Free Press, 1959.

Capital in the American Economy: Its Formation and Financing. Princeton: Princeton University Press for the National Bureau of Economic Research, 1961.

Economic Growth of Nations: Total Output and Production Structure. Cambridge, MA: Belknap Press of Harvard University Press, 1971.

La Croix, Sumner J. and Christopher Grandy. "Financial Integration in Antebellum America: Strengthening Bodenhorn's Results," *Journal of Economic History* 53 (September 1993), pp. 653–8.

Lamoreaux, Naomi R. "Banks, Kinship, and Economic Development: The New England Case," *Journal of Economic History* 46 (September 1986), pp. 647–67.

"Information Problems and Bank's Specialization in Short-Term Commercial Lending: New England in the Nineteenth Century." In *Inside the Business Enterprise: Historical Perspectives on the Use of Information*, pp. 161–95. Edited by Peter Temin. Chicago: University of Chicago Press, 1991.

Insider Lending. Cambridge: Cambridge University Press, 1994.

and Christopher Glaisek. "Vehicles of Privilege or Mobility?: Banks in Providence, Rhode Island, during the Age of Jackson," *Business History Review* 65 (Autumn 1993), pp. 502–27.

Larson, Henrietta. *Jay Cooke: Private Banker*. Cambridge: Harvard University Press, 1936.

Lebergott, Stanley L. "Labor Force and Unemployment, 1800–1960." In *Output, Employment, and Productivity in the United States after 1800*. Edited by Dorothy S. Brady. New York: Columbia University Press, 1966.

Lebsock, Suzanne. *The Free Women of Petersburg: Status and Culture in a Southern Town, 1784–1860*. New York: W. W. Norton & Company, 1984.

Leland, Hayne E. and David H. Pyle. "Informational Asymmetries, Financial Structure, and Financial Intermediation," *Journal of Finance* 32 (May 1977), pp. 371–87.

Lesesne, J. Mauldin. *The Bank of the State of South Carolina*. South Carolina Tricentennial Commission. Columbia: University of South Carolina Press, 1970.

Lewis, Lawrence Jr. *A History of the Bank of North America, The First Bank Chartered in the United States*. Philadelphia: J. B. Lippincott & Company, 1882.

Lucas, Robert. "On the Mechanics of Economic Development," *Journal of Monetary Economics* 22 (1988), pp. 3–42.

Macauley, Frederick. *The Movement of Interest Rates, Bond Yields, and Stock Prices in the United States Since 1856*. New York: National Bureau of Economic Research, 1938.

Machlup, Fritz. "Introduction." In *International Mobility and Movement of*

Capital, pp. 1–24. Edited by Fritz Machlup, Walter S. Salant and Lorie Tarshis. New York: Columbia University Press for National Bureau of Economic Research, 1972.

A History of Thought on Economic Integration. New York: Columbia University Press, 1977.

Mankiw, N. Gregory, David Romer, and David N. Weil. "A Contribution to the Empirics of Economic Growth," *Quarterly Journal of Economics* 107 (May 1992), pp. 407–37.

Martin, Joseph G. *Twenty-One Years in the Boston Stock Market*. Boston: Redding and Company, 1856.

Mathias, Peter. *The First Industrial Nation: An Economic History of Britain, 1700–1914*. New York: Charles Scribner's Sons, 1969.

McCloskey, Donald N. *The Rhetoric of Economics*. Madison, Wisconsin: University of Wisconsin Press, 1985.

Knowledge and Persuasion in Economics. Cambridge: Cambridge University Press, 1996.

and J. Richard Zecher. "How the Gold Standard Worked, 1880–1913." In *Enterprise and Trade in Victorian Britain*. Edited by Donald N. McCloskey. London: George Allen & Unwin, 1981.

"The Success of Purchasing Power Parity: Historical Evidence and its Implications for Macroeconomics." In *A Retrospective on the Classical Gold Standard, 1821–1931*. Edited by Michael Bordo and Anna J. Schwartz. Chicago: University of Chicago Press, 1984.

McKinnon, Ronald I. *Money and Capital in Economic Development*. Washington, D.C.: Brookings Institution, 1973.

McPherson, James M. *Battle Cry of Freedom: The Civil War Era*. New York: Oxford University Press, 1988.

Mikesell, Raymond F. "Comment." In *International Mobility and Movement of Capital*, pp. 83–9. Edited by Fritz Machlup, Walter S. Salant and Lorie Tarshis. New York: Columbia University Press for National Bureau of Economic Research, 1972.

Miller, Harry E. *Banking Theories in the United States Before 1860*. Cambridge: Harvard University Press, 1927 (reprint Clifton: Augustus M. Kelley Publishers, 1972).

Modigliani, Franco and Merton Miller. "The Cost of Capital, Corporation Finance and the Theory of Investment," *American Economic Review* 48 (June 1958), pp. 261–97.

Mokyr, Joel. "Are We Living in the Middle of an Industrial Revolution?," Federal Reserve Bank of Kansas City *Economic Review* 82 (Second Quarter 1997), pp. 31–43.

Mullineaux, Donald J. "Competitive Monies and the Suffolk Bank System: A Contractual Perspective," *Southern Economic Journal* 53 (April 1987), pp. 884–98.

Myers, Margaret G. *The New York Money Market: Volume I, Origins and Development*. New York: Columbia University Press, 1931.

Neal, Larry. "Integration of International Capital Markets: Quantitative Evidence from the Eighteenth to Twentieth Centuries," *Journal of Economic History* 45 (June 1985), pp. 219–26.

"The Integration and Efficiency of the London and Amsterdam Stock Markets in the Eighteenth Century," *Journal of Economic History* 47 (March 1987), pp. 97–115.

The Rise of Financial Capitalism: International Capital Markets in the Age of Reason. Cambridge: Cambridge University Press, 1990.

Nevins, Allan. *History of the Bank of New York and Trust Company, 1784 to 1934.* New York: privately printed, 1934.

Norris, James D. *R. G. Dun & Co., 1841–1900: The Development of Credit-Reporting in the Nineteenth Century.* Westport: Greenwood Press, 1978.

North, Douglass. *The Economic Growth of the United States, 1790–1860.* Engle-wood Cliffs, NJ: Prentice-Hall, 1974.

Institutions, Institutional Change and Economic Performance. Cambridge: Cambridge University Press, 1990.

"Institutional Change in American Economic History." In *American Economic Development in Historical Perspective*, pp. 87–98. Edited by Thomas Weiss and Donald Schaefer. Stanford, CA: Stanford University Press, 1994.

Odell, Kerry. "The Integration of Regional and Interregional Capital Markets: Evidence from the Pacific Coast, 1888–1913," *Journal of Economic History* 49 (1989), pp. 297–310.

Olson, Mancur. *The Logic of Collective Action: Public Goods and the Theory of Groups.* Cambridge, MA: Harvard University Press, 1971.

Parker, William N. "The Finance of Capital Formation in Midwestern Development, 1800–1910." In *American Economic Development in Historical Perspective*, pp. 168–76. Edited by Thomas Weiss and Donald Schaefer. Stanford, CA: Stanford University Press, 1994.

Patrick, Hugh T. "Financial Development and Economic Growth in Underdeveloped Countries," *Economic Development and Cultural Change* 14 (January 1966), pp. 174–89.

Perkins, Edwin J. *Financing Anglo-American Trade: The House of Brown, 1800–1880.* Cambridge: Harvard University Press, 1975.

Pierson, George Wilson. *Tocqueville in America.* (Abridged by Dudley C. Lunt.) Garden City: Anchor Books, 1959.

Pollard, Sidney. "Fixed Capital in the Industrial Revolution in Britain," *Journal of Economic History* 24 (September 1964), pp. 299–314.

Posner, Richard A. *Economic Analysis of Law.* 2d edition. Boston: Little, Brown and Company, 1977.

Poulson, Barry. "Economic History and Economic Development: An American Perspective." In *American Economic Development in Historical Perspective*, pp. 70–83. Edited by Thomas Weiss and Donald Schaefer. Stanford: Stanford University Press, 1994.

Pred, Allan R. *Urban Growth and the Circulation of Information: The United States System of Cities, 1790–1840.* Cambridge: Harvard University Press, 1973.

Puth, Robert C. *American Economic History* 3d Edition. Fort Worth: Dryden Press, 1993.

Ransom, Roger L. and Richard Sutch. *One Kind of Freedom: The Economic Consequences of Emancipation*. Cambridge: Cambridge University Press, 1977.

Redish, Angela. "Why was Specie Scarce in Colonial Economies?: An Analysis of the Canadian Currency, 1796–1830," *Journal of Economic History* 44 (September 1984), pp. 713–28.

Redlich, Fritz. *The Molding of American Banking: Men and Ideas*. 2 parts. New York: Johnson Reprint Company, 1968 (reprint New York: Hafner Publishing Company, 1947).

Robinson, Joan. "The Generalizaton of the General Theory," in *The Rate of Interest and Other Essays*. London: Macmillan, 1952.

Rockoff, Hugh. *The Free Banking Era: A Reexamination*. New York: Arno Press, 1975.

   "Regional Interest Rates and Bank Failures," *Explorations in Economic History* 14 (Winter 1977), pp. 90–5.

   "New Evidence on Free Banking in the United States," *American Economic Review* 75 (September 1985), pp. 886–9.

   "Origins of the Usury Provision of the National Banking Act," unpublished mimeo, Rutgers University, 1988.

Rolnick, Arthur and Warren Weber. "New Evidence on the Free Banking Era," *American Economic Review* 73 (December 1983), pp. 1080–91.

   "The Causes of Free Bank Failures: A Detailed Examination," *Journal of Monetary Economics* 14 (October 1984), pp. 267–91.

Rostow, Walt Whitman. *The Stages of Economic Growth: A Noncommunist Manifesto*. Cambridge: Cambridge University Press, 1963.

Rothenberg, Winifred B. "The Emergence of a Capital Market in Rural Massachusetts, 1730–1838." *Journal of Economic History* 45 (December 1985), pp. 781–808.

Royall, William L. *A History of Virginia Banks and Banking Prior to the Civil War*. New York: Neale Publishing Company, 1907.

Royalty, Dale. "Banking and the Commonwealth Ideal in Kentucky, 1806–1822," *Register of the Kentucky Historical Society* 77 (1979), pp. 91–107.

Schubert, Eric. "Arbitrage in the Foreign Exchange Markets of London and Amsterdam during the 18th Century," *Explorations in Economic History* 26 (March 1989), pp. 1–20.

Schumpeter, Joseph A. *The Theory of Economic Development: An Inquiry into Profit, Capital, Credit, Interest, and the Business Cycle*. Translated by Redvers Opie. Cambridge: Harvard University Press, 1934.

Schwartz, Anna J. "The Beginning of Competitive Banking in Philadelphia, 1782–1809," *Journal of Political Economy* 55 (October 1947), pp. 417–31.

Schweikart, Larry. *Banking in the American South from the Age of Jackson to Reconstruction*. Baton Rouge: Louisiana State University Press, 1987.

Selgin, George A. and Lawrence H. White. "How Would the Invisible Hand Handle Money," *Journal of Economic Literature* 32 (December 1994), pp. 1718–49.

Shaw, Edward S. *Financial Deepening in Economic Development*. New York: Oxford University Press, 1973.

Smiley, Gene. "Interest Rate Movements in the United States, 1888–1913," *Journal of Economic History* 35 (September 1975), pp. 591–620.

Smith, Adam. *An Inquiry into the Nature and Causes of the Wealth of Nations*. New York: Modern Library [1776] 1937.

Smith, Paul F. *Money and Financial Intermediation: The Theory and Structure of Financial Systems*. Englewood Cliffs: Prentice-Hall, 1978.

Smith, Walter Buckingham. *Economic Aspects of the Second Bank of the United States*. New York: Greenwood Press, 1969.

Sokoloff, Kenneth L. "Investment in Fixed and Working Capital During Early Industrialization: Evidence from U.S. Manufacturing Firms," *Journal of Economic History* 44 (June 1984), pp. 545–56.

"Productivity Growth in Manufacturing during Early Industrialization." In *Long-Term Factors in American Economic Growth*. Studies in Income and Wealth, Vol. 51. Edited by Stanley L. Engerman and Robert E. Gallman. Chicago: University of Chicago Press, 1986.

"Invention, Innovation, and Manufacturing Productivity Growth in the Antebellum Northeast." In *American Economic Growth and Standards of Living before the Civil War*, pp. 345–78. Edited by Robert E. Gallman and John Joseph Wallis. Chicago: University of Chicago Press, 1992.

Spencer, Charles Jr. *The First Bank of Boston, 1784–1949*. New York: Newcomen Society, 1949.

Starnes, George T. *Sixty Years of Branch Banking in Virginia*. New York: Macmillan Company, 1931.

Stigler, George J. *The Organization of Industry*. Chicago: University of Chicago Press, 1968.

and Robert A. Sherwin. "The Extent of the Market," *Journal of Law and Economics* 28 (October 1985), pp. 555–85.

Stokes, Howard Kemble. *Chartered Banking in Rhode Island, 1791–1900*. Providence: Preston & Rounds Company, 1902.

"Public and Private Finance." In *State of Rhode Island and Providence Plantations at the End of the Century: A History*, Vol. III, pp. 173–322. Edited by Howard Field. Boston: Mason Publishing Company, 1902.

Sushka, Marie Elizabeth and Brian W. Barrett. "Banking Structure and the National Capital Market, 1869–1914," *Journal of Economic History* 44 (June 1984), pp. 463–77.

Sylla, Richard. "Federal Policy, Banking Market Structure, and Capital Mobilization in the United States, 1863–1913," *Journal of Economic History* 29 (December 1969), pp. 657–86.

The American Capital Market, 1846–1914: A Study of the Effects of Public Policy on Economic Development. New York: Arno Press, 1975.

"Forgotten Men of Money: Private Bankers in Early U.S. History," *Journal of Economic History* 36 (March 1976), pp. 173–88.

"Early American Banking: The Significance of the Corporate Form," *Business and Economic History*, 14 (Second Series) (March 1985), pp. 105–23.

Jack W. Wilson and Charles P. Jones. "U.S. Financial Markets and Long-Term

Economic Growth, 1790–1989." In *American Economic Development in Historical Perspective*, pp. 28–52. Edited by Thomas Weiss and Donald Schaefer. Stanford: Stanford University Press, 1994.

Jack W. Wilson and Robert E. Wright. "America's First Securities Markets, 1790–1830: Emergence, Development, and Integration." Unpublished paper, New York University, 1997.

Temin, Peter. *The Jacksonian Economy*. New York: W. W. Norton & Company, Inc., 1969.

Causal Factors in American Economic Growth in the Nineteenth Century. London: Macmillan Education Ltd., 1975.

Thomas, Brinley. *Migration and Economic Growth: A Study of Great Britain and the Atlantic Economy*. Cambridge: Cambridge University Press, 1954.

Tomlinson, Paul G. *A History of the Trenton Banking Company, 1804–1929*. Trenton: privately printed, 1929.

Tooker, Elva C. *Nathan Trotter: Philadelphia Merchant, 1787–1853*. Cambridge: Harvard University Press, 1955.

Tucker, George. *The Theory of Money and Banks Investigated*. Boston: C. C. Little and J. Brown, 1839 (reprint New York: Greenwood Press, 1968).

Vatter, Barbara. "Industrial Borrowing by the New England Textile Mills, 1840–1860: A Comment," *Journal of Economic History* 21 (June 1961), pp. 216–21.

Wainwright, Nicholas B. *History of the Philadelphia National Bank*. Philadelphia: William F. Fell Company, 1953.

Walker, Amasa. *History of the Wickaboag Bank*. Boston: Crosby, Nichols & Company, 1857.

Warren, George F. and Frank A. Pearson. *Prices*. New York: John Wiley & Sons, 1933.

Webster, Pelatiah. *An Essay on Credit: In Which the Doctrine of Bank, is Considered, and Some Remarks are Made on the Present State of the Bank of North America*. In Krooss and Samuelson, pp. 221–9.

Weiss, Thomas. "Revised Estimates of the United States Workforce, 1800–1860." In *Long-Term Factors in American Economic Growth*. Studies in Income and Wealth, Vol. 51. Edited by Stanley L. Engerman and Robert E. Gallman. Chicago: University of Chicago Press, 1986.

"U.S. Labor Force Estimates and Economic Growth, 1800–1860." In *American Economic Growth and Standards of Living before the Civil War*, pp. 19–75.

"Economic Growth Before 1860: Revised Conjectures." In *American Economic Development in Historical Perspective*, pp. 11–27. Edited by Thomas Weiss and Donald Schaefer. Stanford: Stanford University Press, 1994.

Western National Bank of Baltimore. *A Brief History of a Bank*. Baltimore: privately published, 1938.

Whitney, David R. *The Suffolk Bank*. Cambridge, Mass.: Riverside Press, 1878.

Womack, Roy Douglas. *An Analysis of the Credit Controls of the Second Bank of the United States*. New York: Arno Press, 1978.

Woodman, Harold D. *King Cotton and His Retainers: Financing and Marketing the Cotton Crop of the South, 1800–1925*. Lexington, KY: University of Kentucky Press, 1968.

BIBLIOGRAPHIC SOURCES

Gass, Frances, Eleanor Goehring, and Mary Louise Ogden. *Guide to Reports of State Departments and Institutions Found in the Appendix Volumes of Tennessee House and Senate Journals.* Knoxville: typescript in University of Tennessee Library.

Hassee, Adelaide. *Index of Economic Materials in the Documents of the States of the United States: Kentucky, 1790–1904.* Washington, D.C.: Carnegie Institute, 1919.

Index of Economic Materials in the Documents of the States of the United States: Massachusetts, 1790–1904. Washington, D.C.: Carnegie Institute, 1919.

Index of Economic Materials in the Documents of the States of the United States: New York, 1790–1904. Washington, D.C.: Carnegie Institute, 1919.

Index of Economic Materials in the Documents of the States of the United States: Pennsylvania, 1790–1904. Washington, D.C.: Carnegie Institute, 1919.

Index of Economic Materials in the Documents of the States of the United States: Rhode Island, 1790–1904. Washington, D.C.: Carnegie Institute, 1919.

CITY DIRECTORIES

Directory of the City of Charleston, to Which is Added a Business Directory, 1860. Charleston: W. Eugene Ferslew, 1860.

First Annual Directory for the City of Petersburg to Which is Added a Business Directory for 1859. Petersburg: George E. Furd, 1859.

Longworth's American Almanac, New York Register, and City Directory. New York: T. Longworth & Son, 1842.

New Orleans Annual and Commercial Directory. New Orleans: Michael & Company, 1842.

Richmond, Petersburg, Norfolk, and Portsmouth Business Directory, 1859–60. Richmond: William F. Bartlett, 1859.

Second Annual Directory for the City of Petersburg to Which is Added a Business Directory for 1860. Petersburg: George E. Furd, 1860.

Watertown, North Watertown and Juhelville Business and Residence Directory for 1856–57. Watertown: J. D. Huntington, 1856.

Williams' Memphis Directory, City Guide, and Business Mirror. Memphis: Cleaves & Vaden, 1860.

GOVERNMENT DOCUMENTS

Indiana. State Bank. *Report of the State Bank of Indiana and Condition of its Branches to the Governor.* Indianapolis: Austin H. Brown, 1853.

Kentucky. *House Journal.* (1822, 1825, 1828–1830, 1832–1835, 1838–1840, 1859–1860).

Kentucky. *Senate Journal.* (1823–1840).

Kentucky. *Legislative Documents.* (1841–1852, 1855–1858).

Massachusetts. General Court. "True Abstract of the Returns of Several Banks to the Secretary of the Commonwealth," (1820, 1822–1823, 1827–1829, 1833–1834, 1845–1846).

Massachusetts. General Court. "Report of a Committee of the Massachusetts Senate to Investigate the Affairs of the Penobscot Bank," (December 1809).

Massachusetts. General Court. "Report of the Committee Relative to Penebscot Bank," (1811).

Massachusetts. General Court. "Final Report of the Bank Commissioners." *Senate Document No. 11* (January 1851).

New York. General Assembly. "Annual Report of the Bank Commissioners." *Assembly Documents.* Doc. No. 69 (1831); Doc. No. 102 (1834); Doc. No. 74 (1835); Doc. No. 80 (1836); Doc. No. 78 (1837); Doc. No. 71 (1838); Doc. No. 101 (1839); Doc. No. 44 (1840); Doc. No. 64 (1841); Doc. No. 29 (1842); Doc. No. 34 (1843).

New York. General Assembly. "Annual Report of the Superintendent of the Banking Department." *Assembly Documents* Doc. No. 4 (1856); Doc. No. 5 (1857); Doc. No. 4 (1858); Doc. No. 5 (1859); Doc. No. 3 (1860); Doc. No. 3 (1861).

Ohio. *Senate Journal.* (1834/35–1835/36).

Ohio. "Report of the Auditor of the State . . . Relative to the State and Condition of Certain Banks." *Executive Documents* (1836/37, 1837/38, 1840–1845).

Ohio. "Annual Report of the Board of Bank Commissioners, of the State of Ohio." *Executive Documents.* (1843/44, 1844).

Pennsylvania. *House Journals* (1818, 1832, 1839–1841).

Pennsylvania. *Senate Journal* (1814–1817, 1819–1831, 1833–1838, 1841–1852).

Pennsylvania. *Legislative Documents* (1853–1860).

Rhode Island. General Assembly. "Abstract of the Returns from the Several Banks in the State of Rhode Island, made to the General Assembly," *Acts and Resolves* (1809–1845, 1848, 1850, 1858, 1860).

Tennessee. *House Journal* (1845, 1848–1849, 1851, 1853–1855, 1859).

Tennessee. *Senate Journal* (1842–1843, 1849).

South Carolina. *Reports and Resolutions of the General Assembly of South Carolina.* (1844, 1852–1854, 1860, 1865).

South Carolina. *A Compilation of All the Acts, Resolutions, Reports and Other Documents in Relation to the Bank of the State of South Carolina, Affording Full Information Concerning that Institution.* Columbia, 1848.

United States. Census Office. Eighth Census (1860). Manuscript censuses from various counties in New York, Tennessee, and Virginia.

United States. Census Office. Ninth Census (1870). *A Compendium of the Ninth Census.* Washington, D.C.: Government Printing Office, 1872.

United States. Census Office. Ninth Census (1870). *Statistics of Population.* Washington, D.C.: Government Printing Office, 1872.

United States. Comptroller of the Currency. *Annual Report of the Comptroller of the Currency* (1876).

United States. Department of Commerce. *Statistical Abstract of the United States* 155th ed. Lanham, MD: Bernan Press, 1995.

United States. House. 22d Congress, 1st Session, *Executive Document No. 147*.

United States. House. 22d Congress, 1st Session, *House Report No. 460*.

United States. House. 23rd Congress, 1st Session, *Executive Document No. 498*.

United States. House. 23rd Congress, 2d Session, *Executive Document No. 190*.

United States. House. 24th Congress, 1st Session, *Executive Document No. 42*.

United States. House. 24th Congress, 1st Session, *Executive Document No. 65*.

United States. House. 24th Congress, 2d Session, *Executive Document No. 65*.

United States. House. 25th Congress, 2d Session, *Executive Document No. 79*.

United States. House. 25th Congress, 2d Session, *Executive Document No. 471*.

United States. House. 25th Congress, 3d Session, *Executive Document No. 227*.

United States. House. 26th Congress, 1st Session, *Executive Document No. 172*.

United States. House. 26th Congress, 2d Session, *Executive Document No. 111*.

United States. House. 29th Congress, 1st Session, *Executive Document No. 226*.

United States. House. 29th Congress, 2d Session, *Executive Document No. 120*.

United States. House. 30th Congress, 1st Session, *Executive Document No. 77*.

United States. House. 31st Congress, 1st Session, *Executive Document No. 68*.

United States. House. 32d Congress, 1st Session, *Executive Document No. 122*.

United States. House. 32d Congress, 2d Session, *Executive Document No. 66*.

United States. House. 33d Congress, 1st Session, *Executive Document No. 102*.

United States. House. 33d Congress, 2d Session, *Executive Document No. 82*.

United States. House. 34th Congress, 1st Session, *Executive Document No. 102*.

United States. House. 34th Congress, 3d Session, *Executive Document No. 87*.

United States. House. 35th Congress, 1st Session, *Executive Document No. 107*.

United States. House. 35th Congress, 2d Session, *Executive Document No. 112*.

United States. House. 36th Congress, 1st Session, *Executive Document No. 49*.

United States. House. 36th Congress, 2d Session, *Executive Document No. 77*.

Virginia. *House Journals* (1821–1824, 1827–1831).

Virginia. *House Documents* (1825–1826, 1832–1860).

PERIODICALS

Albany Argus, various issues, 1829–1859.

Bankers' Magazine, various issues, 1848–1861.

Bicknell's Counterfeit Detector, Banknote List, and General Price Current (Philadelphia), title varies various issues, 1830–1857.

Charleston Mercury, various issues, 1836–1859.

Commercial and Shipping List (New York), various issues, 1830–1859.

The Economist, 28 September 1996.

Hunt's Merchants' Magazine and Commercial Review, various issues, 1840–1861.

Journal of Commerce (New York), various issues, 1836–1837.

Merchants and Bankers Register for 1860 (New York), 1860.
Ming's New York Price Current, various issues, 1811–1815.
Missouri Republican, various issues, 1850.
New Orleans Price Current, various issues, 1835–1859.
New York Herald Tribune, various issues, 1839–1860.
New York Price Current, various issues, 1811–1817.
Niles Weekly Register, various issues, 1818–1819.
The (Daily) Picayune (New Orleans), title varies, various issues, 1834–1861.
The Pilot (Boston), 12 October 1812.
Philadelphia Price Current, various issues, 1827–1830.

Index

257